Collector's Guide to

Classic
O-Gauge Trains

David Doyle

©2007 Krause Publications
Published by

krause publications
An Imprint of F+W Publications

700 East State Street • Iola, WI 54990-0001
715-445-2214 • 888-457-2873
www.krausebooks.com

Our toll-free number to place an order or obtain
a free catalog is (800) 258-0929.

Library of Congress Catalog Number: 2006934237

ISBN: 978-089689-457-0

Designed by Donna Mummery
Edited by Justin Moen

Printed in China

CONTENTS

INTRODUCTION

No doubt the first toy train was created not long after George Stephenson's first train rode the rails in 1814. (In 1804 Richard Trevithick built a locomotive that did not operate on rails.) It is not clear which arrived in this country first, toy trains or the real thing (Peter Cooper's Tom Thumb in 1830.) What is clear is that trains have held the imagination of both adults and children for 150 years. It was natural then that these toys move from wooden, cast iron or brass static or push replicas to self-propelled replicas. A few attempts were made to use actual steam power to move the miniatures around the rails, but the hazards of flame, hot water and steam, as well as the expense, prevented these toys from becoming widespread successes. Clockwork or mechanical trains were much safer, and considerably more successful, but required almost constant attention to keep running. The rewinding of the toy and lack of speed and direction control quickly shattered any realism that existed in the imagination of the operator.

Electricity, however, provided a medium through which trains could be run for extended periods of time, and by which the operator could control the speed, direction and stopping of the train. One of the first people to recognize this was Joshua Lionel Cowen, whose electric novelty company in 1901 produced an electrically powered gondola car. It was initially sold as an animated window display with which merchants could call attention to their wares, however the public saw the train as a toy for both adults and children. By the following year, Cowen changed his marketing strategy to match that of the public demand–and Lionel Trains began their journey to domination of the U.S. electric train market.

Cowen, however, was by no means the only purveyor of electric trains; Harry Ives, W.O. Coleman, Louis Marx, Olympian A.C. Gilbert, and a host of others climbed aboard the electric train express. The firms of these men and others created an array of products that fueled the imaginations and filled the Christmas lists of generations of American boys–and some girls too.

In 1906, Lionel began producing trains that rolled on "Standard Gauge" track, which was 1-2-1/8 inches between the railheads. Ives and American Flyer, who due to copyright issues dubbed their trains "Wide Gauge," also produced trains of this same massive size.

Standard-Gauge trains consumed relatively large amounts of raw material, and large shipping and display volumes–all factors leading to high costs. Thus, in 1910, Ives introduced O-Gauge trains to its product line. These trains, which ran on track measuring 1-1/4 inches between the outside rail centers, were much smaller than their Wide-Gauge predecessors. This made them much more economical to produce, transport and merchandise–and much easier for youthful enthusiasts to handle, as well as requiring less space in the home.

By 1915, Lionel entered the O-Gauge market, and by World War II production of Standard Gauge by major manufacturers had ceased.

Though Lionel, American Flyer and Marx made forays into other sizes–namely HO and 00–starting even before WWII, it was to be O-Gauge trains that dominated the marketplace in the 1940s and 50s–the golden age of toy trains.

Increasingly, sophisticated toys were produced–logs and milk cans were unloaded, signal bells rang, cranes unloaded cargo, and rockets were launched. Brightly colored diesel locomotives trailing equally dazzling freight cars plied the miniature rails. But the trend of expanding offerings would not continue forever.

By the late 1950s, electric trains had reached their zenith of popularity as toys. Jet aircrafts captured the imagination of the distant-traveling public, stealing it away from the sleek streamliners like the Super Chief, California Zephyr and 20th Century Limited. Astronauts and pilots replaced engineers as favorites of youth. The newly established

Interstate Highway system allowed the shift of merchandise from rail travel to truck, ending the trips to the local freight house to pick up goods. The Interstate allowed easy travel for millions of shiny new cars being bought in America's burgeoning economy. Miniature cars, in the form of slot outfits, similarly tugged children from the rails.

For those retailers and manufacturers that stayed true to trains, the size of O-Gauge trains–though viewed as compact when introduced in 1910–began to be viewed as a liability. HO-Gauge trains were smaller–HO literally represents "Half O"–but had originally been developed as models for mature hobbyists. Forgetting these origins, HO trains began to be offered as children's playthings, their small size again allowing lower retail prices and appealing to the space-saving consciousness of homeowners.

These trains however lacked the fortitude to survive handling by enthusiastic youngsters, and their track systems did not permit reliable operation unless permanently fastened down. The latter both defeated a certain amount of the space saving, as well as eliminating the creative play value for children of setting up varying track designs–how much fun are glued-together Tinker Toys, Lincoln Logs or American Bricks? Those that did not permanently fasten down the HO tracks were doomed to frequent derailments and unreliable operation. The toy train industry–struggling to compete against new toys–had unwittingly undermined one of its hallmarks–that of being rugged, reliable toys–a reputation created by the O-Gauge trains.

Today, though the number of children who yearn for a train under the Christmas tree now may only be a portion of those who did 50 years ago, there are two other groups whose interest grows. One of these is the adult toy train operator–to the laymen, these enthusiasts are scarcely distinguishable from their cousins, the model railroader. The other group is the toy train collector. These people preserve the toys, and joys, of yesterday. It is for this group this volume has been written.

COLLECTING

Toy train collectors are their own fraternity, eagerly welcoming new buffs with a sincere interest in toy trains. Avail yourself of this knowledge base and friendship no matter if you are an experienced collector or a rookie. Something can always be learned. There is no substitute for experience in this hobby, as in any other. No book, no matter how complete, contains all the answers. Thousands of words and the best illustrations cannot equal the experience gained by holding a piece in your own hands. There is no finer place than in the home of a friend and fellow collector. A piece that is not for sale can be examined, unhurried and questions answered honestly, an excellent preparation for seeking an item in the marketplace.

The advent of Internet auctions has been a boon for collectors, particularly those in remote areas. But for those in more populous areas, there is no substitute for shopping in the company of fellow collectors at hobby shops and train shows, especially for the neophyte. Examining an item personally, with the counsel of more experienced collectors, is especially urged when purchasing expensive, often repaired or forged items.

However, after gaining some experience, working with a trusted and reputable train auction company can provide access to trains that otherwise may take years, or even decades, to acquire.

Enthusiasts have been collecting toy trains perhaps as long as they have been produced. In the United States, the largest and oldest collector's group is the Train Collector's Association, or TCA. Founded in 1954 in Yardley, Pa., the group has grown to over 31,000 members. An annual convention is held at various locations around the country each summer. Smaller, regional groups called Divisions and Chapters dot the nation. Twice each year, one such group, the Eastern Division, hosts the largest toy train show in the world. The York Fairgrounds, in York, Pa. becomes a veritable Mecca for the toy train buff with several buildings encompassing more than 100,000 square feet of toy trains for sale, display or trade. Members of the TCA agree to abide by a code of conduct, assuring fair and honest dealings between members. The nationally recognized Grading Standards were developed by the TCA.

The TCA National Headquarters and the associated National Toy Train Museum is located in Strasburg, Pa. The Train Collectors Association can be reached at its Web site, www.traincollectors.org, or by writing to:

Train Collectors Association
P.O. Box 248
300 Paradise Lane
Strasburg, PA 17579
(717) 687-8623

The second-oldest organization is the Toy Train Operating Society, formed on the West Coast in 1966. Similar in style and purpose to the TCA, traditionally the bulk of the TTOS members and events has been in the west, but has been gradually spreading eastward. The TTOS can be contacted at:

Toy Train Operating Society
25 W. Walnut Street, Suite 308
Pasadena, CA 91103
Phone (626) 578-0673

One of the first, and certainly the largest, Lionel-specific clubs is the Lionel Collector's Club of America. Founded Aug. 1, 1970 by Jim Gates of Des Moines, Iowa, the organization has grown steadily since. The club was founded on the idea that collectors and operators of Lionel trains need an organization of their own. The club's mailing address is:

LCCA Business Office
P.O. Box 479
La Salle, IL 61301-0479

The youngster of these groups is the Lionel Operating Train Society, or LOTS. Founded in 1979 by Larry Keller of Cincinnati, this club's purpose is providing a national train club for operators of Lionel trains and accessories. Like the others, it publishes magazines, swap-lists and a membership directory. LOTS can be reached at:

LOTS Business Office
6376 West Fork Road
Cincinnati, OH 45247-5704

Condition and Rarity

To the collector, condition is everything, and train collectors have established criteria for grading trains. Two systems are currently in use, the older (good, very good, excellent, etc.) system used by the Train Collector's Association for over 50 years, and a newer system, the (C7, C8, C10) system, recently adopted by the TCA. Use of these conditions when describing the condition of collectable trains protects both the buyer and the seller.

These grading standards are as follows:

Fair: Well-scratched, chipped, dented, rusted, warped.

Good, or C2: Small dents, scratches, dirty.

Very Good, or C3: Few scratches, exceptionally clean, no major dents or rust.

Excellent, or C6: Minute scratches or nicks, no dents or rust, all original, less than average wear.

Like New, or C8: Only the slightest signs of handling and wheel wear, brilliant colors and crisp markings; literally like new. As a rule, Like New trains must have their original boxes in comparable condition to realize the prices listed in this guide. Trains in Like New and Mint conditions are the most desirable to collectors, and their prices are not only higher, but also considerably more volatile than those of lesser condition.

Mint, or C10: Brand new, absolutely unmarred, all original and unused. Items dusty or faded from display, or with fingerprints from handling, cannot be considered mint. Although Lionel test ran their locomotives briefly at the factory, items "test run" by consumers cannot be considered mint. Most collectors expect mint items to come with all associated packaging with which they were originally supplied.

As one can imagine, Mint pieces command premium prices. The supply is extremely limited, and the demand among collectors is great, so often the billfold of the buyer, rather than a more natural supply and demand situation, limits the price of such pieces.

In addition to the categories stated above, two other classifications are important in the toy train hobby; restored and reproduction.

Restored: A number of the trains found in the marketplace have been restored. The rugged steel construction of many of the items has insured that the item itself has survived, even if its brilliant enamel coating did not. Fortunately, many of these worn and scuffed items have been rescued from the trash bin, disassembled, stripped of their old finish, and a new one applied. Coupled with mechanical repairs and polished or replaced brightwork, these trains now shine with all their previous glory. Unfortunately, some of the more larcenous types of our society choose to represent these restored items as excellent condition originals–often painting them in the more desirable color combinations to boot. Under those circumstances, remember, it's not the train that is cheating. It's the seller.

No values are assigned in this book for restored items. The quality of restorations vary widely, ranging from spectroscopically matched paints applied to carefully stripped cars to "close enough" off the rack spray paints applied sometimes even directly over the old paint. Also, some collectors loath restored items, no matter how well done, or how honestly marked as restored. These factors combine to make assigning values to restored items virtually impossible. Use your own judgment, and remember, no matter how scarce an original is in a given color, the value of a restored item is not affected by color.

Further, collecting prewar trains is becoming an old enough hobby that some early restorations are 50 years old, and have acquired a patina of their own. For neophytes contemplating a major purchase, it is extremely important that you have absolute confidence in the seller, and hopefully the assistance of an experienced collector as well. If you are looking to add a specific item to your collection, it is extremely helpful to visit other collectors and carefully examine an original in advance. This will help you, much more than photos in this or any other book, know what an item should look like.

Reproduction: Reproductions allow enthusiasts to enjoy operating trains that otherwise they could not locate, could not afford, or would feel too risky to operate. A number of firms, Joe Mania Trains, Williams Reproductions, Kramer Reproductions, MTH and even Lionel have built excellent reproductions. Their products are clearly, but discretely marked as reproductions. Unfortunately, other firms and individuals have reproduced items, particularly early trains, without any indication that they are not of original manufacture. These items are much more akin to being forgeries intended to deceive for great financial gain, rather than a reproduction built to permit enjoyment. None of the national train collecting organizations knowingly allows these items into their shows, or meets, but occasionally they do slip in, as they often do at independent shows.

Values for forgeries are not given in this book, as they are worthless on the legitimate market.

Demand: Demand is one of the key factors influencing values. The postwar Santa Fe F-3 Diesel was the most produced locomotive in Lionel's history, yet clean examples still command premium prices due to demand.

Rarity: or scarcity, is also a factor influencing the value of trains. Low production quantities or extreme fragility cause some items to be substantially more difficult to find than others. When scarcity is coupled with demand the result is a premium price, while other items, extremely scarce, command only moderate prices due to lack of demand, or appreciation, on the part of collectors.

Supply: A short-term extension of rarity, whether actual or temporary, also affects price. If only one sought after item is at a given show, the seller is unlikely to negotiate or reduce his price. If, however, multiple sellers at a given event have identical items, no matter how rare, the temporary market glut can bring about temporarily reduced prices.

Lastly, the **buyer's intent** will effect what they are willing to pay. A collector who intends to add a piece to their permanent collection will obviously pay more for an item than a dealer who is purchasing for resale.

Trains in less than Very Good condition are not generally considered collectable.

As mentioned earlier, Mint condition trains are too uncommon to establish pricing on, as is the case for many prewar trains in Like New condition.

The prices listed are what a group of collectors would consider a reasonable market value when dealing at a train show, or "meet." Listed is a price they would be willing to pay to add that piece to their collection. When buying at a specialized train auction with Internet access, one can expect to pay more as the pool of potential buyers is greater. The savings in fuel often offset this increased cost by reducing lodging and time that would otherwise be spent tracking a given item down over time searching from show to show.

When contemplating a sale to a dealer, you should expect to receive 30 to 50 percent less than the value listed, with the poorer condition the trains the greater the amount of discount, due to the greater difficulty the dealer will have selling them. Remember that these prices are only a guideline. You are spending your money—what an item is worth to you is of greater importance than what it is worth to the author. Conversely, the publisher does not sell trains, this is not a mail-order catalog, and you should not expect a dealer or collector to "price match."

Boxes

Manufacturers boxed their products to ease handling and protect the trains en route and once at the market. They were strictly utilitarian, and throughout much of the postwar era, no thought was given to eye appeal. During the prewar era, it was intended that attentive, trained salespeople sell the trains. Self-service, and thus consumer oriented packaging, was not a factor.

Scattered throughout this book are photos of selected pieces with their original packaging. Items produced over an extended period of time sometimes used a variety of boxes during their production run, so boxes for a given piece can legitimately vary from those shown in this book. Beware, however that many unknowing (or uncaring) collectors and dealers often place items in the improper vintage box in an effort to "upgrade" the packaging.

One reason for this is that relatively speaking few boxes survive. The boxes, being pasteboard, were more fragile than the sturdy trains, and inherently would have a lower survival rate. Plus, people were buying TRAINS, not boxes—many of the boxes went out with the trash Christmas morning. Even in the early days of collecting, boxes, especially set boxes and outer master cartons, were considered bulky nuisances and were thrown away. Today, any given box is scarcer than its intended contents, and clean trains in their original boxes command a premium price in the marketplace. Even the boxes themselves have developed a collector market, but remember; to be proper the box must be not only the same stock number, but also the same vintage as the train inside.

HOW OLD IS MY TRAIN?

Unlike certain other collectibles, the age of a toy train is not a factor in its value. That is, an older train is not inherently more valuable than a newer train. It is rather the variations in construction throughout an item's production run that effect its scarcity, and thus value. Some toy trains are marked on the sides with "New" or "Built" dates. These dates are often totally irrelevant to when a piece was actually produced, and are decorative only. For the collector, establishing the production date of these trains is done as a curiosity, or when trying to properly and precisely recreate a given train set, rather than as part of the valuing process.

ACKNOWLEDGMENTS

Since its inception in 1910, a wide range of manufacturers has produced O-Gauge trains. Each of these firms naturally strove to create a loyal customer base, and though today many of these firms no longer exist, or at best produce trains, this loyalty remains, now entrusted to generations of collectors. Thus, creating a volume of this nature required the help and cooperation of many collectors, businessmen and enthusiasts, who I am privileged to thank, and call friends.

Many collectors and businesses shared photographs with me or allowed me to make my own images of rare and important pieces in their collections. Many knowledgeable collectors and dealers graciously reviewed the manuscript and offered corrections, criticism and commentary, and provided valuable insight on values for the items listed herein. Every effort has been made to present complete and accurate information here, and any errors herein are purely my own.

As with all my books on toy trains, collectors John and Bill Autry welcomed me with open arms, allowing me to photograph their collection not only in place, but trusting me with dozens of items to take to the Krause photo studio as well. Their generosity will not be soon forgotten.

Greg Stout, of Stout Auctions, who arguably handles the largest train collections in the country, granted us unlimited access for photography, and as a result, saved many, many hours of work and miles of driving. His phenomenal knowledge and amazing memory were tremendous assets in this project.

Train collecting is a passion for the entire Tschopp family, and they all pitched in on this project. Brothers Bob and John opened their postwar Lionel collection for photography and shared their knowledge. Their sister, Mary Burns and her husband Terry, put in a long, long day helping photograph the couple's fabulous prewar Lionel collection. Teen-ager Bobby, the newest collector of the family, tirelessly located Lionel and Kusan trains for photography.

Photos for the Marx portion of this book would have been sparse indeed had not Ron Williams allowed me to photograph his collection. Unfortunately, space allows us to show but a small part of his vast array of trains.

Jim Nicholson is a true train collector–all sizes, all brands–and he graciously gave our photographers complete access to his amazing collection.

The Kusan and AMT chapters would not have been complete without the help of Joseph Lechner, Peter Attona and Jim Wagner. John LaLima of East Coast Train Parts provided valuable insights, and Emmo Hein of Mid-South Hobbies allowed us to photograph various items from both his store inventory, and personal collection. Jack Sommerfeld likewise allowed us to photograph from his collection and inventory at Sommerfeld's Trains.

The late Gary Lavinous and his team of dedicated volunteers stayed until near midnight at the National Toy Train Museum helping me photograph many of the most rare pieces shown in this volume. Though their day was nearing 18 hours long, they dismantled display cases to allow access, not only without complaining, but with genuine enthusiasm.

Parts with Character shared much knowledge and experience with me, as well as allowing needed photos to be taken.

My old friend, Jeff Kane of www.ttender.com, loaned several items from his collection for photography, as well as sharing part of his vast knowledge acquired through his years of supplying repair parts.

A handful of collectors chose to remain anonymous. Their anonymity, however, does not lessen the value of their contributions of photographs and information to this work — thank you.

HOW TO USE THIS BOOK

1. ⟶

3. ↘

2. ⟶   C5   C7   C8

2350: While difficult to locate, the version w/white "N," orange "H," white "NEW HAVEN," as well as painted nose markings, is not as sought after as the two versions listed above.   **$500**   **$800**   **$1,300** ⟵ 4.

1.) Photo: In some listings, photos are supplied to better help identify and verify what Model you possess.

2.) Listing Name: Items will be listed by Model number. In most instances, if the model number does not appear on the item, the number is listed in parenthesis.

3.) Listing Description: Located directly after the Listing Name is a brief description of the listing, giving vital information to better help identification.

4.) Values: Values are listed in the columns to the right of the description. Values for each condition are in U.S. Dollars.

> **C5 *formerly known as Good*:** Signs of play wear scratches, dents, minor surface rust, evidence of heavy use.

> **C6 *formerly known as VG=Very Good*:** Few scratches, exceptionally clean, no major dents or rust.

> **C7 *formerly known as EX=Excellent*:** Minute scratches or nicks, no dents or rust, all original, less than average wear.

> **C8 *formerly known as LN=Like New*:** Only the slightest signs of handling and wheel wear, brilliant colors and crisp markings; literally like new. As a rule, Like New trains must have their original boxes in comparable condition to realize the prices listed in this guide.

Items shown in italics are the most common version. Items in bold are the most desirable. Prices are similarly coded.

Editor's note: The Train Collectors Association has changed its rating system for the condition of toy trains. Rather than Good, Excellent, Like New, etc., ratings now range from C1 through C10, with C10 being the highest, or former Mint condition. Most commonly collected are trains in C5 through C8 condition, and pricing throughout this book reflect these ratings.

AMERICAN FLYER

The company that is best remembered today as American Flyer was founded in Chicago about 1907. William Hafner, an experienced toymaker, developed a clockwork-powered train. His friend, William O. Coleman, gained control of a struggling hardware manufacturer, the Edmonds-Metzel Manufacturing Co., and that firm's excess capacity was turned to toy production. Hafner, also a superb salesman, secured orders totaling $15,000 from Montgomery Ward and G. Sommers & Co., and the company was firmly in the toy business. Beginning in 1908, Edmonds-Metzel trains were marketed as "American Flyer," and in 1910, the firm's name was changed as well. Edmonds-Metzel was gone, as was hardware production, but American Flyer trains were in full swing.

By 1913, the collaboration between Hafner and Coleman, which had created the successful line, began to fail, resulting in Hafner leaving American Flyer. Hafner went on to form his own company: Hafner Manufacturing Co.

American Flyer introduced other types of toys to its product line, but the 1918 introduction of electric trains (the line previously had

consisted of clockwork O-Gauge trains) set the company on its
course for the next five decades. But the joy of a new product was
dampened by the death of William O. Coleman. With the passing of
his father, W.O. Coleman Jr. took the helm of the company.

In 1925, Flyer augmented its production of O-Gauge trains with
the introduction of larger Wide-Gauge trains. These trains operated
on the same track as did Lionel's Standard-Gauge train, but could not
be marked as such because Standard Gauge was Lionel's proprietary
trade name.

Three years later, one of Flyer's chief competitors, Ives, filed
bankruptcy, setting the stage for the latter firm's takeover by a
partnership of Lionel and American Flyer. This partnership lasted until
1930, when Lionel became sole owner of Ives. However, even with
one competitor eliminated, Flyer still faced stiff competition. Toward
the upper end the Chicago firm loomed Lionel; for the economy
market, they faced off against the formidable Louis Marx organization.
The stiff competition forced American Flyer to withdraw from the
declining Wide-Gauge market after 1936.

A needed infusion of money and talent came in 1938 when Coleman sold out to famous Olympic athlete and Erector Set proprietor, A. C. Gilbert. Gilbert moved production to Connecticut, and redesigned the line to 1/64 scale proportions the following year. At the same time, the much smaller HO-Gauge line was introduced. HO literally stands for Half Oh, and was considerably more realistic than even the redesigned O-Gauge line. HO remained part of the American Flyer line through 1963, even though in later years subcontractors such as Tru-Scale, Mantua or Varney produced much of the line.

Like other U.S. train manufacturers, Gilbert suspended production during WWII, its facilities used instead for war production. At the conclusion of hostilities, American Flyer retooled its trains for the new S-Gauge. Advertising of the period touted the realism of the two-rail track the new trains ran on, much to the chagrin of both Lionel and Marx, who continued to rely on three-rail track.

Despite the scale-like appearance of the new product line, and Gilbert's marketing talent, American Flyer never achieved more than the number two-market position against the juggernaut of Lionel. The declining market for electric trains, and A.C. Gilbert's passing in 1961, led to the sale of the venerable firm to oil tycoon cum entertainment magnate Jack Wrather. Wrather was flush with cash from his successful "Lassie" and "Lone Ranger" television series, but sorely lacked experience in the toy market. Production of American Flyer trains ceased in 1966, and in 1967 Lionel gained ownership of the tooling and brand in exchange for liquidating the remaining inventory of American Flyer trains.

Since 1979, Lionel has offered a few American Flyer items almost every year, but this effort is a far cry from the glory days of Chicago or New Haven.

	C5	C7	C8
1 Locomotive: wind-up.	$50	$100	$150
1 Transformer: 25-watt.	15	20	30
1 Transformer: 35-watt.	19	25	35
2 Locomotive: cast iron, wind-up.	70	140	200
1-1/2 Transformer: 45-watt.	23	30	40
1-1/2B Transformer: 50-watt.	30	40	60
2 Transformer: 75-watt.	38	50	75
1-1/2 Transformer: 50-watt.	30	40	60
3 Locomotive: wind-up.	45	90	125
4 Locomotive: 0-4-0, wind-up.	60	125	175
4A Locomotive: wind-up.	70	140	200
8B Transformer:	42	55	75
8B Transformer: 100-watt, w/bulb covers.	53	70	100
8B Transformer: 100-watt, w/out bulb covers.	45	60	95
8B Transformer: w/uncoupler, track, manual and buttons.	53	70	100
9 Locomotive: 0-4-0, wind-up.	60	120	175
10 Locomotive: 0-4-0, cast iron, wind-up.	50	100	150
10 Locomotive: 1925, electric.	120	240	350
11 Locomotive: 0-4-0, wind-up.	90	180	275
12 Locomotive: cast iron.	50	100	150
12 Smoke Cartridges:	—	4	10
13 Locomotive and Tender: 0-4-0, wind-up, black, orange and green.	75	150	225
14 Locomotive: 0-4-0, wind-up.	45	90	150
15 Locomotive: wind-up.	35	70	100
16 Locomotive: 0-4-0, electric.	55	110	150
18B Transformer:	90	120	175
19B Transformer: 300-watt w/volt and amp.	75	100	150
28 Locomotive: 0-4-0, wind-up.	40	85	115
29 Locomotive: cast iron, first electric, and wind-up.	75	150	225
34 Locomotive: 0-4-0, wind-up.	70	140	225
40 Locomotive: 0-4-0, wind-up.	70	140	225
92 Switch Tower:	60	80	125
96 Station: c. 1931.	30	40	60
104 Kenilworth Station:	18	25	40
105 Pullman:	30	60	100
119 Hiawatha Locomotive: tin-plate, wind-up, w/tender.	60	120	175
119 Hiawatha Locomotive: tin-plate, electric.	90	180	225
119 Hiawatha Locomotive: w/tender.	350	700	1,000
119 Tender:	30	60	100
120 Tender:	40	80	125
121 Tender: black and white, marked "No. 121."	30	60	100
152 Locomotive: wind-up.	45	90	135
228 Log Car:	20	40	65
229 Boxcar:	20	40	65
230 Dump Car:	20	40	65
231 Tank Car:	20	40	65

406 Log Car

407 Sand Car

408 Boxcar

410 Tank Car

410 Tank Car

411 Caboose

415 Floodlight Car

425 Locomotive

429 Locomotive

	C5	C7	C8
323 Coach:	$60	$100	$150
328 Tender:	30	60	100
356 Tender: Comet.	40	80	125
401 Locomotive: 2-4-2.	88	175	250
401 Locomotive: 2-4-4, Pennsylvania.	35	70	100
403 Locomotive: 2-4-4.	65	125	200
404 Pullman:	30	60	100
405 Observation Car:	30	60	100
406 Log Car: 1939, green or orange.	18	35	50
407 Sand Car: 1939, green.	20	40	60
408 Boxcar: 1939-40, orange.	20	45	70
409 Dump Car:	30	65	100
410 Locomotive:	55	110	170
410 Tank Car: 1939-40, silver tank, green frame; or green on blue frame.	25	55	80
411 Caboose: 1939-40, similar to 3211, red.	20	40	60
412 Milk Car:	48	95	150
415 Floodlight Car: 1939.	45	90	150
416 Wrecker Car:	100	200	300
419 Locomotive: streamliner.	135	275	400
420 Locomotive: American Flyer Lines.	120	250	375
420 Locomotive: die-cast, w/tender.	100	200	300
421 Tender:	35	70	100
422 Locomotive: 2-4-2.	125	250	375
423 Locomotive:	90	175	250
424 Locomotive: 2-4-4.	60	125	185
425 Locomotive: see 427.	100	200	300
427 Locomotive: 1939-40, 2-6-4.	200	400	600
429: see 431.			
431 Locomotive: 1939-40, 0-6-0.	425	850	1,275
432 Locomotive: 4-4-2.	300	600	900
434 Locomotive: 4-4-2.	350	700	1,050
436 Locomotive: 4-6-2.	550	1,100	1,650
437 Locomotive: 2-4-2.	280	560	850
449 Locomotive: 2-6-4.	840	1,680	2,520
472 Unloading Car: 1940-41, Army, w/Tootsietoy armored car.	60	115	175
474 Dump Car: automatic.	100	200	300
476 Gondola: 1940-41, green.	25	50	75
478 Boxcar: 1940-41, 1946, white w/red roof.	20	40	60
480 Tank Car: 1940, yellow, Shell, or silver and blue.	25	50	75
481 Wrecker Car: 1941, black or red frame.	40	80	120
482 Lumber Car: 1940-41, green or black.	30	65	95
483 Girder Car: 1941, black w/orange girder.	25	50	75
484 Caboose: 1940-46, red.	15	35	50
486 Hopper: 1940-41, yellow.	40	80	120
488 Floodlight Car:	50	100	150
490 Whistle Car: 1940-41, gray.	40	75	115
490B Whistle Car: 1940, blue.	40	75	115
492R Mail Pickup Car: 1941, red.	30	60	90
492G Mail Pickup Car: 1941, green.	30	60	90

472 Unloading Car

476 Gondola

478 Boxcar

480 Tank Car

480 Tank Car

481 Wrecker Car

482 Lumber Car

482 Lumber Car

483 Girder Car

484 Caboose

486 Hopper

490 Whistle Car

490B Whistle Car

492R Mail Pickup Car

	C5	C7	C8
492T Mail Pickup Car: 1941, tuscan.	$30	$60	$90
494R Baggage Car: 1940-41, red.	30	60	90
494G Baggage Car: 1940, green.	30	60	90
494B Baggage Car: 1940-41, blue.	30	60	90
494T Baggage Car: 1941, tuscan.	30	60	90
495R Coach Car: 1940-41, red.	35	70	100
495RL Coach Car: 1940-41, red, illuminated.	35	70	100
495G Coach Car: 1940-41, green.	35	70	100
495GL Coach Car: 1940-41, green, illuminated.	35	70	100
495B Coach Car: 1940-41, blue.	35	70	100
495BL Coach Car: 1940-41, blue, illuminated.	35	70	100
495T Coach Car: 1941, tuscan.	35	70	100
495TL Coach Car: 1941, tuscan, illuminated.	35	70	100
496RL Pullman: 1941, red, illuminated.	90	175	275
496GL Pullman: 1941, green, illuminated.	90	175	275
496T Pullman: 1941, tuscan.	90	175	275
496TL Pullman: 1941, tuscan, illuminated.	90	175	275
497R Observation Car: 1941, red.	50	95	150
497RL Observation Car: 1941, red, illuminated.	50	95	150
497GL Observation Car: 1941, green, illuminated.	50	95	150
497T Observation Car: 1941, tuscan.	50	95	150
497TL Observation Car: 1941, tuscan, illuminated.	50	95	150
504 Gondola: 1939-41, die-cast gray or tuscan.	100	200	300
504 Tender: Choo-choo and smoke unit.	25	50	75
506 Boxcar: 1939-41, Baltimore and Ohio, white.	50	100	150
508 Hopper: 1939-41, Virginian.	65	130	200
510 Cattle Car: 1939-41, Missouri Pacific, brown.	40	75	115
512 Tank Car: 1939-41, Texaco, silver or gray.	40	75	115
513 Observation Car:	15	25	40
514 Wrecker Car:	100	200	300
515 Automobile Car:	15	30	45
515 Coach Car: tin-plate, lithographed, yellow, red, black and orange, early.	15	25	40
516 Caboose: 1939-41, illuminated, UP or NYC.	45	85	125
518 Baggage Car:	25	50	75
519 Pullman:	25	50	75
521 Baggage-Club Car: 1939-41, tuscan.	100	200	300
524 Pullman: 1939-41, tuscan.	300	600	900
531 Locomotive: 4-6-4.	450	900	1,350
534 Locomotive: 4-8-4.	1,400	2,800	4,250
545 Locomotive: 1940, 4-4-2.	50	100	150
553 Locomotive: steam.	55	110	175
553 Tender:	40	75	115
555C Tender:	30	60	90
555 Tender: black.	20	40	60
556 Locomotive: Royal Blue, 1940-41, 4-6-2.	55	115	175
558C Tender: w/chugger.	35	65	100
558 Tender: w/out chugger.	25	50	75
559 Locomotive: 1940-41, 4-6-2, Pennsylvania K5.	175	350	525
561 Steam Locomotive: 1940-41, 4-6-2, Pennsylvania K5.	105	210	325
563C Locomotive: w/tender.	75	150	225

494B Baggage Car

495G Coach Car

495B Coach Car

504 Gondola

506 Boxcar

508 Hopper

510 Cattle Car

512 Tank Car

516 Caboose

521 Baggage-Club Car

524 Pullman

545 Locomotive

	C5	C7	C8
564 Locomotive: 4-6-4.	$1,250	$2,500	$2,750
564C Tender:	25	50	75
565 Locomotive:	75	150	225
568 Locomotive: 4-8-4.	1,500	3,000	4,500
570 Steam Locomotive: 1940-41, 4-6-4, New York Central J3, 3/16.			
	150	300	450
571 Steam Locomotive: 3/16 scale, 4-8-4.	200	400	600
572 Steam Locomotive: see 571.			
574B Locomotive: 0-8-0.	1,000	2,000	3,000
574 Locomotive: 0-8-0, switcher.	700	1,400	2,100
575B Locomotive: 0-8-0.	600	1,200	1,800
597 Passenger and Freight Station:	35	70	100
616 Locomotive: wind-up.	75	150	225
617 Locomotive: 2-4-2.	50	100	150
622 Locomotive:	40	80	125
640 Steam Locomotive: 1936, 0-4-2, black.	100	150	225
641 Locomotive: 2-4-2.	250	500	750
816 Locomotive: wind-up, three cars.	300	600	900
830 Locomotive: wind-up, two cars.	140	275	425
832 Locomotive: wind-up, three cars.	140	275	425
960T Locomotive: two cars.	175	350	525
961T Locomotive: 0-4-0, three cars.	140	275	425
964T Locomotive: three cars.	200	400	600
970T Hiawatha Set: includes locomotive tender, two coaches and observation car.			
	335	670	1,000
1025 Railway Express Mail Car:	30	60	90
1026 Passenger Car:	15	25	40
1045 Transformer: 25-watt.	15	20	35
1093 Locomotive: 1930-31.	220	440	675
1094 Locomotive:	350	700	1,100
1096 Box Cab Locomotive: 1925-27, 0-4-0, w/square headlight, rubber stamped.			
	75	150	225
1097 Engine: 0-4-0, lithographed, orange, green and red, w/nickel trim.			
	75	150	225
1102 Coach:	35	70	100
1103 Locomotive:	325	650	975
1103 Passenger Car:	30	60	100
1104 Baggage:	30	60	100
1105 Baggage Car: marked "American Express."	60	120	175
1105 Canadian National Railways Dominion Flyer: lithographed, red and black, w/nickel trim.			
	30	60	100
1106 Coach: lithographed, brown and black, marked "Dominion Flyer."			
	40	80	125
1106 Lumber Car: 1930, black.	20	35	60
1106 Parlor Car: lithographed, yellow, black and green.			
	30	60	100
1106 Parlor Car: lithographed, green w/black roof, four wheels.			
	30	60	100
1107 Coach Car: lithographed.	20	35	60
1108 Baggage Car: lithographed.	25	45	75
1109 Sand Car: lithographed, red.	20	35	60
1110 Boxcar:	25	50	75

556 Locomotive

559 Locomotive

561 Steam Locomotive

570 Steam Locomotive

1093 Locomotive

1096 Box Cab Locomotive

1107 Coach Car

1111 Caboose

	C5	C7	C8
1111 Caboose: 1919-35.	$25	$50	$75
1112 Boxcar: 1919-35, NYC Reefer, lithographed 1115 on side.			
	30	60	100
1112 Boxcar: 1930, lithographed, yellow.	35	70	110
1113 Gondola: 1925, lithographed, green.	20	35	60
1114 Caboose: lithographed, red, green and white, w/brass trim.			
	25	50	75
1115 Automobile Boxcar: later.	40	80	125
1115 Boxcar: see 1112.			
1116 Gondola:	25	50	75
1116 Sand Car:	60	120	200
1117 Caboose:	35	70	110
1118 Tank Car: lithographed, gray-white and black.	45	90	150
1119 Stock Car:	40	80	125
1120 Caboose:	25	50	75
1120 Observation Car: 1923-29.	25	50	75
1120 Passenger Car: 1923-29.	25	50	75
1121 Locomotive: w/whistle and tender, 2-4-0.	30	60	100
1122 Bluestreak Passenger Car:	25	50	75
1123 Passenger Car: tuscan.	20	40	60
1123 Passenger Car:	20	40	60
1124 Pullman:	60	120	200
1127 Caboose:	15	30	50
1128 Tank Car:	15	30	50
1141 Log Car:	40	80	125
1146 Log Car:	40	80	125
1147 Observation Car:	50	100	150
1157 Observation Car:	50	100	150
1200 Baggage Car: lithographed, four-wheel.	30	60	100
1200 Baggage Car: lithographed, eight-wheel.	30	60	100
1201 Locomotive: 1920-24, steeple cab, black or dark green.			
	45	90	140
1201 Passenger Car: lithographed, red w/black roof.	30	60	100
1202 Baggage Car: Express.	35	65	100
1202 Baggage Car: Electric Service.	40	80	125
1203 Coach Car: lithographed, eight-wheel, early.	35	65	100
1203 Passenger Car: lithographed, blue w/black roof.			
	35	65	100
1204 Baggage Car:	60	120	200
1205 Baggage Car: American Railway Express.	30	60	100
1205 Mail Car: 1924-26.	30	60	100
1206 Passenger Car: 1922-26, red or orange.	40	75	125
1206 Pullman:	40	75	125
1207 Observation Car: 1926.	40	75	125
1208 Locomotive:	80	160	250
1209 Observation Car:	60	120	200
1211 Locomotive: 1920-24, steeple cab, black or dark green.			
	45	90	150

1112 Boxcar

1115 Automobile Boxcar

1116 Gondola

1120 Observation Car

1120 Passenger Car

1201 Locomotive

1121 Locomotive

1205 Baggage Car

1205 Mail Car

	C5	C7	C8
1211 Passenger Coach:	$30	$60	$100
1212 Observation Car:	100	200	300
1213 Pullman:	60	120	200
1214 Baggage:	60	120	200
1217 Locomotive: 0-4-0, electric.	60	120	200
1218 Engine: 0-4-0, black, lettering on side, w/nickel and brass trim.			
	60	120	200
1218 Locomotive: 1920-25, red, black and yellow.	60	120	200
1218 Locomotive: 0-4-0, black, red and yellow, electric.			
	75	150	225
1219 Coach Car:	20	40	60
1223 Coach Car:	20	40	60
1225 Locomotive: 1919, 0-4-0, cast iron.	100	200	300
1257 Observation Car:	120	240	375
1270 Locomotive:	100	200	300
1286 Pullman:	45	90	150
1287 Observation Car: Chicago.	45	90	150
1290 Transformer:	30	40	100
1306 Passenger Car: 1922-26, four- or eight-wheel, blue, green, red or brown.			
	25	50	75
1322RT Locomotive: four cars.	550	1,100	1,700
1620 Pullman:	50	100	150
1621 Pullman:	65	135	200
1622 Observation Car:	65	135	200
1641 Hiawatha Coach: 1936-37.	50	150	250
1642 Hiawatha Observation: 1936-37.	50	150	250
1681 Locomotive: 2-6-4.	250	500	750
1683 Locomotive:	700	1,400	2,100
1684 Locomotive:	600	1,200	1,800
1686 Steam Locomotive: 1937, 4-4-2, streamlined.			
	110	220	350
1687 Locomotive: 2-4-2.	350	700	1,100
1688 Locomotive: 2-4-2.	150	275	425
1710 Locomotive:	75	150	225
1730RW Streamliner: 1935, Union Pacific, 51 in. long.			
	200	425	625
1736 Freight Set: B & O.	250	475	750
1835TW Tender:	75	150	225
2005 Triangle Light:	45	70	120
2010 Double Arc Lamppost: 12-1/2 in. high.	35	70	110
2020 Electric Loco: 4-4-4.	200	400	600
2020 Water Tank:	50	100	150
2029 Whistle Unit: remote control.	30	60	100
2043 Semaphore:	75	225	400
3000 Baggage: lithographed, black and two-tone green.			
	50	100	150
3001 Pullman: 1922-24, Illini.	50	100	150
3001 Pullman: 1922-24, Illini.	50	100	150
3004 Caboose: illuminated.	60	120	200
3005 Observation Car: Illini.	30	60	100
3006 Flatcar:	10	20	30
3007 Sand Car:	250	500	750
3008 Boxcar: 1925-27, lithographed, GN, ART, B & O, or Nickel Plate.			
	250	500	750

1206 Passenger Car

1207 Observation Car

1211 Locomotive

1218 Engine

1218 Locomotive

1306 Passenger Car

1641 Hiawatha Coach

1306 Passenger Car

1642 Hiawatha Observation

1686 Steam Locomotive

	C5	C7	C8
3009 Dump Car: 1934-35, decaled set.	$5	$10	$15
3010 Tank Car: gray w/black nickel trim.	50	100	150
3011 Locomotive:	100	175	275
3012 Auto Car:	50	100	150
3012 Boxcar: rubber stamped, decaled set.	15	30	45
3012 Locomotive: 0-4-0, lithographed, headlight in cab, electric.	100	200	300
3013 Gondola: decaled set.	25	50	75
3013 Locomotive:	400	800	1,250
3014 Caboose: decaled set.	25	50	75
3014 Locomotive:	550	1,100	1,700
3015 Auto Car:	25	50	75
3015 Boxcar:	20	40	60
3015 Locomotive: 1927, green.	150	275	425
3016 Sand Car:	25	50	75
3017 Caboose: eight-wheel.	15	25	40
3018 Tank Car: 1934-35, eight-wheel.	75	175	250
3018 Tank Car: 1930-32, yellow and black, w/copper trim.	30	65	100
3019 Dump Car: eight-wheel.	15	35	50
3019 Dump Car:	15	35	50
3019 Electric Loco: dark green, black frame and maroon windows, rubber stamped, headlight.	200	400	600
3020 Engine: 4-4-4, maroon and black, w/nickel trim.	250	500	750
3020 Engine: 4-4-4, black and yellow, w/nickel trim.	200	400	600
3025 Crane Car:	50	100	150
3045 Wrecker Car:	70	140	210
3046 Lumber Car: eight-wheel.	20	40	60
3080 Mail Car:	40	80	125
3081 Pullman: Illini.	40	80	125
3085 Observation Car: Columbia.	40	80	125
3100 Locomotive: 0-4-0 red, black, gold, w/brass trim and plates.	60	120	200
3102 Locomotive: 1926, lithographed.	50	100	150
3102 Tanker:	20	40	60
3103 Locomotive: 1930.	100	200	325
3105 Locomotive: blue.	140	240	400
3107 Engine: 0-4-0.	75	150	225
3107RC Locomotive:	250	500	750
3107 Lumber Car:	15	30	50
3109 Engine: 0-4-0, green, brown, w/brass trim.	200	300	400
3110 Locomotive: 1928-29, 0-4-0, w/headlight.	125	250	375
3111 Gondola:	20	40	60
3112 Boxcar: lithographed.	45	90	140
3112 Engine and Baggage Car: baggage car marked "United States Mail Railway Post Office."	125	250	375
3112 Hopper:	25	50	750
3113 Locomotive:	110	220	330
3113 Locomotive: 0-4-0, two-tone blue w/two-tone blue coaches marked "Nationwide Lines" made for J.C. Penney Co., extremely rare; set complete in original boxes.	500	1,000	1,400

3001 Pullman

3005 Observation Car

3008 Boxcar

3015 Locomotive

3018 Tank Car

3020 Engine

3020 Engine

3025 Crane Car

3100 Locomotive

3103 Locomotive

3105 Locomotive

3107 Engine

	C5	C7	C8
3113 Locomotive: 0-4-0, two-tone blue w/two-tone blue coaches marked, "American Flyer Bluebird," American Flyer Lines lettering.			
	$500	$1,000	$1,500
3115 Engine: 1928-30, 0-4-0, peacock blue, w/brass trim.			
	60	120	190
3116 Engine: 0-4-0, turquoise and black, w/brass trim.			
	200	400	600
3117 Engine: 0-4-0, red w/brass trim.	150	300	450
3140 Club Car:	70	140	225
3141 Coach Car: red, black and gold, w/brass trim.			
	50	90	150
3141 Pullman: red and black, w/brass trim.	50	90	150
3142 Observation Car: red, black and gold, w/brass trim.			
	50	90	150
3150 Baggage Car:	50	90	150
3151 Passenger Car:	30	55	90
3152 Observation Car: two-tone orange, w/brass trim.			
	50	100	150
3152 Passenger Car:	60	120	200
3160 Passenger Car:	60	120	200
3161 Passenger Car:	75	150	225
3162 Observation Car: turquoise, blue and gray, w/brass trim.			
	30	60	100
3171 Pullman: beige and green, w/brass trim.	20	40	60
3172 Observation Car: beige and green, w/brass trim.			
	20	40	60
3176 Pullman:	25	50	75
3177 Observation Car:	30	60	90
3178 Coach:	200	400	600
3180 Club Car: beige and green, w/brass trim, marked "Potomac."			
	40	75	120
3180 Club Car: two-tone red, green, w/brass trim.			
	25	50	75
3181 Pullman: beige and green, w/brass trim, marked "Potomac."			
	40	75	120
3182 Locomotive: 0-4-0.	200	400	600
3182 Observation Car: beige and green, w/brass trim, marked "Potomac."			
	40	75	120
3184 Locomotive: 0-4-0.	250	500	750
3185 Locomotive: turquoise/teal blue.	225	450	700
3186 Locomotive:	400	800	1,250
3187 Locomotive: 1928-32, red.	300	600	900
3188 Locomotive: 0-4-0.	250	500	750
3189 Tender: 1933, tin.	75	150	225
3190 Locomotive: 0-4-0, remote control reverse.	50	100	150
3191 Locomotive: 2-4-2.	160	320	500
3192 Locomotive: 1937.	40	80	125

3109 Engine

3110 Locomotive

3113 Locomotive

3115 Engine

3141 Pullman

3142 Observation Car

3150 Baggage Car

3151 Passenger Car

3152 Observation Car

3161 Passenger Car

3162 Observation Car

3171 Pullman

	C5	C7	C8
3192 Tender:	$55	$110	$175
3195 Locomotive: cast iron.	65	130	200
3197 Locomotive: 0-4-0.	250	500	750
3198 Locomotive: cast iron.	90	180	275
3201 Caboose:	25	50	75
3206 Flatcar: orange, w/lumber.	45	90	150
3207 Gondola:	20	35	60
3208 Boxcar: 1938, orange and blue.	55	110	175
3210 Tank Car: 1938, silver and green.	45	90	150
3211 Caboose:	40	75	120
3212 Milk Car: 1938.	40	80	125
3213 Floodlight Car:	75	150	225
3216 Log Car: 1937.	30	65	100
3219 Dump Car: 1938.	40	80	125
3280 Club Car: turquoise/teal blue.	90	180	275
3280 Club Car: two-tone blue, w/brass trim, marked "Golden State."	180	360	550
3281 Pullman: green and two-tone red, marked "Jeffersonian."	60	120	200
3281 Pullman: turquoise/teal blue, 1928-31, 1933-34.	90	180	275
3281 Pullman Car: two-tone blue, w/brass trim, marked "Golden State."	180	360	550
3282 Observation Car: two-tone blue, w/brass trim, marked "Golden State."	180	360	550
3282 Observation Car: turquoise/teal blue.	90	180	275
3302 Locomotive: 2-4-2.	250	500	750
3304 Locomotive: 2-4-2.	150	300	450
3307 Locomotive: bell in cab.	100	200	300
3308 Locomotive: 2-4-2.	150	300	450
3309 Locomotive: 2-4-2.	200	400	600
3310 Locomotive: 2-4-2.	100	200	300
3313 Locomotive: 2-4-2.	200	400	600
3315 Locomotive:	350	700	1,100
3316 Locomotive: 2-4-2.	30	60	100
3316 Tender:	20	40	60
3323 Locomotive: 2-4-2.	250	500	750
3324 Locomotive: 2-4-2.	250	500	750
3326 Locomotive: 2-4-2.	65	135	200
3380 Baggage Car: red w/dark red roof and brass window inserts and decals, eight-wheel, lighted.	60	120	190
3381 Coach Car: red w/dark red roof and brass window insert and decal, eight-wheel, lighted.	60	120	190
3382 Observation Car: red w/dark red roof and brass window insert and decal, eight-wheel, lighted.	60	120	190
3541 Pullman:	70	140	225
3542 Observation Car:	70	140	225
3579 Pullman:	40	80	125
3750 Coach:	50	100	150
3751 Coach:	50	100	150
3752 Observation Car:	75	150	225

3172 Observation Car

3187 Locomotive

3212 Milk Car

3280 Club Car

3281 Pullman

3281 Pullman Car

3282 Observation Car

3282 Observation Car

3310 Locomotive

1205 Baggage Car

1286 Pullman

	C5	C7	C8
4002 Locomotive: 2-6-4, black and white, w/copper trim, w/tender.			
	$50	$100	$150
4321 Locomotive: 0-6-0, black and white, w/nickel trim, w/tender.			
	115	225	350
4403 Locomotive:	75	150	225
4603 Locomotive: 2-4-4.	150	300	450
4615 Locomotive: 2-4-2.	350	700	1,100
4629 Locomotive:	150	300	450
4677 Locomotive:	300	600	950
4890 Pullman:	40	80	125
5130 Observation Car:	45	90	150
5160 Caboose: Union Pacific.	25	50	75
5640 Hudson: 4-6-4, w/tender.	350	700	1,100
9217 Street Lamp: green metal.	15	30	45
9910 Locomotive: cast aluminum, electric, Burlington Zephyr.			
	265	525	800
9910 Locomotive: wind-up, Burlington Zephyr.			
	85	175	275
9910 Locomotive: tinplate, electric, Burlington Zephyr.			
	125	275	400
9911 Baggage Car:	150	300	450
9912 Observation Car:	150	300	450
9913 Pullman:	150	300	450
9914 Locomotive:	400	800	1,200
9915 Locomotive:	600	1,200	1,800
22006 Transformer: 25-watt.	45	60	110
25671 Track Trip:	2	4	6
26672 Track Trip:	2	4	6
26782 Trestle Set:	25	45	70

1287 Observation Car

AMT

American Model Toys (later Auburn Model Trains) was incorporated in May 1948 by John "Jack" W. Ferris in Fort Wayne, Ind. Ferris was not a newcomer to the manufacturing of toy trains–he had been involved in the industry as far back as the late 1920s. His first firm, Scale Model Railways, was ultimately sold to Megow. The first products of his new firm, commonly known as AMT, were sand-cast O-Gauge aluminum passenger cars. These illuminated passenger cars included two Roomette Pullmans and an Observation, and were painted with the colors and markings of the New York Central and Pennsylvania railroads. Very early in the company's history the firm relocated from Ft. Wayne about 25 miles to Auburn, Ind.

With no other comparable O-Gauge streamlined passenger cars on the market, Ferris' fledgling firm flourished. After only a brief period producing the sand-cast cars, production switched to using extruded aluminum bodies with die-cast frames. These changes were made at the urging of Carter Collier, AMT's chief engineer. These cars, which came in eight styles–Baggage, Mail, Crew Combination, Day Coach, Pullman Bedroom-Roomette, Diner, Vista Dome, and Observation–had smooth roofs and included interior illumination. The series was offered in the markings of the Santa Fe and New York Central railroads, an obvious

attempt to capitalize on the success of Lionel's streamlined F-3 diesels, introduced in 1948.

Building on the success of these O-Gauge streamliners, the firm began offering HO-Gauge counterparts in 1951. The following year, AMT introduced a series of large colorful boxcars. These boxcars, much larger than the 3464-series cars Lionel was offering at the time and much more elaborately decorated, no doubt pushed Lionel into the creation of their famous 6464 boxcars. However, as had been the case with the streamliners, AMT briefly enjoyed a monopoly and good sales, which lead to the offering of additional types of freight cars in 1953. These cars included Stock, Refrigerator, Depressed Center Flat, and Cabooses.

The second major breakthrough of 1953 was AMT's introduction of their model of a Budd Rail Diesel Car (RDC). Though not a spectacular seller for the Indiana firm, it did precede a similar offering from Lionel by three years.

Bigger news however was AMT's introduction of its own locomotive, patterned after the EMD F-7. Powered by a seven-pole Pittman motor and equipped with traction tires, these locomotives proved to have excellent performance.

Alas, despite its fine products, the firm was under assault by Lionel,
who viewed them as a threat, and hampered by its own liberal credit and
sales policies with distributors. Thus, when Nashville-based Kusan Corp.
approached Ferris in 1953 with an offer to purchase, it was well received.
Ultimately the entire AMT operation, including inventory and tooling
were moved south, where they continued to be sold, with some changes,
under the KMT logo.

Today, AMT continues to have a small but loyal following of
collectors who prize the colorful and well-made trains.

	C5	C7	C8

AMT Sand-Cast Passenger Cars

These cars, the first offered by AMT, were all illuminated and equipped with
sprung trucks.

Pennsylvania
1001 Pullman: City of Altoona.	$75	$125	$175
1002 Pullman: City of Fort Wayne.	75	125	175
1003 Observation: Skyline View.	75	125	175

New York Central
1004 Pullman: City of Toledo.	75	125	175
1005 Pullman: City of Buffalo.	75	125	175
1006 Observation: Manhattan Island.	75	125	175

Extruded Aluminum Cars

About 1949-50, AMT began manufacturing their streamlined passenger
cars with extruded aluminum bodies, rather than the sand castings used
previously. Among notable variations include the length of the nameplates on
the cars. Except for C & NW plates, the bulk of AMT's nameplates were 4-1/4
in. long, though some occasionally turn up with four-inch plates. Further, the
Bedroom-Roomette cars could also be purchased with prototypically correct
"Pullman" lettering rather than a specific road name–today this variation is
difficult to locate.

The window glazing came most often in blue plastic, but some had
two-piece acetate windows, the outer layer clear, the inner frosted. The vista
domes too came in blue, which often warp, or white, which are frequently
found cracked. Also, cars were available new with either smooth or fluted roofs.
Originally, the fluted roof cars were lower cost, but today on the collector market
they command a slight premium. The prices listed below are for the smooth-roof
versions. Finally, catalog number, rather than the number on the side of the car
lists the cars below.

"Texas Special" Set: Aluminum cars with red painted trim wearing the markings of
the Missouri-Kansas-Texas and Frisco jointly operated Texas Special passenger train.
1001 Mail Express: Number plate reads "3407."	75	125	200
1002 Roomette: "BOWIE."	75	125	200
1003 Diner: Number plate reads "DINER."	75	125	200
1004 Vista Dome: "CROCKETT."	75	125	200
1005 Observation: "SAM HOUSTON."	75	125	200

	C5	C7	C8
1006 Day Coach: Number plate reads "3160."	$75	$125	$200
1007 Crew Combination: Number plate reads "5260."	75	125	200
1008 Baggage: Number plate reads "4170."	75	125	200
2001 Mail Express: Number plate reads "3407."	40	75	125
2002 Roomette:			
(Type I) Number plate reads "INDIAN LAKE."	40	75	125
(Type II) Number plate reads "INDIAN SCOUT."	40	75	125
2003 Diner: "DINER."	40	75	125
2004 Vista Dome: "BUENA VISTA."	40	75	125
2005 Observation: "INDIAN ARROW."	40	75	125
2006 Day Coach: Number plate reads "3160."	40	75	125
2007 Crew Combination: Number plate reads "5264."	40	75	125
2008 Baggage: Number plate reads "4170."	40	75	125
New York Central Set: Large letterboard reads "NEW YORK CENTRAL." w/smaller plates carrying numbers and car names.			
3001 Mail Express: Number plate reads "3407."	40	75	125
3002 Roomette:			
(Type I) "CITY OF DETROIT."	40	75	125
(Type II) "CITY OF ERIE."	40	75	125
(Type III) "CITY OF UTICA."	40	75	125
3003 Diner: "DINER."	40	75	125
3004 Vista Dome: "BUENA VISTA."	40	75	125
3005 Observation: "SENECA FALLS."	40	75	125
3006 Day Coach: Number plate reads "3160."	40	75	125
3007 Crew Combination: Number plate reads "5260."	40	75	125
3008 Baggage: Number plate reads "4170."	40	75	125
Pennsylvania Set: Large letterboard reads "PENNSYLVANIA" w/smaller plates carrying numbers and car names.			
4001 Mail Express: Number plate reads "3407."	40	75	125
4002 Roomette:			
(Type I) "CITY OF PITTSBURGH."	40	75	125
(Type II) "FORT WAYNE."	40	75	125
4003 Diner: "DINER."	40	75	125
4004 Vista Dome: "CITY OF NEW YORK."	40	75	125
4005 Observation: "CITY OF CHICAGO."	40	75	125
4006 Day Coach: Number plate reads "3160."	40	75	125
4007 Crew Combination: Number plate reads "5260."	40	75	125
4008 Baggage: Number plate reads "4170."	40	75	125
Southern Set: All cars bear a large plate on each side reading "SOUTHERN" and small plates w/additional lettering.			
5001 Mail Express: Number plate reads "3407."	75	125	200
5002 Roomette:			
(Type I) "CATAWBA RIVER."	75	125	200
(Type II) "POTOMAC RIVER."	75	125	200
(Type III) "DAN RIVER."	75	125	200
5003 Diner: "DINER."	75	125	200
5004 Vista Dome: "GEORGIA."	75	125	200
5005 Observation: "CRESCENT CITY."	75	125	200

Santa Fe Set: Large letterboard reads "SANTA FE" w/smaller plates carrying numbers and car names.

6755 Southern

8644 Pennsylvania

34922 Santa Fe

3162 Southern

9241 Santa Fe

	C5	C7	C8
5006 Day Coach: Number plate reads "3160."	$75	$125	$200
5007 Crew Combination: Number plate reads "5260."	75	125	200
5008 Baggage: Number plate reads "4170."	75	125	200

Chicago & Northwestern Set: These cars were attractively painted in the yellow and green scheme of the CNW. The "CHICAGO & NORTHWESTERN" nameplates on these cars are significantly larger than the nameplates on the other cars. Once again, smaller plates were used for names and numbers.

6001 Mail Express: Number plate reads "3407."	80	150	250
6002 Roomette: "NORTHERN PINES."	80	150	250
6003 Diner: "DINER."	80	150	250
6004 Vista Dome: "NORTHERN STREAMS."	80	150	250
6005 Observation: "NORTHERN STATES."	80	150	250
6006 Day Coach: Number plate reads "3160."			

Too rarely traded to establish accurate pricing.

6007 Crew Combination: Number plate reads "5260."	80	150	250
6008 Baggage: Number plate reads "4170."	80	150	250

Baltimore & Ohio Set: Large letterboard is marked "BALTIMORE & OHIO" and small plates have additional lettering.

7001 Mail Express: Number plate reads "3407."

Too rarely traded to establish accurate pricing.

	C5	C7	C8

7002 Roomette: "YOUNGSTOWN."
Too rarely traded to establish accurate pricing.

7003 Diner: "DINER." Too rarely traded to establish accurate pricing.

7004 Vista Dome: "CAPITOL CITY."
Too rarely traded to establish accurate pricing.

7005 Observation: "WAWASEE." Too rarely traded to establish accurate pricing.

7006 Day Coach: Number plate reads "3160."
Too rarely traded to establish accurate pricing.

7007 Crew Combination: Number plate reads "5260."
Too rarely traded to establish accurate pricing.

7008 Baggage: Number plate reads "4170."
Too rarely traded to establish accurate pricing.

AMT F-7 Diesel Locomotives

322 Santa Fe: F-7 A-unit, catalog number F2. Painted in Santa Fe's freight paint scheme of dark blue and yellow w/yellow lettering. Typically AMT production has a slightly humped body.

	C5	C7	C8
Powered	$100	$140	$180
Dummy	50	70	110

1733 New York Central: F7 A-unit, catalog number F3. These locos were painted in the two-tone gray "lightning stripe" scheme of the New York Central. The lettering was white.

Powered	120	160	200
Dummy	55	80	130

2019 Missouri, Kansas & Texas (The Texas Special): F7 A-unit, catalog number F1. Finished in the red, silver and black paint scheme worn by the "Texas Special" passenger train. The upper portion of the nose was painted to simulate an antiglare panel.

Powered	120	160	225
Dummy	75	125	175

5400 Chicago & Northwestern: F7 A-unit, catalog number F6. Finished in yellow and green paint scheme. Fuel tank skirts are yellow.

Powered	140	190	250
Dummy	80	140	200

6755 Southern: F7 A-unit, catalog number F5; green and gray paint; w/yellow lettering, gray roof, black fuel tank skirts.

Powered	125	160	225
Dummy	70	110	160

8644 Pennsylvania: F7 A-unit, catalog number F4, bright tuscan red.

Powered	120	150	210
Dummy	60	100	150

Baltimore & Ohio: F7 A-unit, catalog number F7; painted dark blue, gray, and yellow w/yellow lettering.

Powered	180	300	400
Dummy	100	150	200

CB & Q Burlington: F7 A-unit: silver, red, and black paint; AMT production.
Too rarely traded to establish accurate pricing.

Boxcars

Introduced in 1951, these boxcars represented a substantial improvement over competitive products. Well detailed, some of these cars were also colorfully decorated.

2227 Canadian Pacific: Cataloged as number 8007, this car was painted tuscan w/ white lettering.

	15	25	40

4382 Minneapolis & St. Louis "Merchandiser": Cataloged as number 9004, this car had yellow lettering on green body paint. Its doors were green as well.

	15	30	45

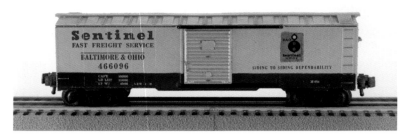

466096 Baltimore & Ohio "Sentinel"

	C5	C7	C8
13057 Nickel Plate: Cataloged as number 8006, this car was painted tuscan w/white lettering.	$15	$25	$40
19509 Great Northern: Cataloged as number 8002, these cars wore tuscan paint; w/white lettering. Black doors were installed.	15	25	40
25439 Erie: Assigned catalog number 8003, this car was painted tuscan and decorated w/black and white markings.			
(Type I) Lettered "CU FT 3769," black doors.	10	20	35
(Type II) Lettered "CU FT 3730," black doors.	20	40	60
(Type III) Lettered "CU FT 3770," black doors.	25	45	65
(Type IV) Reporting marks printed in two columns, fitted w/tuscan doors.	30	50	75
30565 New York, New Haven & Hartford: Cataloged as number 8005; black doors and white lettering highlighted this otherwise tuscan boxcar.	15	25	40
34922 Santa Fe: Assigned catalog number 8004, this tuscan boxcar w/black doors was lettered in white.	10	20	30
56312 Pennsylvania Merchandise Service: Cataloged as number 9002, the distinctive white band and red lettering of the "Merchandise Service" logo runs across the top of this brown boxcar.	20	30	45
153902 Southern: The AMT catalog listed this tuscan w/white lettering car as number 8001.	15	25	40
174479 New York Central "Pacemaker": Cataloged as number 9001, this car wore the distinctive red and gray "Pacemaker" paint scheme.	15	25	40
466096 Baltimore & Ohio "Sentinel": The brilliant blue and silver "Sentinel" paint scheme adorned AMT's catalog number 9003.	20	30	45
523977 Canadian National: Cataloged as number 8008, this tuscan boxcar was decorated w/green and white lettering.	25	40	55

	C5	C7	C8

Rail Diesel Cars (RDCs)

The AMT Rail Diesel Cars had plastic bodies housing a seven-pole electric motor. Introduced in 1953, it continued to be offered after the Kusan takeover. All were numbered "3160" on their bodies.

	C5	C7	C8
New York Central: Catalog number 1-33.	$75	$110	$150
Pennsylvania: Catalog number 1-44.	60	90	125
Santa Fe: Catalog number 1-22.	80	110	140
Southern: Catalog number 1-55.	75	110	150

Following up on the success of their boxcars, in 1953 AMT launched a line of new scale-sized freight cars.

Cabooses

Cabooses came with either black or yellow frames and steps, with the yellow steps warranting a premium of about 20 percent over the prices listed here.

	C5	C7	C8
104 Santa Fe: This caboose, painted in traditional red paint, was assigned catalog number C22. Its lettering was white.	30	45	65
832 Pennsylvania: This caboose, painted in traditional red paint, was assigned catalog number C24. Its lettering was white.	30	45	65
1216 New York Central: This caboose too was painted in traditional red paint. Its catalog number was C23. Its lettering was white.	30	45	65
3162 Southern: Yet another red caboose w/white lettering, this car was given catalog number C25.	40	55	85
90079 Chesapeake & Ohio: Cataloged as number C26, this red-painted caboose had white lettering.	45	65	100

Depressed-Center Flatcars

	C5	C7	C8
412 Monon: Cataloged as number 7351, this sand-cast aluminum car was painted gray w/red lettering.	20	45	75

Gondolas

	C5	C7	C8
51297 Louisville & Nashville: This shiny black car w/white lettering was given catalog number 7651.	15	35	60

Refrigerator Cars

	C5	C7	C8
1008 Gerber's: Cataloged as number 7251, this multi-colored car had sides painted blue and white, its roof red, ends white, and the lettering blue.	20	40	70
9241 Santa Fe: Cataloged w/number 7252, this car had yellow sides and ends, and a red-brown roof. The lettering was black.	20	35	65

Stock Cars

	C5	C7	C8
32066 Chicago, Burlington & Quincy: This tuscan-sided car w/black and white markings was given catalog number 7151.	15	25	35
47150 Missouri, Kansas & Texas: Assigned catalog number 7150 was this yellow-sided car w/black roof and white lettering.	20	30	45
140449 Atlantic Coast Line: This tuscan car was given catalog number 7152. It had white lettering.	15	25	35

DORFAN

Dorfan produced trains only from 1924-1933, but during that time it was one of the Big Four of American train making, along with Ives, Lionel and American Flyer.

Julius and Milton Forcheimer worked for their cousin's firm of Joseph Kraus & Co. in Nürnberg, Germany until 1923. At that time, Julius left his position in production and Milton his in sales departments, and moved to the United States. They brought with them not only the German firm's chief engineer, John C. Koerber, but also, to a certain extent the company name. Joseph Kraus & Co. marketed their trains as the "Fandor" line, named after Milton and Julius' mothers, Fanny and Dora. Once in America, the names were reversed and Dorfan was born.

The experience afforded by this management team, coupled with the booming American toy market of the 1920s, put the new company in a prime position. Eager to set themselves apart from other toy train makers, the firm introduced the die-cast zinc-alloy locomotive body. This material afforded most of the heft of cast iron toys, but was considerably more resilient. In fact, Dorfan referred to the material as "unbreakable." Dorfan's products however did have some problems. In fact, Dorfan's claims to fame, and infamy, were one and the same.

Zinc-alloy die-casting was a relatively new science at the time, and not fully understood. Cleanliness and purity of material are very important to the quality of die-casting. Impurities in the alloy over time cause the metal to expand, become very fragile and eventually crumble. Sadly, this was the case with the bulk of Dorfan's castings. Accordingly, it is very, very difficult today to find Dorfan locomotives with intact, solid castings. Fortunately for the operator, replacement reproduction body castings have been produced by a number of small firms, allowing the well-engineered Dorfan mechanisms to continue to operate.

Dorfan produced trains in both "Wide Gauge"—running on the same size track as Lionel's Standard Gauge, and "1-3/8-in." or Narrow Gauge track—equal to Lionel's O-Gauge.

However, despite the company's originality and the quality of its product, the stock market crash of 1929 and the Depression were fatal to the company. Production ceased about 1934, and the remaining inventory relocated to the company offices, from which it was liquidated through 1936.

Dorfan's Innovations

Die-cast locomotive bodies.

Easily assembled locomotive construction sets.

Upright lamppost.

Switchboard or "Panel Board."

Lacquered lithographed cars.

Sets to build both locomotive and motor from same parts.

Double-track O-Gauge working hopper car.

Inserted window frames in passenger cars (inserted from outside of car).

One-unit removable drive wheels and axles.

First automatic circuit breaker.

Die-cast trucks.

Die-cast car wheels.

Ball-bearing locomotive.

O-Gauge derrick car.

Die-cast steam-outline electric locomotive.

Remote-controlled train-stop signals.

Directional remote control for locomotives.

Steam-type locomotives with separate polished metal domes and stacks.

Model position-light signals.

Model signal bridge.

Remote control uncoupler.

410 Bridge

605 Hopper

3931 Electric Locomotive

610 Derrick

	C5	C7	C8
50 Electric Locomotive: Narrow-Gauge, red.	$150	$200	$250
51 Electric Locomotive: 1925-33, 0-B-0, "Take-Apart" locomotive, red, brown, maroon, dark green, turquoise, orange, or olive.	80	150	200
52 Electric Locomotive: 1928-33, 0-B-0, "Take-Apart" locomotive dark green, orange, blue, or olive.	75	150	225
53 Electric Locomotive: 1927-33, 0-B-0, red, blue, black, or apple green.	225	325	425
53-RC Electric Locomotive: 1930-33, 0-B-0, red, blue, black, or apple green.	225	325	425
54 Locomotive: 0-B-0, 1930-33, silver-blue, w/or w/out air tanks.	150-175	275-325	375-425
54-RC Locomotive: 0-B-0, 1930-33, silver-blue, w/or w/out air tanks.	150-175	275-325	375-425
54 Locomotive: 0-4-0, silver and gray, w/brass trim.	180	360	550
55 Electric Locomotive: 0-B-0, 1928-33, black, blue or red.	175	250	350
70 Automatic Electric Crane: 1929-30.	1,200	1,900	2,750
84: see 604.			
145 Electric Locomotive: 0-B-0, 1925-?, Narrow-Gauge, orange or red.	150	200	275
154 Steam Locomotive: 0-4-0, 1929-30, Narrow-Gauge, black.	150	200	275
155 Steam Locomotive: 0-4-0, 1925-30, Narrow-Gauge, red.	125	175	250
156 Steam Locomotive: 0-4-0, 1928-30, Narrow-Gauge, black.	150	200	275
157 Steam Locomotive: 0-4-0, 1928-30, Narrow-Gauge, black, blue or green.	150	200	275
160 Tender:	35	70	100
310 Tunnel: 1925-30, lithographed folding tunnel, 7-3/8-in. long.	20	40	65
319 Tunnel: 1930, 8-1/4 in. long, composition.	15	30	40
320 Tunnel: 1925-30, eight in. long, lithographed, folding, sign reads "Dorfan Heights."	15	30	40
321 Tunnel: 1927-30, 11-1/4 in. long, composition.	15	30	40
322 Tunnel: 1927-30, 12-1/4 in. long, composition.	15	30	40
323 Tunnel: 1927-30, 14-1/4 in. long, composition.	20	35	50
330 Semaphore: 1925-27, seven in. tall.	10	20	30
340 Danger Signal: 1925-30, seven in. tall, w/diamond-shaped warning signs.	10	20	30
350 Telegraph Pole: 1925, seven in. tall, w/two insulators on crossarm.	8	12	20
351 Lamppost: 1925, non-operating, seven in. long.	5	10	15
355 Pullman: 1925-30, Narrow-Gauge, four wheels, 5-1/2 in. long, yellow w/orange roof, red w/black roof, or orange w/black roof, dark red.	20	45	65
356 Pullman: 1930, Narrow-Gauge, four wheels, 6-3/4 in. long.	30	55	85
370 Telegraph Pole: 1926-30, seven in. tall, w/two insulators on crossarm.	8	12	20
375 Crossover: 45-degree, two-rail, Narrow-Gauge.	5	10	15
385 Pair of Manual Turnouts: two-rail, Narrow-Gauge.	10	20	30
400 Automatic Block Signal: Narrow-Gauge, 1925-30.	20	40	80

	C5	C7	C8
401 Control Block Signal: Narrow-Gauge, 1926-30.	$20	$40	$80
402 Semaphore: 1927-30, Narrow-Gauge, olive green, 12 in. tall.	15	35	70
405 Switchboard: 1925-26, control stand w/six knife switches.	15	25	50
406 Bell Signal: 1928-30, 8-1/2 in. tall grade crossing signal w/bell, Narrow-Gauge.	15	30	60
406 Power Switch House: 1926-27, structure contains a 405.	125	250	400
407 Switchboard: 1926-30, control stand w/six knife switches.	15	25	50
410 Bridge: 1925-30, Narrow-Gauge, green base w/red girders and orange deck, 30 in. long.	30	70	150
411 Bridge: 1926-30, Narrow-Gauge, 40 in. long due to double center span.	50	150	300
412 Electra Bridge: 1927-30, Narrow-Gauge, 40 in. long due to double center span, lights of four corner posts.	100	275	500
415 Telegraph Pole: 1927-30, 8-1/2 in. tall, w/two insulators on crossarm.	8	12	20
416 Warning Signal: 1927-30, 8-1/2-in. tall grade crossing signal, Narrow-Gauge.	20	30	40
417 Position-Light Signal: 1930.	30	50	100
417 Newark Central Station: 1927-29, illuminated, three-story, lithographed.	125	200	400
418 Signal Bridge w/One-Position-Light Signal: 1930.	125	250	500
418 Montclair Station: 1927-29, non-illuminated, two-story, lithographed.	75	125	200
419 Signal Bridge w/Two-Position-Light Signal: 1930.	150	300	600
420 Boulevard Light: 1925-30, seven in. tall.	10	15	25
421 Automatic Crossing Gate: 1929-30, Narrow-Gauge.	20	40	75
424 Station: 1930, non-illuminated, two-story, lithographed.	75	125	200
425 Station: 1930, illuminated, w/flag and clock, cream or blue-gray w/red roof.	60	100	150
426 Station: 1930, illuminated, three-story, lithographed.	125	200	400
427 Station: 1930, illuminated, 18-1/2 in. long, 9-1/2 in. deep, cream, two clock faces fenced roof w/flagpole.	400	1,000	1,500
430 Lamppost: 1925-30, 8-1/2 in. tall, 14 volts.	10	15	25
431 Lamppost: 1930, 13-1/2 in. tall, 110 volts.	15	25	50
432 Flagpole: 1930, 20-1/2 in. tall, U.S. flag can be raised and lowered.	1,200	5,000	9,000
433 Lamppost: 1930, 13-1/2 in. tall, 14 volts.	15	25	50
465 Track Binders (clips): 1928-30, fits both narrow and wide gauge track per dozen.	35	50	75
470 Pullman: 1925-30, Narrow-Gauge, four wheels, 6-3/4 in. long, dark red body and roof (1925), dark red w/black roof (1926-30), green w/yellow roof (1929-30), or green body and roof (1930); lettered "5402" along w/one of the names Franklin, Hamilton, Washington, Jefferson.	30	50	70
475 Crossover: 1925-30, Narrow-Gauge, 45-degree, three-rail.	15	25	40
480 Pullman: 1925-27, Narrow-Gauge, four wheels, 6-3/4 in. long, brown w/brass plates in 1925, or orange w/decal lettering in 1926-27.	40	60	85

	C5	C7	C8
485 Turnouts: 1925-30, Narrow-Gauge, three-rail, pair.	$15	$35	$75
485-L Turnouts: 1925-30, Narrow-Gauge, three-rail, pair w/signal lights.	25	50	90
490 Pullman: 1925-30, Narrow-Gauge, eight wheels, 7-1/4 in. long, dark green, olive green, red, blue, or **turquoise, lettering w/plates** or decal.	25-40	40-70	80-110
491 Observation: 1926-29, Narrow-Gauge, eight wheels, 7-1/4 in. long, olive green, red, blue, or **turquoise, lettering w/plates** or decal.	25-40	40-70	80-110
492 Baggage Car: 1928-30, eight wheels, 10 in. long, green, green and red or green and black.	60	120	175
493 Pullman: 1928-30, eight wheels, 10 in. long, green, green and red or green and black.	40	65	110
494 Observation: 1928-30, eight wheels, 10 in. long, green, green and red or green and black.	50	85	125
495 Pullman: 1928-30, eight wheels, 7-1/4 in. long, lettered Atlanta, Boston or Seattle, maroon, orange, blue or red.	20	45	70
496 Pullman: 1928-30, eight wheels, 10 in., lettered "Boston," green, green and red or green and black.	65	110	150
496 Pullman: 1929-30, eight wheels, nine in. long, blue, red or silver-blue.	35	60	100
497 Observation Car: 1929-30, eight wheels, nine in. long, blue, red or silver-blue.	35	60	100
498 Pullman: 1930, eight wheels, 7-1/4 in. long, red, olive green, turquoise or brown.	40	60	85
499 Observation Car: 1930, eight wheels, 7-1/4 in. long, red, olive green, turquoise or brown.	40	60	85
600 Gondola: 1926-30, Narrow-Gauge, yellow.	20	30	50
601 Boxcar: 1926-30, Narrow-Gauge, NYC, tan.	20	35	65
602 Boxcar: 1926-30, Narrow-Gauge, UP, green.	20	35	65
603 Boxcar: 1926-30, Narrow-Gauge, Pennsylvania, red.	20	35	65
604 Tank Car: 1926-30 Narrow-Gauge, red.	25	45	75
605 Hopper: 1926-30, Narrow-Gauge, gray.	20	30	45
606 Caboose: 1926-30, Narrow-Gauge, red.	20	45	75
607 Caboose: 1928-30, Narrow-Gauge, red.	45	65	90
609 Lumber Car: Narrow-Gauge, 1929-30.	35	65	125
610 Derrick: Narrow-Gauge, 1929-30.	65	150	300
770 Steam Locomotive: 4-4-0. Exceptionally rare.			
3677 Caboose: see 606.			
3919 Electric Locomotive: 0-B-0, 1930, orange.	275	700	1,100
3931 Tank Car: see 604.			
3931 Electric Locomotive: 2-B-2, 1930, green, black or ivory.	1,200	1,800	3,000
5402 Coach: see 470.			
11201: see 605.			
11701: see 805.			
14048: see 600.			
29325 Tank Car: see 804.			
121499 Boxcar: see 801.			
126432 Boxcar: see 602.			
253711 Gondola: see 800.			
486751 Caboose: see 606 or 806.			
517953 Boxcar: see 603.			
S182999 Boxcar: see 601.			

HAFNER

The name Hafner is often met with blank looks from many train collectors, which is unfortunate given the deep involvement of the Hafner family with the toy train industry.

William Hafner's first involvement with toy manufacturing was through the Toy Auto Co., which he founded in 1901. This Chicago firm produced mechanical (windup) replicas of early American cars. The firm operated under the name of William F. Hafner Co. from 1902 into 1907.

About 1905, Hafner began tinkering with O-Gauge trains, powered by the clockwork motor he had perfected in his miniature automobiles. Lacking capital to develop this aspect of the business, it remained little more than a curiosity for Hafner. This was soon to change though. In 1907, William Hafner took examples of his mechanical trains and called on Steinfield Bros. of New York City. Steinfield, a major toy distributor, was impressed with Hafner and his trains, and he left their offices with an order for $15,000 worth of trains—a respectable sum, especially in context of the times.

While Hafner was still under-capitalized, word of his hefty Eastern order reached William O. Coleman, Sr., owner of Burley and Co.—a noted china and porcelain distributor in Chicago. Coleman also had a financial interest in a local hardware-manufacturing firm, Edmonds-Metzel.

A deal was struck, Hafner joined Coleman's Edmonds-Metzel firm the same year and Edmonds Metzel set about manufacturing Hafner's trains. Soon the popularity of the trains was such that they became Edmonds-Metzel's sole product. By 1910, it had been decided that the endeavor was worthy of a more evocative name, and the name American Flyer Manufacturing was selected.

	C5	C7	C8
Caboose: No. 3057.	$8	$12	$16
Caboose: No. 41021.	10	14	18
Caboose: No. 81932.	8	12	16
Gondola: No. 91746.	4	8	12
Hopper: No. 91876.	12	18	25
Locomotive: No. 109.	20	40	60
Locomotive: No. 112.	40	75	100
Locomotive and Tender: No. 1010, black and silver or red and silver.			
	15	30	45
Locomotive and Tender: No. 115041.	15	30	45
Locomotive and Tender: No. 2000.	15	40	60

As too often happens with such organizations, the relationship was short lived and in 1914 William Hafner left American Flyer. Hafner set up shop, still in Chicago, producing his own line of trains, which he branded Overland Flyer.

Hafner's new business prospered—the interruption of European imports due to World War I no doubt helping the fledgling firm—and soon the company relocated to larger facilities. While trains were the bulk of Hafner's products, they were not the only toys—or even goods—that were produced. Full-sized lawn chairs, tools and Christmas tree stands joined miniature cars and submarines.

The growing company relocated yet again in 1930 to 1010 North Kolmar Ave. in Chicago. It would be there that John Hafner, William's son, would bring production to a halt in March 1951.

Electing not to embrace the electric train craze that swept the nation, Hafner remained true to William's clockwork mechanism until the end. Hafner did not believe his firm had the wherewithal for the complexities of electric train production. This led to an unlikely alliance, with Hafner's clockwork trains being imported and sold overseas by none other than the Lionel Corp.

While on paper the firm merged in 1950 with Chicago plastic's manufacturer Wallace A. Erickson Co., effectively the merger achieved little. When John Hafner decided to cease production in 1951, the remaining inventory, tools and dies were sold to the All Metal Products Co. of Wyandotte, Mich.—ending the long chapter of toy trains known as Hafner and opening the short chapter known as Wyandotte.

	C5	C7	C8
Overland Flyer Set: green.	$90	$125	$175
Overland Flyer Set: red and cream.	75	100	125
Santa Fe Boxcar:	10	15	25
Santa Fe Refrigerator Car:	10	15	25
Tanker: No. 1010.	10	14	20
Tender: No. 78100.	4	8	12
Tender: No. 90131.	4	8	12
Train Set: freight, w/No. 2000 Locomotive.	60	120	140
Union Pacific Streamliner Train Set: No. M10000.	75	100	150

HOGE

Unlike the firms listed in this volume, Hoge Manufacturing Co. (pronounced "Hoagy") never actually manufactured trains. Rather, they commissioned Mattatuck Manufacturing Co. of Waterbury, Ct. to produce the items, which Hoge then sold through its New York sales office. Mattatuck Manufacturing Co. was, and is, a diversified firm producing a wide array of products ranging from handcuffs to automotive wiring harnesses.

Hampden Hoge formed his company in Manhattan in December 1909, with an eye towards office products. From the beginning into the 1930s, Hoge produced staples and staplers, thumbtacks, clocks, and other items found in the workplace. In less than 10 years, Hampden Hoge had left the firm he began, and to which he had given his name. A little over 10 years beyond that, in 1931, famed toy seller Henry Katz dissolved his own firm and joined Hoge Manufacturing Co., heading its new toy division.

During the first year, Hoge contracted with Mattatuck to produce the company's trains, and two types of O-Gauge train sets were produced. As the 1930s advanced the company's offerings expanded. Clockwork and electric trains were produced, including steam locomotives and diesel streamliners. Particularly sought after today is a 1935-36 Animated Circus Set. Like many of Hoge's offerings, the circus set is lithographed. Then in 1939, just as quickly as the firm decided to enter the toy train market, the decision was made to leave it.

Subsequently Mattatuck Manufacturing acquired Hoge, but toy train production was not resumed.

	C5	C7	C8
Burlington Zephyr Streamline Coach: five-rail, automatic bell.			
	$300	$450	$600
Circus Train: No. 750, 1932.	400	600	800
Observation Car: No. 881.	15	22	30
Pullman: No. 881.	15	22	30
Streamliner: No. 900.	90	135	180
Tom Thumb Boxcar: No. 1902.	45	68	90
Tom Thumb Flatcar:	35	53	70
Tom Thumb Locomotive: No. 881, electric.	20	30	40
Union Pacific Streamline Coach: sheet brass, three-piece unit.			
	300	450	600

No. 900 Streamliner

IVES

MADE IN
THE IVES
SHOPS

Edward Ives formed E.R. Ives & Co. in 1868, when he was but 29 years old. The firm, which went through six name changes, was originally located in Plymouth, Conn., but in 1870 relocated to the more cosmopolitan Bridgeport. Ives' toys were originally made primarily of paper and designed to operate by air currents rising from a warm stove. Soon, however, wood, tin and even cast iron began to be used in the growing line of toys, which were now often powered by clockwork mechanisms. Despite stiff competition from foreign manufacturers, the business prospered. But just before Christmas 1900, a catastrophic fire swept through the Ives plant, reducing it to rubble. Regrouping in a new facility, the firm was back on its feet by 1901 and introduced one of its most famous lines of toys—trains. Complete railway systems were produced, with track, switches, tunnels, and buildings, with the company's reliable clockwork motor powering the locomotives. These trains ran on O-Gauge track. That changed in 1910 as Ives began manufacturing electric trains as well.

In addition to the relatively small O-Gauge trains, Ives produced
1-Gauge trains. Large trains this size, though popular in Europe, never
really caught on in the U.S., and in 1920, two years following Edward Ives'
death, 1-Gauge was replaced by Wide-Gauge. Ives' Wide-Gauge trains
ran on the same size track as Lionel's Standard-Gauge, but that term was
trademarked, forcing Ives (and American Flyer) to term theirs Wide-Gauge.

With Edward's son Harry at the helm, Ives pushed forward, fighting
against a blitz of advertising—not all of it truthful—from Lionel. In 1924,
the firm patented a remote control reversing switch, which was superior
to any on the market. The familiar sequence of action: forward–neutral–
reverse–neutral–forward is recognized as standard even today. In fact,
the Ives mechanisms in general were of superb quality. Nevertheless,
Lionel's ad campaign was taking its toll. In an effort to build its market
position, Ives began selling its entry-level sets at a loss. It hoped to bring
consumers into the Ives camp, and then sell additional track, cars and

accessibility, all of which were profitable. This strategy failed however, and in 1927, acting as chairman of the board, Harry Ives brought in Charles R. Johnson as president. But even with new blood, the company continued its downward spiral. In 1928, Ives filed for bankruptcy, with liabilities of $188,303.25. Johnson, with $245,000 worth of Christmas season stock in hand, petitioned the court to allow a private sale and quick settlement. For unknown reasons, this petition was denied, and on July 31, 1928, American Flyer and Lionel jointly purchased the Ives brand—but not the plant or tooling—for the princely sum of $73,250. Presumably this price reflected the liens of the creditors. It is believed that the Lionel-Flyer strategy was to keep the company out of the hands of other investors, who potentially could rebuild it into a formidable player in the toy train market. Harry Ives was retained as chairman through 1929, at which time he left the company. He died seven years later.

After the joint takeover, the Ives line used an amalgam of their designs, and those of the new co-owners. In 1930 Lionel took over American Flyer's stake in Ives. It is thought that the reasoning behind this was to provide Flyer with some needed tooling, which came from discontinued Lionel designs. Secondly, it gave Lionel possession of the coveted Ives reversing mechanism. The Ives operation, then existent in name only, was moved into the Lionel plant. It continued to be marketed by Lionel as a low-end product until 1933, when it was re-badged Lionel-Ives before being dropped the next year.

Lionel protected its claim to the Ives name for decades subsequent to this by manufacturing their ubiquitous track clips—used to hold pieces of sectional track together on floor setups—with the IVES name embossed in them, an ignominious end to a once proud name.

	C6	C8
Train Set: cast-iron, big six locomotive w/tender and two gondolas.	$1,875	$2,500
0 Locomotive: 1903-1905, 2-2-0; tin body, embossed boiler bands, black and red lithograph; four-wheel painted tender w/cast-iron wheels; arched windows on each side.	225	450
0 Locomotive: 1906, 2-2-0; tin body, embossed boiler bands; blue and white or green and white lithograph, some red and white; F.E. No. 1 tender, four-wheels, two windows per cab side w/number beneath.	200	400
0 Locomotive: 1907-1909, 2-2-0; cast-iron body, wheel arrangement reverse bicycle type, w/drivers in front; lithographed plates under cab windows "IVES No. 0," rectangular cab window; separate tin boiler bands; dummy headlight; F.E. No. 1 tender w/tin wheels.	175	350
0 Locomotive: 1910-1912, 2-2-0; cast-iron body w/lithographed number boards beneath cab windows; large drive wheels behind smaller tin wheels; dummy headlight, two separate boiler bands; F.E. No. 1 tender.	150	300

	C6	C8

0 Locomotive: 1913-1915, 2-2-0; black cast-iron body, separate boiler bands, dummy headlight; same wheel arrangement as previous year, same general engine; number stamped beneath rectangular window; No. 1 tender. $125 $250

00 Locomotive: 1930, 0-4-0; black or red cast-iron boiler, no boiler band; two rectangular windows per cab side marked "IVES No. 00" beneath; tin wheels; dummy headlight in boiler front; No. 9 tender. 145 290

1 Tender: 1903-1905, hand painted; four cast-iron wheels, tin body. 100 200

1 Locomotive: 1906, 2-2-0; painted and lithographed tin in blue and white or green and white; embossed boiler bands; two rectangular windows on both sides of cab w/ number beneath; F.E. No. 1 tender w/tin wheels. 200 400

1 Tender: 1906-1909, F.E. No. 1, four tin wheels, tin body, red lithograph. 75 150

1 Locomotive: 1907-1909, 2-2-0; black painted cast-iron w/two separate boiler bands, dummy headlight; drive wheels in front w/two small tin wheels trail behind; lithographed plates below rectangular cab window reads "IVES No. 1," four-wheel F.E. No. 1 tender. 175 350

1 Locomotive: 1910-1912, 2-2-0; drive wheels behind small tin wheels, two separate boiler bands; rectangular cab window w/lithograph number board beneath; dummy headlight; four-wheel F.E. No. 1 tender. 150 300

1 Tender: 1910-1913, tin body lithographed "F.E. No. 1," four tin wheels. 55 110

1 Tender: 1914, tin body lithographed "IVES No. 1," four tin wheels. 50 100

1 Locomotive: 1926-1928, 0-4-0; cataloged in black w/one separate tin boiler band, tin wheels, no side rods; rectangular cab window stamped "IVES No. 11" beneath; four-wheel No. 11 tender in NYC & HR livery; dummy headlight in boiler front. 125 250

1 Locomotive: 1929, 0-4-0, same basic design as previous year, but now cataloged w/handbrake. 135 270

2 Locomotive: 1906, 2-2-0; painted tin body, embossed boiler bands; two rectangular cab windows on either side w/number painted beneath; F.E. No. 1 tender w/tin wheels. 200 400

2 Locomotive: 1907-1909, 2-2-0; black painted cast-iron w/two separate boiler bands, dummy headlight; drive wheels are in front of tin trailing wheels; rectangular cab window on both sides, plates below lithographed "IVES No. 2," F.E. No. 1 tender. 175 350

2 Locomotive: 1910-1912, 2-2-0, black cast-iron boiler w/two separate boiler bands, dummy headlight; drive wheels behind small tin wheels now; rectangular window on both sides of cab, plates below lithographed "IVES No. 2," F.E. No. 1 tender. 150 300

2 Locomotive: 1913-1915, 2-2-0; black cast-iron boiler, same general engine as previous year, stamped number now; Ives No. 1 tender. 135 270

3 Locomotive: 1903-1905, 2-2-0; painted tin body, lithographed roof, embossed boiler bands; same as No. 0, w/stronger spring; one arched cab window per side, stack is only detail on boiler top; painted tender w/cast-iron wheels. 225 450

3 Locomotive: 1906, 2-2-0; painted and lithographed tin in blue and white or green and white; embossed boiler bands; two rectangular windows per cab side w/number painted beneath; F.E. No. 1 tender w/tin wheels. 200 400

3 Locomotive: 1907-1909, 2-2-0; reverse bicycle wheel pattern w/large drive wheels in front; black cast-iron body w/two separate boiler bands, dummy headlight; lithographed plate below rectangular cab window reads "Ives No. 3," F.E. No. 1 tender. 175 350

3 Locomotive: 1910-1911, 2-2-0; black cast-iron body w/dummy headlight, two separate boiler bands; drive wheels now behind small tin wheels; rectangular cab window per side, lithographed "IVES No. 3" on plate below; F.E. No. 1 tender. 150 300

	C6	C8

3 Locomotive: 1912, 0-4-0; black boiler, two separate boiler bands, dummy headlight; four cast-iron wheels w/drive rods; rectangular cab window lithographed "IVES No. 3" on plate below; F.E. No. 1 tender w/tin wheels. $125 $250

4 Locomotive: 1910-1912, 2-2-0; black cast-iron boiler w/two separate boiler bands, drive wheels behind small tin wheels; dummy headlight; w/rectangular cab window lithographed "IVES No. 4" on plate below; F.E. No. 1 tender. 125 250

4 Locomotive: 1912, 0-4-0; black cast-iron boiler w/two separate boiler bands, dummy headlight; four cast-iron wheels w/drive rods; rectangular cab window lithographed "IVES No. 4" on plate below; F.E. No. 1 tender w/tin wheels. 115 230

5 Locomotive: 1913-1916, 0-4-0; black cast-iron body, separate boiler bands; cast-iron wheels, dummy headlight on top of boiler; single rectangular cab window stamped "IVES No. 5" below; No. 1 tender. 110 220

5 Locomotive: 1917-1922, 0-4-0; black cast-iron body, tin wheels, two separate boiler bands, dummy headlight in center of boiler front; two rectangular windows on both sides of cab stamped "IVES No. 5" below; No. 11 tender. 85 170

6 Locomotive: 1913-1916, 0-4-0; black cast-iron body, cast-iron wheels w/straight side rods, dummy headlight on top of boiler; singular rectangular cab window stamped "IVES No. 6" below; Ives No. 1 tender. 85 170

6 Locomotive: 1917-1925, 0-4-0; black cast-iron body w/cast-iron wheels w/straight drive rods; dummy headlight in center of boiler front; two rectangular windows on both sides of cab stamped "IVES No. 6" below; No. 11 tender. 85 170

6 Locomotive: 1926-1928, 0-4-0; black cast-iron body w/die-cast wheels w/straight drive rods; dummy headlight in boiler front center; two rectangular cab windows on both sides stamped "IVES No. 6," NYC & HR No. 11 tender. 85 170

6 Locomotive: 1929, 0-4-0; black boiler, die-cast wheels w/straight drive rods, dummy headlight in boiler front; same engine as previous year, but now a handbrake has been added; two rectangular cab windows per side stamped "IVES No. 6" below; No. 12 tender. 85 170

9 Tender: 1930, same basic body and frame as No. 11 w/out rivet or spring detail; plain, flat surface; four tin wheels; often no stamping of legend on tender. 50 100

10 Locomotive: 1930, 0-4-0; came w/Pequot set; black cast-iron body, tin wheels, w/out drivers; rectangular cab window marked "IVES No. 10" below; No. 11 tender. 175 350

10 Locomotive: 1931-1932, 0-B-0; tin body, center cab electric style locomotive, often in peacock blue or cadet blue; St. Paul-type of engine, headlights at both ends, pantograph and bell or whistle on top of motor hoods; two windows and one door on either side and one door per end; same as 10-E w/automatic reverse. 140 285

11 Locomotive: 1904-1905, 2-2-0; black cast-iron body w/tapered boiler, integral boiler bands, and dummy headlight on front top of boiler; rectangular cab window w/red area beneath; L.V.E. No. 11 tender. 175 350

11 Tender: 1904-1913, LVE No. 11 tin body, four tin wheels, and red lithograph. 58 115

11 Locomotive: 1906-1907, 0-4-0; black cast-iron body w/four separate boiler bands, gold trim, red area below rectangular cab window; four cast-iron wheels, dummy headlight on top of boiler. Boiler tapers towards the front like those on American Standard locomotives; LVE No. 11 tender. 165 330

11 Locomotive: 1908-1909, 0-4-0, black cast-iron boiler w/three separate bands; straight boiler w/dummy headlight on top; red area below cab; L.V.E. No. 11 tender. 160 320

11 Locomotive: 1910-1913, 0-4-0. black boiler and cab, lithographed plates beneath arched cab windows say "IVES No. 11," cast-iron wheels, three separate boiler bands; L.V.E. No. 11 tender; dummy headlight on boiler top. 155 310

11 Locomotive: 1914-1916, 0-4-0, black cast-iron boiler, two boiler bands, cast-iron wheels; two square windows per cab side, w/"IVES No. 11" stamped beneath them; dummy headlight on boiler top, Ives No. 11 tender. 138 275

	C6	C8

11 Tender: 1914-1930, tin body w/four tin wheels, marked "NYC & HR," Ives No. 11.
$48 / $ 95

12 Tender: 1928-1930, tin body, four tin wheels; same basic tender as No. 11, but w/ coal load. 45 90

17 Locomotive: 1904-1905, 2-2-0, black cast-iron boiler tapers towards front; dummy headlight on boiler top, four separate boiler bands; rectangular cab window w/red area beneath; L.V.E. No. 11 tender, handbrake in cab. 228 455

17 Locomotive: 1906-1907, 0-4-0, same body casting as No. 11, but has a handbrake located inside cab; black body, four separate boiler bands; gold trim, red area beneath cab rectangular window, cast-iron wheels, dummy headlight; boiler tapers towards front; L.V.E. No. 11 tender. 218 435

17 Locomotive: 1908-1909, 0-4-0, black straight cast-iron body, w/three separate bands; dummy headlight on top; same as No. 11 of the period; L.V.E. No. 11 tender; handbrake. 205 410

17 Locomotive: 1910-1913, 0-4-0, same as No. 11; black boiler cab, arched cab windows w/"IVES No. 17" beneath; cast-iron wheels, straight side rods, three separate boiler bands; dummy headlight on boiler top, L.V.E. No. 11 tender; handbrake in cab. 190 380

17 Locomotive: 1914-1916, 0-4-0, same as No. 11 of the same period; black cast-iron body, two square windows per side, w/"IVES No. 17," stamped beneath; dummy headlight on boiler top; "IVES No. 11" tender, cast-iron wheels w/straight side rods; handbrake in cab. 180 360

17 Locomotive: 1917-1925, 0-4-0, black boiler and cab w/dummy headlight in boiler center front, separate boiler band; handbrake in cab; NYC & HR No. 17 tender; straight side rods; single cab window w/"IVES No. 17" stamped beneath. 180 360

17 Tender: 1917-1927, four-wheels of tin, tin body, stamped lettering says "IVES No. 17" or "NYC & HR," comes w/coal load. 45 90

17 Locomotive: 1926-1927, 0-4-0, black cast-iron body w/one boiler band; die-cast wheels w/straight side rods, one arched cab window w/"IVES No. 17" stamped beneath; headlight back on top of boiler now; NYC & HR No. 17 tender; handbrake. 175 350

17 Locomotive: 1928-1929, 0-4-0, black cast-iron body w/one boiler band; die-cast wheels w/straight side rods, one arched cab window w/"IVES No. 17" stamped beneath; headlight back on top of boiler now; NYC & HR No. 12 tender w/coal load; handbrake. 175 350

19 Locomotive: 1917-1925, 0-4-0, black cast-iron boiler and cab w/handbrake, two arched windows and "IVES No. 19" beneath; cast-iron wheels w/straight drive rods, single separate boiler band; dummy headlight centered in boiler front; NYC & HR No. 17 tender. 225 450

19 Locomotive: 1926-1927, 0-4-0, black cast-iron body w/one boiler band, dummy headlight on top of boiler; one boiler band separate; two arched cab windows marked "IVES No. 19" beneath; die-cast wheels w/straight drive rods; No. 17 NYC & HR tender. 200 400

19 Locomotive: 1928-1929, 0-4-0, black cast-iron body w/one boiler band, dummy headlight on top of boiler; one boiler band separate; two arched cab windows marked "IVES No. 19" beneath; die-cast wheels w/straight drive rods; No. 12 tender. 200 400

20 Locomotive: 1908-1909, 0-4-0, cast-iron body w/separate boiler bands; red area beneath two cab windows; dummy headlight on top of boiler; cast-iron wheels w/ straight drive rods; reverse lever, brake speed governor; four-wheel; No. 25 tender. 220 440

20 Locomotive: 1910-1914, 0-4-0, straight boiler, cast-iron body w/grab rails on boiler sides. Dummy headlight on top of boiler, two rectangular cab windows w/lithographed plate marked beneath "IVES No. 20," speed governor, reverse and brake; cast-iron wheels w/straight drive rods; eight-wheel. 195 390

C6   C8

20 Locomotive: 1915-1916, 0-4-0, straight boiler, cast-iron body w/grab rails on boiler sides. Dummy headlight on top of boiler, two rectangular cab windows w/lithographed plate stamped beneath "IVES No. 20," speed governor, reverse and brake; cast-iron wheels w/straight drive rods; eight-wheel; No. 25 tender.
         $195 $390

20 Livestock Car: 1928-1929, Standard-Ga., American Flyer body on two four-wheel Ives trucks; sliding doors, brass plates; green body, red roof or orange body, red roof.
         190   380

20 Gondola: 1928-1929, Standard-Ga., American Flyer body on two four-wheel Ives trucks.   158   315

20 Caboose: 1928-1929, Standard-Ga., American Flyer body on two four-wheel Ives trucks; red body, mirror roof; brass trim and plates.   140   280

20 Gondola: 1928-1929, Standard-Ga., black American Flyer body mounted on two four-wheel Ives trucks; brass plates and trim.   135   270

20 Boxcar: 1928-1929, Standard-Ga., American Flyer body on two four-wheel Ives trucks; brass plates, sliding doors; yellow body w/blue roof or green body w/red roof.
         190   380

25 Locomotive: 1903, 4-4-0; black cast-iron body w/four cast boiler bands, dummy headlight on top of boiler, boiler tapers towards front; cast-iron wheels; three square windows on both sides of cab w/red area painted beneath; reverse and handbrake; hand-painted tin tender w/four cast-iron wheels.   325   650

25 Locomotive: 1904, 4-4-0; black cast-iron body w/six separate boiler bands; dummy headlight on boiler top; three square cab windows on both sides of cab w/red area painted beneath; tin pony wheels; reverse brake; L.V.E. No. 11 tender w/tin wheels.
         300   600

25 Locomotive: 1905, 4-4-0; black cast-iron tapering boiler w/six separate boiler bands, dummy headlight on top of boiler; three square cab windows on both sides w/gold frame and gold stripes beneath; tin pony wheels; handbrake and reverse; L.V.E. No. 11 tender w/red square outline on roof.   295   590

25 Locomotive: 1906-1907, 4-4-2; black body, boiler tapers toward front, w/four separate boiler bands, dummy headlight on top of boiler; three square windows on both sides of cab w/gold frames and stripes, gold outline on roof; tin pony wheels; handbrake and reverse; four-wheel L.V.E. No. 25 tender, no side rods.
         275   550

25 Locomotive

	C6	C8

25 Tender: 1906-1909, four tin wheels; black tin body w/red lithographed spring detail and side boards; L.V.E. No. 25 black lettering on red background. $150 $300

25 Locomotive: 1908-1909, 4-4-2; same general characteristics and casting as previous year; three square cab windows w/gold frames and two gold stripes beneath; gold square outline on cab roof; handbrake and reverse; L.V.E. No. 25 tender, no side rods.   263   525

25 Locomotive: 1910, 4-4-2; black cast-iron body, w/straight boiler, three separate boiler bands, stanchions for grab rails are cast into body; dummy headlight on top of boiler; two rectangular windows on both sides of cab, lithographed plate below reads "IVES No. 25," handbrake and reverse; tin pony wheels; eight-wheel No. 25 tender; angled side rods.   238   475

25 Tender: 1910-1912, eight tin wheel, black body marked "Limited Vestibule Express" in white framed in gold, blue painted interior.   150   300

25 Locomotive: 1911-1914, 4-4-2; black cast-iron boiler, w/three separate boiler bands, dummy headlight on top front of boiler, grab rails are connected by cotter pins; two rectangular windows on both sides of cab w/plate below lithographed "IVES No. 25," red and gold trim; tin wheels on pony truck, cast-iron drivers w/angled side rods; handbrake and reverse; L.V.E. tender.   388   775

25 Tender: 1913-1914, eight-wheel, black tin body marked "Limited Vestibule Express" in white framed in gold.   150   300

25 Locomotive: 1915-1916, 0-4-0; body casting and general detail same as previous model, some have tin pony or spoked cast-iron wheels; handbrake and reverse; latter version of tender, either marked "IVES No. 25" or "No. 25."   225   450

25 Tender: 1915-1920, eight-wheel, black tin body, sides marked "IVES No. 25" in white, back marked "No. 25" in white.   145   295

25 Tender: 1928-1930, die-cast body w/coal load, two four-wheel trucks w/die-cast wheels; tool boxes cast into tender sides.   150   300

30 Locomotive: 1921-1927, 0-4-0 clockwork; w/electric center cab; green or red tin body on cast frame like 3250 series; cast-iron wheels until 1924, die-cast after 1925.   200   400

30 Locomotive: 1928, 0-B-0, clockwork w/electric box cab w/headlight and whistle; same body as 3258; stamped tin frame, tin lithographed body.   200   400

32 Locomotive: 1921-1927, 0-4-0, clockwork; electric center cab; same body as the 3253 loco w/handrails; one door stamped "32 N.Y.C. & H.R.," the other "The IVES Railway Lines," cast-iron frame w/tin body; cast-iron wheels until 1924, die-cast from 1925-1927.   225   450

50 Baggage Car: 1901-1905, four cast-iron wheels, hand-painted red, green or blue body and roof, clerestory w/white painted side.   175   350

50 Baggage Car: 1906-1907, red, white or yellow body lithographed to simulate wood; four tin wheels, steps, vestibules; unpunched door on each side, one marked "Limited Vestibule Express Baggage Car," the other "United States Mail Exp. Service," black roof w/clerestory frame w/red lithographed spring detail; vestibules separate.   195   390

50 Baggage Car: 1908-1909, four-wheel; red lithographed frame has spring detail and striped steps; white/silver body; sides marked "Limited Vestibule Express," "United States Mail Baggage Car" and "Express Service No. 50," three doors on both sides and one on each end; black roof w/clerestory; vestibules part of body.   150   300

50 Baggage Car: 1910-1913, four tin wheels; lithographed yellow tin body w/open frame, black roof and clerestory; sides marked "Pennsylvania Lines," punched center door marked "Baggage No. 50" and "Express Mail," two doors lithographed on other side; wood sheathing on sides.   83   165

50 Baggage Car: 1914, four tin wheels, lithographed tin body and frame; same general car as previous year, but now marked "The Ives Railway Lines."   75   150

52 Passenger Car

60 Baggage Car

60 Baggage Car

	C6	C8

50 Baggage Car: 1915-1930, four tin wheels; red, yellow, green, and tan tin body lithographed to resemble steel, tin frame; marked "The Ives Railway Lines" below roof line and "Baggage No. 50" and "U.S. Express Mail" on each side; open center doors and two lithographed doors w/open windows on side; black frame w/spring detail over wheels, black roof w/small clerestory strip. Because so many of these cars were made, the molds were rendered useless. $25 $50

51 Passenger Car: 1901-1905, four cast-iron wheels, hand-painted tin body w/six windows on each side and vestibules at each end; roof w/clerestory strip w/white accents; red, blue or green body w/horizontal white or cream stripe beneath windows. 175 350

51 Passenger Car: 1906-1907, four tin wheels, red lithographed spring detail on frame w/vestibule at each end; lithographed body marked "Mohawk," "Hiawatha" or "Iroquois" and "Limited Vestibule Express" below roof line; roof w/clerestory strip. 195 390

51 Passenger Car: 1908-1909, four tin wheels, tin lithographed white body w/red detail, w/black frame w/red lithographed detail; body marked "Limited Vestibule Express" below roof line; six windows marked "Brooklyn" below windows on lithographed plate; vestibules part of car. 170 260

51 Passenger Car: 1910-1913, four tin wheels, tin body lithographed to resemble wood grain sheathing; black, green or gray frame w/holes over axle area; body marked "Pennsylvania Lines" below roof line; seven windows marked "Newark" below; doors replaced vestibules at end of car; roof w/clerestory strip. 95 190

51 Passenger Car: 1914, four tin wheels, tin body, roof w/clerestory strip; same car as previous year's but w/"The Ives Railway Lines" lettered below roof line. 75 150

C6   C8

51 Passenger Car: 1915-1930, four tin wheels, tin body lithographed to simulate steel; simple frame w/spring detail over axles; came in variety of colors: red, green, orange, yellow and tan; seven windows and two doors on each side; body marked "IVES Railway Lines" below roof line and "51 Chair Car 51" below windows. $25 $50

52 Passenger Car: 1908-1910, four tin wheels, tin body lithographed to simulate wood; four windows w/transoms and two doors on each side; marked "Limited Vestibule Express" below roof line and "Buffalo" below windows; roof w/clerestory strip; same body used for No. 801 trolley in 1910; cataloged as "Drawing Room Car." 125   250

52 Passenger Car: 1911-1913, four tin wheels, tin body lithographed to simulate wood siding; green, gray or black frame w/holes above axles; five windows and two doors on each side; body marked "Pennsylvania Lines" below roof line and "Washington" below windows; roof w/clerestory strip. 100   200

52 Passenger Car: 1914, four tin wheels, tin body lithographed to simulate wood siding; green, gray or black frame w/holes above axles; five windows and two doors on each side; body marked "Pennsylvania Lines" below roof line and "The Ives Railway Lines" above windows; roof w/clerestory strip. 95   190

52 Passenger Car: 1915-1930, four tin wheels, tin body lithographed to simulate steel; five windows and two doors on each side; marked "The Ives Railway Lines" below roof line and "52 Parlor Car 52" below windows; roof w/clerestory strip. 45   90

53 Freight Car: 1910-1914, four tin wheels, white body, frame w/holes over axle; open doorway on both sides; marked "Pennsylvania Lines" on one side of doorway and "P.A.R.R. Co." and "No. 53" on the other. 90   180

53 Freight Car: 1915-1930, same as previous frame w/spring-detail frame. 68   135

54 Gravel Car: 1903-1904, four cast-iron wheels, hand-painted tin body. 100   200

54 Gravel Car: 1905-1909, four tin wheels, tin body lithographed to simulate wood; red lithographed spring detail on frame. 95   190

54 Gravel Car: 1910-1914, four tin wheels, tin lithographed body on frame w/holes over axle; body marked "No. 54." 55   110

54 Gravel Car: 1915-1930, four tin wheels, tin body lithographed simulated wood; later frame w/spring detail; body marked lithographed "No. 54." 40   80

55 Stock Car: 1910-1914, four tin wheels, yellow tin body lithographed to simulate wood; frame w/holes above axle; marked "Livestock Transportation" below roof line; no doors, just doorway on each side. 50   100

55 Stock Car: 1915-1930, four tin wheels, tin body lithographed to simulate wood; later frame w/spring detail, marked "Livestock Transportation" above doorway. 40   80

56 Caboose: 1910-1914, four tin wheels, white or red tin body lithographed to simulate wood; single open door on each side, w/window on each side of door; small cupola on roof; frame w/holes over axles; marked "Pennsylvania Lines" above door. 113   225

56 Caboose: 1915-1930, four tin wheels, tin body lithographed to simulate wood; frame w/spring detail; open door; marked "Pennsylvania Lines" over door and "Caboose No. 56" on both sides. 100   200

57 Lumber Car: 1910-1914, four tin wheels, tin frame w/hole over axles; painted tin body, w/lumber load. 40   80

57 Lumber Car: 1915-1930, four tin wheels, later frame w/spring detail; painted tin body w/lumber load. 30   60

60 Baggage Car: 1905-1909, four tin wheels; tin body lithographed to simulate wood; tin roof w/clerestory strip; sliding lithographed door; sides marked "United States Mail Exp. Service," "Limited Vestibule Express Baggage Car" and "No. 60." 325   650

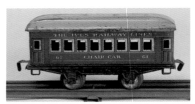

61 Chair Car

62 Parlor Car

64 Merchandise Car

65 Livestock Car

	C6	C8

60 Baggage Car: 1910-1913, eight wheels, red, blue, white, rose or yellow tin body lithographed to simulate wood; sliding lithographed door; truss rods on frame w/single support in middle; tin roof w/separate clerestory strip; flat truss rods in 1910 and 1911, later rounded; marked "Limited Vestibule Express" below roof line, "Express Service Baggage" to left of door and "United States Mail" to right.   **$135 $270**

60 Baggage Car: 1914-1915, same as previous year, marked "The Ives Railway Lines" below roof line.   **120   240**

60 Baggage Car: 1915-1920, eight wheels, tin roof w/clerestory strip, green or red tin body lithographed to simulate steel sides w/rivet detail; lithographed in single-sliding door single in middle of side; truss rods on each side of frame; marked "The Ives Railway Lines" below roof level and "Express Service Baggage" to left of door and "U.S. Mail" to right of door.   **75   150**

60 Baggage Car: 1921-1923, eight wheels, tin roof and body, same as previous year, w/out truss rods on the frame.   **70   140**

60 Baggage Car: 1924-1930, eight-wheel, tin roof w/clerestory strip; red, red-brown or blue-green lithographed w/out rivet detail and gold trim and brass journals; same general car as before, w/truss rods.   **110   220**

61 Passenger Car: 1905-1909, four tin wheels; yellow, red, blue, buff and white bodies; tin body lithographed to simulate wood; vestibules part of body; body marked "Limited Vestibule Express" below roof line, "Express" below eight windows.   **345   690**

61 Passenger Car: 1910-1913, eight-wheel, white, blue, yellow, red, or rose tin lithographed to simulate wood; truss rod on each side of frame and door at each end of side where vestibules were previously; tin roof w/separate clerestory strip, body marked "Limited Vestibule Express" below roof line and "Yale" below eight windows.   **155   310**

61 Passenger Car: 1914-1915, green, body marked "The Ives Railway Lines" above windows and "61 Chair Car 61" below eight windows.   **150   300**

61 Chair Car: 1916-1920, , eight-wheel; green, red or olive tin body lithographed to simulate steel w/rivet detail; truss rods on frame; door at each end of side; one-piece roof w/clerestory strip; body marked "The Ives Railway Lines" above windows and "61 Chair Car 61" below eight windows.   **75   150**

                                                            C6   C8

61 Chair Car: 1921-1923, same car as previous year; green or red body lithographed to
simulate steel; w/out truss rods on frame. $68 $135

61 Chair Car: 1924-1930, same car as previous year; eight-wheel; red, red-brown or
blue-green body lithographed to simulate steel w/out rivet detail, frame w/truss rods.
                                                             68   135

62 Parlor Car: 1905-1909, four-wheel, yellow, red, blue, buff, and white tin body
lithographed to simulate wood; tin one-piece roof; three windows and two doors per
side; "Limited Vestibule Express" below roof line and "Princess" below windows.
                                                             395   790

62 Parlor Car: green, body marked "The Ives Railway Lines" above windows and "62
Parlor Car" below windows.   175   350

62 Parlor Car: 1910-1913, eight wheels; red, white, blue, yellow, or rose tin body
lithographed to simulate wood; truss rods on frame; tin roof w/separate clerestory strip;
five windows and two doors per side; marked "Limited Vestibule Express" below roof
line and "Harvard" below windows.   180   360

62 Parlor Car: 1914-1915, same as previous year, w/"The Ives Railway Lines" above
windows.   150   300

62 Parlor Car: 1916-1920, eight-wheel; tin lithographed steel w/rivet detail; frame
w/truss rods; one-piece tin roof w/clerestory strip; five windows and two doors on each
side; marked "The Ives Railway Lines" below roof line and "Parlor Car" below the
windows.   75   150

62 Parlor Car: 1921-1923, same car as previous year but w/out truss rods on frame;
eight-wheel; one-piece tin roof w/clerestory strip.   68   135

62 Parlor Car: 1924-1930, same car w/out rivet detail; eight-wheel; red-brown, red,
emerald green or blue-green; one-piece roof w/clerestory strip; five windows, two
doors on each side; marked "The Ives Railway Lines" above windows and "62 Parlor
Car 62."   68   135

63 Gravel Car: 1904-1907, four-wheel; tin body painted w/vertical stripes w/cast-iron
wheels.   70   140

63 Gravel Car: 1908-1909, four-wheel; tin lithographed body simulates wood w/tin
wheels.   50   100

63 Gravel Car: 1910-1911, eight-wheel; dark green lithographed body w/incomplete
lithographed on each end. Flat truss rods on frame.   48   95

63 Gravel Car: 1912, eight-wheel; dark green body w/complete lithographed at ends,
flat truss rods on frame.   35   70

63 Gravel Car: 1913-1914, eight-wheel; Kelly green body, same as previous year, w/
half-round truss rods.   35   70

63 Gravel Car: 1915-1916, eight-wheel; gray lithographed w/pinkish tones; w/rounded
truss rods; marked "63" on sides.   30   60

63 Gravel Car: 1917-1920, eight-wheel; gray lithographed tin body w/out pinkish
coloration; rounded truss rods.   25   50

63 Gravel Car: 1921-1923, eight-wheel; gray lithographed body, no truss rods on frame.
                                                             25   50

63 Gravel Car: 1924-1929, eight-wheel; gray lithographed body, rounded truss rods on
frame, journal slots on trucks.   25   50

63 Gravel Car: 1930, eight-wheel; gray lithographed body, rounded truss rods on
frame, brass journals on trucks.   25   90

64 Merchandise Car: 1908-1909, four-wheel; painted frame and roof, single sliding
door; body marked "Fast Freight Line" to left of door and "General Merchandise Car"
to right.   95   190

64 Merchandise Car: 1910-1912, eight-wheel; lithographed tin body to simulate
wood; tin roof, white w/lithographed blue and red stripes; T-trucks and flat truss
rods on frame; single sliding door in middle of side; body marked "General Mdse.
Car No. 64," "Union Line" w/star logo to left of door and "Merchandise Car No. 64
Pennsylvania Line" to right of door.   90   180

66 Tank Car

69 Lumber Car

	C6	C8

64 Merchandise Car: 1910-1930, there are many variations of this car, and different years and different lithograph ink provided a rich palette of colors in each given herald. Because the heralds are listed at the end of the chapter, only the major changes in the car will be listed here; Union Star lines was the first, others weren't cataloged until 1913. All were produced between 1913 and 1930.

64 Merchandise Car: 1913-1917, eight-wheel, tin body lithographed to simulate wood; frame w/rounded truss rods; painted tin roof; all heralds available. $100 $200

64 Merchandise Car: 1918, eight-wheel; same car, new trucks w/no detail, w/flat sides; all heralds available. 100 225

64 Merchandise Car: 1919-1920, eight-wheel; same car, trucks w/rivet detail, no journal slots. 150 250

64 Merchandise Car: 1921-1923, eight-wheel; same car, w/out truss rods on side frames. 100 200

64 Merchandise Car: 1924, eight-wheel; same car, w/side frame truss rods. 90 180

64 Merchandise Car: 1925-1928, eight-wheel; same general cars, trucks w/journal slots. 100 200

64 Merchandise Car: 1929-1930, same general car, red roof, trucks w/brass journals. 100 200

65 Stock Car: 1908-1909, four-wheel; body lithographed w/rivet detail; roof striped w/brake wheel at one end; horizontal slots punched out; striped lithographed door below "Livestock Transportation." 63 125

65 Livestock Car: 1910-1912, eight-wheel; white or gray-white body lithographed to simulate wood; dark green frame w/flat truss rods; striped lithographed roof w/catwalk; punched out sides; single sliding door on each side below "Livestock Transportation." 55 110

65 Livestock Car: 1913-1917, eight-wheel; painted orange body w/single sliding door on each side; painted roof w/catwalk; T-trucks; sides marked "Livestock," "Transportation" and "The Ives R.R."; c. 1916-1917 car changed to yellow lithographed body w/lithographed door; some doors have slots punched in them. 38 75

65 Livestock Car: 1918, eight-wheel; lithographed body in orange-yellow to simulate wood detail; trucks w/out detail; gray painted roof w/catwalk; sides marked "Livestock," "Transportation" and "The Ives R.R." 25 50

65 Livestock Car: 1919-1920, same as previous year, eight-wheel, trucks w/detail. 25 50

65 Livestock Car: 1921-1923, same as previous year, eight-wheel, w/out truss rods on side frames. 23 45

65 Livestock Car: 1924, same as previous years, w/truss rods. 23 45

65 Livestock Car: 1925-1928, same as previous years, eight-wheel, trucks w/journal slots. 23 45

65 Livestock Car: 1929-1930, same as previous years, w/brass journals on trucks; some lithography is now more orange than orange-yellow; roof is now painted red. 23 45

	C6	C8

66 Tank Car: 1910-1912, eight-wheel; flat truss rods on frame; painted dome and tank body mounted right onto frame, w/stripes, rivet detail and "Tank Line" painted on sides; T-trucks; red or green body. $75 $150

66 Tank Car: 1913-1915, eight-wheel; frame w/round truss rods; T-trucks; black tank body on saddles w/gold band painted around each end of tank; no lettering on sides, and "TL No. 66" stamped on each end; short dome. 48 95

66 Tank Car: 1916-1917, eight-wheel; T-trucks; gray painted body on saddles mounted to frame; black dome; sides are lettered "66 Standard Oil 66," "Air Brake," "Made In The Ives Shops" and "Cap'y 100000 Gals," ends stamped "66." 30 60

66 Tank Car: 1918, flat truck; same characteristics as previous year, changed "Cap'y 100000 Gals" to read "Cap'y 10,000 Gals." 23 45

66 Tank Car: 1919-1920, eight-wheel, same as previous year, without type D-2 trucks. 23 45

66 Tank Car: 1921-1923, eight-wheel, same as before, w/out truss rods on frame sides. 20 60

66 Tank Car: 1924, eight-wheel, same, w/out truss rods on frame. 23 45

66 Tank Car: 1925-1928, eight-wheel; orange body, black dome; body mounted to frame by saddles; sides marked "66 Standard Oil 66," "Air Brake," "Made In The Ives Shops" and "Cap'y 10,000 Gals," ends marked "66," trucks w/journal slots. 23 45

66 Tank Car: 1929-1930, eight-wheel; same car as before previous years; trucks w/brass journals. 150 300

67 Caboose: 1910-1912, eight-wheel; white body lithographed to simulate wood sheathing; some main roofs are lithographed w/stripes, some are painted; single lithographed sliding door on each side; sides marked "Pennsylvania Lines," "Caboose No. 67," window to right of door marked "No. 67" below; flat truss rods on frame. 105 210

67 Caboose: 1913-1917, eight-wheel; lithographed body w/single sliding door on each side; gray painted tin roof w/red cupola and red roof; body is red or brown-red; white lettering below roof line reads "The Ives Railway Lines," window to left of door marked "Caboose 67" below; window to right of door marked "Caboose 67," ends of car marked "The Ives Miniature Railway System" and "PARR/67," rounded truss rods on frame. 43 85

67 Caboose: 1918, eight-wheel; same as previous years w/type D-1 trucks; marked "The Ives Railway Line" below right window. 38 75

67 Caboose: 1919-1920, eight-wheel; same as before w/type D-2 trucks. 38 75

67 Caboose: 1921-1923, eight-wheel; same as before, no truss rods on frame sides. 38 75

67 Caboose: 1924, eight-wheel; same as before, w/truss rods back on frame. 38 75

67 Caboose: 1925-1928, eight-wheel; same car as previous years, w/type D-3 trucks w/out journals. 38 75

67 Caboose: 1929-1930, eight-wheel; same basic car as previous years, but more of a red-orange cast to lithography and yellow lettering; green cupola roof; trucks w/brass journals. 38 75

68 Reefer: 1910-1912, eight-wheel; lithographed white body; lithographed roof w/ catwalk; lithographed and sliding doors; T-trucks; flat truss; sides marked "Merchants Dispatch Transportation Company," "Refrigerator No. 68" and "Refrigerator No. 68 Dairy Line Express." 155 310

68 Reefer: 1913-1917, eight-wheel; same car as previous; white body w/painted roof; truss rods on frame are rounded; no brake wheel on roof. 143 285

	C6	C8

68 Reefer: 1918, eight-wheel; same as previous year, but flat side type D-1 trucks.
$138 $275

68 Reefer: 1919-1924, eight-wheel; same as previous year, type D-2 trucks.
138 275

68 Reefer: 1925-1928, eight-wheel; same as previous year; w/type D-3 trucks.
138 275

68 Observation Car: 1925-1930, eight-wheel; emerald green and blue-green body tin lithographed to simulate steel; tin roof w/clerestory strip; brass observation platform; one door and five windows on both sides; brass journals; sides marked "The Ives Railway Lines." 60 100

68 Reefer: 1929-1930, eight-wheel; same as previous years, w/red roof and trucks w/ brass journals. 138 275

69 Lumber Car: 1910-1912, eight-wheel; black painted body w/six red stakes, lumber load held on by three chains over the top; flat truss rods on side frame; T-trucks.
65 130

69 Lumber Car: 1913-1917, eight-wheel; black painted body, six red stakes, rounded truss rods; lumber load held on by three chains; T-trucks. 50 100

69 Lumber Car: 1918, eight-wheel; black painted body, red stakes; lumber load held on by chains; flat trucks; rounded truss rods. 45 90

69 Lumber Car: 1919-1920, eight-wheel; painted body; lumber load held on by chains; rounded truss rods. 45 90

69 Lumber Car: 1921-1923, eight-wheel; red-brown painted body and stakes; lumber load held on by three chains; trucks; frame w/out truss rods. 45 90

69 Lumber Car: 1924, eight-wheel; red-brown body and stakes; lumber load held on by three chains; frame has truss rods. 45 90

69 Lumber Car: 1925-1928, eight-wheel; maroon or tan painted body and stakes; lumber load held on by three chains. 45 90

69 Lumber Car: 1929-1930, eight-wheel; green painted body and stakes; some have short lumber load, others have regular both held on by three chains; trucks w/brass journals. 45 90

70 Baggage Car: 1904-1909, 1-Ga., eight-wheel; wheat and yellow tin body lithographed to simulate wood sheathing; tin wheels, black trucks w/red striping; black tin roof w/white clerestory strip; two doors and two mail windows on each side. sides marked "Twentieth Century Limited Express," "U.S. mail," and "Baggage and Express." 325 650

70 Baggage Car: 1910-1915, 1-Ga., eight-wheel; white, yellow or brown body lithographed to simulate wood; tin wheels, tin roof w/clerestory strip; center doors on both sides and end, window next to each side door; sides marked "Twentieth Century Limited Express" or "New York Central Lines," "Baggage Express No. 70," "New York and Chicago," "United States Mail," steps beneath each side end door; still cataloged in 1916. 250 500

70 Baggage Car: 1923-1925, eight-wheel; red lithographed body simulates steel; tin roof w/clerestory strip; sliding door in center and small door at each end of side; sides marked "The Ives Railway Lines," "Express Baggage Service," "60," and "U.S. Mail."
30 60

70 Caboose: 1929-1930, eight-wheel; tin roof w/red roof cupola 1929, green in 1930; catalog shows No. 67 in cut for 1929, but 1930 the car was made w/a red Lionel body.
270 540

71 Combination Car: 1904-1909, 1-Ga., eight-wheel; yellow or wheat tin lithographed to simulate wood; tin roof, black w/white painted clerestory strip; black trucks w/ red striping; door at each end of side w/six windows between them; sides marked "Twentieth Century Limited Express," "Saint Louis," "Baggage," and "No. 71."
375 750

	C6	C8

71 Combination Car: 1910-1915, 1-Ga., eight-wheel; yellow or brown tin body lithographed to simulate wood; tin roof w/clerestory strip; two doors and three double windows on each side; white, marked "Twentieth Century Limited Express," "Baggage," "New York," "Chicago," and "Buffet Car." **$300** **$600**

71 Combination Car: 1916-1920, 1-Ga., eight-wheel; brown tin body lithographed to simulate steel; tin roof w/clerestory strip separate; two doors per side, three double windows and one small window; marked "The Ives Railway Lines," "Baggage," "No. 71," "New York and Chicago." **300** **600**

71 Chair Car: 1923-1925, eight-wheel; red lithographed body simulates steel w/out rivet detail; tin roof w/clerestory strip; eight windows; marked "The Ives Railway Lines," "71," "Chair Car" and "71." **30** **60**

72 Parlor Car: 1904-1909, 1-Ga., eight-wheel; tin body lithographed to simulate wood; tin black roof w/white clerestory sides; black trucks w/red striping; door at each end of side w/four double windows between them; sides marked "Twentieth Century Limited Express," "No 72" and "San Francisco." **488** **975**

72 Parlor Car: 1910-1915, 1-Ga., eight-wheel; white, yellow or brown tin body lithographed to simulate wood; tin roof w/clerestory strip; four double windows, three small windows, and a door at each end of side, steps below door; sides marked "Twentieth Century Limited Express," "No. 72," "Chicago," "No. 72." **488** **975**

72 Parlor Car: 1916-1920, 1-Ga., eight-wheel; brown tin body lithographed to simulate steeple; tin roof w/clerestory strip separate; four windows, three small windows and two doors w/steps below on each side; sides marked "The Ives Railway Lines," "No. 72" and "Washington." **425** **850**

72 Drawing Room Car: 1923-1925, eight-wheel; red tin body lithographed to simulate steel w/out rivet detail; tin roof w/clerestory strip; five windows, two doors per side; marked "72," "Drawing Room Car" and "72," "The Ives Railway Lines." **45** **90**

72 Accessory: 1928-1930, Standard-Ga., pole wagon for circus set. **45** **90**

73 Observation Car: 1916-1920, 1-Ga., eight-wheel; brown tin lithographed to simulate steel; tin roof w/separate clerestory strip; four double windows, three small windows and one door on each side; sides marked "The Ives Railway Lines," "No. 73," "Observation," and "No. 73." **300** **600**

73 Observation Car: 1923-1925, eight-wheel; red tin body lithographed to simulate steel w/out rivet detail; tin roof w/clerestory; five windows and one door per side; brass platform at rear; sides marked "Observation," "73" and "The Ives Railway Lines." **45** **90**

80 Telegraph Poles: 1906-1930, early examples attached right to track ties, later ones stood on their own stands. **7** **14**

87 Flagpole: 1923-1930. **50** **100**

88 Lamp Bracket: 1923-1930, to attach to stations to illuminate them. **10** **20**

89 Water Tower: 1923-1929, orange body, black frame and ladder; movable spout on counterweight; side marked "The Ives Railway Lines." **50** **100**

89 Water Tower: 1930, larger model, yellow tank w/decal mounted on Lionel base; brass plate on base marked "The Ives Railway Lines," later reproduction has rectangular border around this lettering. **175** **350**

90 Drop Bridge: 1929-1930, w/trip lever, for mechanical track. **135** **270**

90 Bridge: 1912-1922, two simulated stone approaches w/culvert formed under juncture; meant for mechanical trains. **45** **90**

90-3 Bridge: 1912-1922, two simulated stone approaches w/culvert formed under juncture; meant for electrical trains. **45** **90**

91-3 Bridge: 1912-1922, two approach ramps w/double viaduct center; stonework design; for electrical trains. **45** **90**

	C6	C8
91 Bridge: 1912-1922, two approach ramps w/double viaduct center; stonework design; for mechanical trains.	$45	$90
91 Bridge: 1923-1930, two approach ramps w/double viaduct center; earthen design; for mechanical trains; 21 in. long.	45	90
91-3 Bridge: 1923-1930, two approach ramps w/double viaduct center; earthen design; for electrical trains; 21 in. long.	45	90
92 Bridge: 1912-1922, two approach ramps w/double viaduct center; stonework; for mechanical trains; 42 in. long.	60	120
92-3 Bridge: 1912-1922, two approach ramps w/double viaduct center; stonework; for electrical trains; 42 in. long.	60	120
92 Bridge: 1923-1930, w/semaphore signal; two approach ramps w/double viaduct center and railings on sides; for mechanical trains; earthen design.	50	100
92-3 Bridge: 1923-1930, w/semaphore signal; two approach ramps w/double viaduct center and railings on sides; for electrical trains; earthen design.	50	100
97 Swing Drawbridge: 1906-1912, two stonework approaches w/revolving center span; lattice-type girders on trestles; for mechanical track, 31 in. long.	130	175
97 Bridge: 1929-1930, Standard-Ga., two approach ramps w/three center spans w/ girders.	65	130
98 Bridge: 1906-1907, two approach ramps, stonework, double viaduct center; lattice-type girders on trestle; for mechanical trains; 31 in. long.	65	130
98 Bridge: 1908-1912, two approach ramps, stonework sides, double stonework viaduct; flat stamped girders on trestle; plain-sided center base, straight corner braces; for mechanical track, 31 in. long.	45	90
98 Bridge: 1911-1920, two approach ramps of stone or earthen design; one single viaduct center span of stonework design; flat stamped trestle sections; for mechanical 1-Ga. track, 42 in. long.	50	100
98-3 Bridge: 1911-1922, two approach ramps of stone or earthen design; one single viaduct center span of stonework design; flat stamped trestle sections; for electrical track, 42 in. long.	45	90
98 Bridge: 1913-1922, two approach ramps of stone or earthen design; one single viaduct center span of stonework design; flat stamped trestle sections; for mechanical track.	45	90
98 Bridge: 1923-1930, two approaches of earthwork design w/square stones along track, center span of flat steel trestles set upon stonework base; for mechanical track, 31 in. long.	45	90
98-3 Bridge: 1923-1930, two approaches of earthwork design w/square stones along track, center span of flat steel trestles set upon stonework base; for electrical track, 31 in. long.	45	90
99 Bridge: 1906-1907, two approach ramps, stonework, double viaduct center; w/two center spans; lattice-type girders on trestle; for mechanical trains, 41 in. long.	75	150
99 Bridge: 1908-1912, same as contemporary No. 98 but w/two center spans, 41 in. long.	65	130
99-3 Bridge: 1911-1922, two approach ramps of stone or earthen design; two viaduct center span of stonework design; flat stamped trestle sections; for electrical track, 41 in. long.	50	100
99 Bridge: 1913-1922, two approach ramps of stone or earthen design; two viaduct center span of stonework design; flat stamped trestle sections; for mechanical track, 41 in. long.	60	120
99-3 Bridge: 1926-1928, same as No. 98 of these years, 41-1/4 in. long.	50	100
100 Bridge: 1906-1917, two approach sections forming a single viaduct between the center juncture; painted groundwork, for mechanical track, 21 in. long.	35	70

	C6	C8

100-3 Bridge: 1910-1917, two approach sections forming a single viaduct between the center juncture; painted groundwork, for electrical track, 21 in. long. $40 $80

100 Accessory Set: 1930-1932, includes clock, telegraph poles, crossing gate, crossing signal, single and double semaphore; 10 pieces. 55 110

101 Bridge: 1906-1922, bridge; two approaches, one center span w/two viaducts, railings on both sides of track, for mechanical trains, 31 in. long. 50 100

101-3 Bridge: 1910-1922, two approach ramps, center section w/two viaducts, railings on both sides of track, for electrical track, 31 in. long. 50 100

102 Tunnel: 1928, papier-mâché, 18 in. long. 15 30

103 Tunnel: 1910-1927, papier-mâché, six in. long. 12 25

103 Tunnel: 1928-1930, papier-mâché, eight in. long. 12 25

104 Tunnel: 1906-1927, papier-mâché, 8-1/2 in. long. 25 50

104 Tunnel: 1928-1930, papier-mâché, 10 in. long. 25 50

105 Tunnel: 1906-1912, papier-mâché, 11 in. long. 12 25

105-E Tunnel: 1913-1919, papier-mâché, 11 in. long. 12 25

105 Tunnel: 1913-1922, 1924-1927, papier-mâché, 14 in. long. 12 25

105 Tunnel: 1928, papier-mâché, 12 in. long. 12 25

106 Tunnel: 1906-1912, papier-mâché, 14 in. long. 15 30

106-E Tunnel: 1910-1912, papier-mâché, 16 in. long. 15 30

106 Tunnel: 1913-1928, papier-mâché, 16 in. long. 15 30

106 Tunnel: 1929-1930, papier-mâché, 19 in. long. 15 30

107 Semaphore: 1905-1917, w/check; arm on post, w/a signal and brake attachment at the base to stop mechanical train. 30 60

107-S Semaphore: 1907-1930, single arm w/wire attached to signal to operate manually. 10 20

107-D Semaphore: 1907-1930, double arm w/wires to operate signals manually. 14 28

107 Tunnel: 1929-1930, papier-mâché, 23 in. long. 18 35

108 Semaphore: 1908-1917, 1-Ga., w/check; arm on post w/a signal and brake attachment at the base to stop mechanical train. 25 50

109 Double Semaphore Tower: 1906-1922, two signals mounted on upright base, early examples had ladder going up to platform, later ones deleted this feature. 35 70

110 Track Bumper: 1906-1928, for sidings, to keep trains from derailing; early examples were just a post w/two pieces of track angled up from road surface and attached to either side of the post; later ones were a more elaborate system w/a sprung bumper for the train touch against. 12 25

110-1 Track Bumper: 1917, for sidings, to keep trains from derailing; early examples were just a post w/two pieces of track angled up from road surface and attached to either side of the post; later ones were a more elaborate system w/a sprung bumper for the train touch against, for 1-Ga. mechanical track. 20 40

110 Bridge Span: 1931-1932, Standard-Ga., Lionel No. 110. 30 60

111 Track Elevating Post: 1904-1907, made for mechanical track for elevated railways; see set section at end of chapter. 20 40

111 Crossing Sign: 1912-1928. 10 20

111 Crossing Sign: 1929, Lionel No. 0-68. 10 20

112 Track Plates: 1906-1932, for connecting track together at ends beneath ties. 1 1

112-1 Track Plates: 1912-1920, 1-Ga., for connecting track together. 1 1

113 Passenger Station: 1906-1911, red body lithographed w/cast-iron door frames and window frames; lithographed roof w/shingles and base w/tiles; sign above; marked "Ticket Office" on one side of window and "Telegraph Office" on the other. 163 325

115 Freight Station

122 Passenger Station

	C6	C8

113 Passenger Station: 1912-1928, painted base and roof w/red brick lithographed body; w/people in windows; front and back are identical on some models w/two doors and three windows; others have one door and two windows; tin chimney on roof.
$88 $175

113-3 Passenger Station: 1924-1928, same as 113, w/No. 88 lamp brackets to illuminate it externally; most stations w/factory illumination have a distinctly yellow cast to the lithographed brickwork; tin chimney.   88   175

114 Passenger Station: 1906-1911, lithographed roof w/simulated shingles, lithographed base simulating tiles; lithographed yellow body w/red cast-iron door on window frames; some examples have lithographed plate on base w/Ives name on it, others marked "Passenger Station," "Ticket Office" and "Telegraph Office" on plates on body; cast-iron chimney on roof.   95   190

114 Passenger Station: 1912-1916, lithographed roof w/simulated shingles and w/lithographed base simulated tiles; body lithographed w/clerk in window on front and back, ladies in one end window and gentlemen in other; two doors on front and back of station; tin chimney on roof.   73   145

114 Passenger Station: 1917-1922, same as previous year, w/painted, not lithographed, roof and base; tin chimney.   65   130

114 Passenger Station: 1923-1928, same as previous years, roof has stamped shingle pattern; station body is shorter than previous years; tin chimney.   65   130

	C6	C8

115 Freight Station: 1906-1911, lithographed block base w/ramp and platform, small yellow lithographed station set on platform; sliding door w/lithographed plate on one side and lettered "Freight," the other side lettered "Station," body lithographed to simulate wood, roof lithographed to simulate shingles; cast-iron chimney on roof.
$145 $290

115 Freight Station: 1912-1916, lithographed block base w/ramp and platform; yellow lithographed body w/open door on front and back; clerk lithographed in window w/handcart carrying Ives packages; scale w/blue shadow lithographed on front and back of building; brown and green door and window trim; tin roof w/tin chimney; clerk visible in end windows.
700   1,400

115 Freight Station: 1917-1922, early examples have yellow lithographed bodies w/painted roof and flat base; painted base and roof; most are the new white lithographed body, but w/same appearance as the last version.
70   130

115 Freight station: 1923-1928, generally the same as previous years, but w/corrugated tin roof and tin chimney; roof has vertical embossed ridges between the gutter and the roof ledge; may not have been made for all five years, but examples w/this roof seem to have an orange shadow beneath the scales, as opposed to the standard blue shadow on other models of the same station.
70   130

116 Passenger Station: 1906-1911, roof w/simulated shingles, lithographed base simulates tiles; body is lithographed yellowish brick w/cast-iron doors and windows; roof has bay gable front and back marked "Grand Central Station" U-shaped bay on front and back of station w/window on each side of U; marked "Ticket Office" above one window and "Telegraph Office" above other; two cast-iron chimneys on roof.
500   1,000

116 Passenger Station: 1912-1916, lithographed roof w/single pattern, bay gable front and back marked "Grand Central Station"; roof w/one, two or three cast-iron chimneys; lithographed base simulates tiles; lithographed body now w/rectangular bay in center w/windows on each side, window in center w/clerk sitting at desk; doors are now part of station body, and have lithographed stained glass pattern.
175   350

116 Passenger Station: 1917-1928, lithographed body is as previous year; roof and base are now painted; bay gable at front and rear is marked "Union Station," first examples in 1917 had a variety of combinations of old and new parts.
175   350

116-3 Passenger Station: 1926-1928, same as the contemporary No. 116 station, w/two or four No. 88 lamp brackets mounted to the exterior for illumination.
160   320

117 Passenger Station: 1906-1911, covered; two base pieces w/lithographed tile pattern; roof supported by eight posts; train passed through between bases; lithographed sign on roof reads "Suburban Station," one bench between center two posts on each base.
550   1,100

117 Passenger Station: 1912-1922, covered; two base pieces, each w/four posts supporting painted tin roof; train passes through between bases; one bench on each base.
450   900

117 Passenger Station: 1923-1928, covered; two base pieces, each w/three posts supporting painted tin roof; two benches per base; train passes between bases.
450   900

118 Platform Station: 1905, covered, small lithographed base w/one post supporting lithographed roof; two lithographed plates read "Suburban" and "Station."
125   250

118 Platform Station: 1906-1912, covered; small lithographed base w/one post supporting lithographed roof; single lithographed plate reads "Suburban Station" on single lithographed plate.
95   190

119 Platform Station: 1905, covered; lithographed tile floor w/two posts supporting lithographed shingle roof; two lithographed plates read "Suburban" and "Station."
125   250

125-81 MKT Merchandise Car

124 Reefer   129 Drawing Room Car

	C6	C8

119 Platform Station: 1906-1912, covered; lithographed tile floor w/two posts supporting lithographed shingle roof; one lithographed plate reads "Suburban Station." — $100 — $200

119 Platform Station: 1913-1914, covered; painted floor w/two posts supporting painted roof w/no lettering. — 75 — 150

120 Platform Station: 1905, covered; lithographed tile base w/candy-stripe railing on three sides w/four wooden posts supporting lithographed shingled roof; two lithographed reads "Suburban" and "Station," came w/the plates lettered "Passenger" and "Station." — 135 — 270

120 Platform Station: 1906-1911, covered; lithographed tile base w/painted railing on one side and both ends; four posts supporting lithographed shingle roof; lithographed sign reads "Suburban Station." — 125 — 250

120 Platform Station: 1912-1916, covered; painted base w/painted railing on one side and both ends; four posts supporting painted roof w/no lettering; some of these still had lithographed roof w/lithographed sign reading "Suburban Station." — 110 — 220

121 Platform Station: 1906-1909, covered; two lithographed bases simulating tilework, one bench apiece, four posts apiece supporting roof made of metal ribs w/32 pieces of stained glass among them; lattice border around bottom of roof. — 600 — 1,200

121 Platform Station: 1910-1916, covered; two lithographed covered; bases simulating tilework, two benches on each base; three posts on each base supporting roof w/metal ribs and eight separate pieces of glass; lattice border around bottom of roof. — 200 — 400

121 Platform Station: 1917-1927, covered; two painted bases w/three supporting posts and two benches on each; metal ribbed roof w/eight pieces of glass; no lattice border. — 160 — 320

121 Caboose: 1929, eight-wheel; red American Flyer body No. 3211 w/Ives trucks w/brass journals; four side windows w/brass inserts and brass end railings. — 100 — 200

121 Caboose: 1930, eight-wheel; Lionel No. 817; red body w/short green cupola roof and trucks w/brass journals; brass end railings and window inserts; w/brass plates marked "121" and "Ives Lines." — 85 — 170

	C6	C8

122 Passenger Station: 1906-1916, combination of the No. 116 passenger station of these years and the No. 121 glass dome of the same period; glass dome was attached to a special shortened roof on one side of the station, and had one supporting base for the other side; see descriptions of No. 116 and No. 121. **$200** **$300**

122 Passenger Station: 1917-1923, combination of No. 116 and No. 121 of the same years; glass dome is supported on one side by posts coming up from a specially widened base on the No. 116 station, and by a normal No. 121 base on the other side; see contemporary No. 116 and No. 121 for further description. **200** **300**

122 Tank Car: 1929-1930, eight-wheel; orange Lionel No. 815 body, Ives journals w/ brass trucks; brass domes, hand rail and ladders; brake wheel at both ends. **90** **180**

123 Double Station: 1906-1923, combination of two No. 116 stations w/a No. 121 glass dome. For more see No. 122, No. 116, and No. 121 for description. **200** **300**

123 Lumber Car: 1910-1912, eight-wheel; black flat truss rod frame w/eight red painted stakes, lumber load held on by four chains, nine in. long. **70** **140**

123 Lumber Car: 1913-1917, eight-wheel; black body, red stake; lumber load held on w/four chains, round truss rods on frame, nine in. long. **55** **110**

123 Lumber Car: 1918-1924, eight-wheel; tan or brown painted body and stakes, lumber load held on by four chains, round truss rods, nine in. long. **55** **110**

123 Lumber Car: 1925-1928, eight-wheel; tan, brown-red or maroon body and stakes; lumber load held on by four chains, round truss rods, nine in. long. **50** **100**

123 Lumber Car: 1929-1930, eight-wheel; green body and stakes; lumber load held on by four chains; rounded truss rods, trucks w/brass journals, nine in. long. **50** **100**

124 Reefer: 1912-1917, eight-wheel; uncataloged, but first ones came w/lithographed roof w/stripes and catwalk; white body lithographed to simulate wood; sliding door in center of each side; side marked "Merchants Dispatch Transportation Company" and "Refrigerator No. 124 Dairy Express Line," rounded truss rods w/two posts. **100** **200**

124 Reefer: 1918-1924, eight-wheel; uncataloged, but first ones came w/lithographed roof w/stripes and catwalk; white body lithographed to simulate wood; sliding door in center of each side; door lithographed "Refrigerator No. 124" on sides; the second "e" is often misspelled as an "f." **95** **190**

124 Reefer: 1925-1928, eight-wheel; uncataloged, but first ones came w/lithographed roof w/stripes and catwalk; white body lithographed to simulate wood; sliding door in center of each side; door lithographed "Refrigerator No. 124" on sides; the second "e" is often misspelled as an "f." **95** **190**

124 Reefer: 1929-1930, eight-wheel; uncataloged, but first ones came w/lithographed roof w/stripes and catwalk; white body lithographed to simulate wood; sliding door in center of each side; trucks w/brass journals; door lithographed "Refrigerator No. 124" on sides; the second "e" is often misspelled as an "f." **95** **190**

125 Merchandise Car: 1905-1909, eight-wheel; yellow body lithographed to simulate wood; red lithographed roof w/horizontal stripes; inboard trucks; single sliding lithographed door marked "Fast Freight Line" to left and "General Merchandise Car" to right. **338** **675**

125 Merchandise Car: 1910-1912, eight-wheel; white body lithographed to simulate wood sheathing w/vertical stripes; w/catwalk; T-trucks, flat truss rods on sides of frame; single sliding door on each side, door marked "General Mcdse. Car No. 125," sides marked "Union Line" and "Merchandise Car No. 125 Pennsylvania Lines." **155** **310**

125 Merchandise Car: 1913-1917, eight-wheel; same description as before but w/gray painted roof; some w/Marklin-type trucks. **138** **275**

	C6	C8

125 Merchandise Car: 1915-1930, eight-wheel; in 1915, the catalog states beneath the Union Star cut, that "No. 125 shows a Star Union Car. Under this number comes a large assortment of freights w/the heralds of different roads." $250 $500

125 Merchandise Car: 1918, eight-wheel; same description as before but w/gray painted roof. 138 275

125 Merchandise Car: 1919-1924, eight-wheel; same description as before but w/gray painted roof. 125 250

125 Merchandise Car: 1925-1928, eight-wheel; same description as before but w/gray painted roof. 125 250

125 Merchandise Car: 1929-1930, eight-wheel; same description as before but w/red painted roof; trucks w/brass journals. 118 235

125-81 MKT Merchandise Car: 1915-30. 200 400

126 Caboose: 1904-1905, four-wheel; gray lithographed body, black and red roof; sliding lithographed door; sides marked "Fast Freight," "No. 126" and "Caboose." 135 270

126 Caboose: 1906-1909, four-wheel; buff-colored lithographed body, black and red lithographed roof; same general characteristics as previous years. 125 250

127 Stock Car: 1904-1909, eight-wheel; gray lithographed body simulating wood, black and red horizontal striped lithographed roof; inboard trucks; sliding door on each side; marked "Livestock Transportation." 145 290

127 Stock Car: 1910-1912, eight-wheel; gray body lithographed to simulate wood; frame w/flat truss rods; lithographed cross braces on diagonal on car sides; w/catwalk and lithographed roof w/vertical stripes; sliding lithographed door, marked "Livestock Transportation." 95 190

127 Stock Car: 1913-1917, eight-wheel; yellow lithographed body w/gray painted roof; Marklin truck style; lithographed sliding door, w/"Livestock" on diagonal to left, and "Transportation" on diagonal to right; side marked "The Ives RR." 50 100

127 Stock Car: 1918, eight-wheel; yellow lithographed body w/gray painted roof; w/type D-1 trucks; lithographed sliding door, w/"Livestock" on diagonal to left, and "Transportation" on diagonal to right; side marked "The Ives RR." 45 90

127 Stock Car: 1919-1924, eight-wheel; yellow lithographed body w/gray painted roof; w/type D-2 trucks; lithographed sliding door, w/"Livestock" on diagonal to left, and "Transportation" on diagonal to right; side marked "The Ives RR." 45 90

127 Stock Car: 1925-1928, eight-wheel. Yellow lithographed body w/gray painted roof; w/type D-3 trucks; lithographed sliding door, w/"Livestock" on diagonal to left, and "Transportation" on diagonal to right; side marked "The Ives RR." 45 90

127 Stock Car: 1929-1930, eight-wheel. Same lithographed pattern as previous models, but more of a yellow-orange; 1930 has some very orange examples; red roof; brass trucks have journals. 45 90

128 Gravel Car: 1905-1909, eight-wheel; gray body lithographed to simulate wood; inboard trucks. 125 250

128 Gravel Car: 1910-1911, eight-wheel; dark green body w/white lithographed striping, incomplete on each side; dark green frame w/flat truss rods, T-trucks; marked "New York Central." 60 120

128 Gravel Car: 1912, eight-wheel; dark green w/lithographed striping; w/frame has rounded truss rods; two support posts; marked "New York Central." 55 110

128 Gravel Car: 1913-1915, eight-wheel; lighter green lithographed body w/same general pattern as previous models; Marklin trucks; two support posts in body. 50 100

128 Gravel Car: 1916-1917, eight-wheel; gray lithographed body w/reddish brown lithographed detail; two support posts across inside of body. 50 100

128 Gravel Car: 1918, eight-wheel; gray lithographed body w/reddish-brown lithographed detail; rounded truss rods, type D-1 trucks; two support posts inside body. 50 100

	C6	C8

128 Gravel Car: 1919-1924, eight-wheel; gray lithographed body w/reddish-brown lithographed detail; rounded truss rods, type D-2 trucks; two support posts inside body. $50 $100

128 Gravel Car: 1925-1928, eight-wheel, gray-lithographed body w/reddish-brown lithographed detail; rounded truss rods, type D-3 trucks; two support posts inside body. 50 100

128 Gravel Car: 1929, eight wheels; gray lithographed body w/reddish-brown lithographed detail; rounded truss rods, brass journals on the type D-4 trucks; two support posts inside body. 50 100

128 Gravel Car: 1930, eight-wheel; gray lithographed body w/reddish-brown lithographed detail; frame w/rounded truss rods; brass journals on type D-4 trucks; some bodies have a lithograph that is almost white, and many examples are not punched for the two support rods across the inside of the body. 50 100

129 Parlor Car: 1904-1909, eight-wheel; yellow body lithograph to simulate wood (also cataloged in red); lithograph roof, some w/stripes, some have a black roof w/lithographed clerestory; inboard trucks; two doors and five windows on each side; sides marked "Limited Vestibule Express" and "Philadelphia." 300 600

129 Drawing Room Car: 1910-1912, eight-wheel; green body lithographed to simulate wood; dark green frame w/flat truss rods, T-trucks; gray roof w/green or red clerestory strip separate; door at each end of side and four double windows; marked "Limited Vestibule Express," "Saratoga" and "129." 70 140

129 Drawing Room Car: 1913-1917, eight-wheel; green body lithographed to simulate wood; rounded truss rods on the side frame; Marklin trucks; gray roof w/green or red clerestory strip separate; door at each end of side and four double windows; marked "Limited Vestibule Express," "Saratoga" and "129." 70 140

129 Drawing Room Car: 1918-1924, eight-wheel; green body lithographed to simulate steel; gray roof is one-piece w/clerestory strip, although some used up the existing supply of two-piece roofs; type D-2 trucks; four double windows and door at each end; marked "The Ives Railway Lines," "129" and "Saratoga." 70 140

129 Drawing Room Car: 1925-1926, eight-wheel; green body lithographed to simulate steel; gray roof is one-piece w/clerestory strip, although some used up the existing supply of two-piece roofs; w/type D-3 trucks; four double windows and door at each end; marked "The Ives Railway Lines," "129" and "Saratoga." Saratoga car was used in 1926 in the "Green Mountain Express" set as an observation car by bending it behind the last set of windows and adding a brass observation railing. Also cataloged in orange in 1926. 70 140

129 Drawing Room Car: 1927-1929, eight-wheel; orange body lithographed to simulate steel w/out rivet detail; orange one-piece roof w/clerestory strip; trucks; four double windows on both sides w/a door at each end of side; marked "The Ives Railway Lines," "Saratoga" and "129." 63 125

129 Drawing Room Car: 1930, eight-wheel; orange body lithographed to simulate steel w/out rivet detail; orange one-piece roof w/clerestory strip; trucks w/brass journals; four double windows on both sides w/a door at each end of side; marked "The Ives Railway Lines," "Saratoga" and "129." 63 125

130 Combination Car: 1904-1909, eight-wheel; yellow lithograph body; black lithographed roof w/red stripes and painted and lithographed clerestory (some roofs are just painted); inboard trucks; baggage door at one end of side, passenger door w/steps at other end of side and six windows between them; sides marked "Limited Vestibule Express," "Buffet," "Baggage" and "New York." 150 300

130 Combination Car: 1910-1912, eight-wheel; green body lithographed to simulate wood; gray roof w/red or green clerestory strip; T-truck and flat truss rods on side frames; baggage door at one end of side, passenger door w/steps at other end of side and three double windows between them; side marked "Limited Vestibule Express," "130," "Buffet" and "130." 70 140

130 Combination Car

132 Observation Car

C6 **C8**

130 Combination Car: 1913-1917, eight-wheel; green body lithographed to simulate wood; gray roof w/red or green clerestory strip; Marklin trucks and rounded truss rods on side frames; baggage door at one end of side, passenger door w/steps at other end of side and three double windows between them; side marked "Limited Vestibule Express," "130," "Buffet" and "130." $70 $140

130 Combination Car: 1918-1924, eight-wheel; green body lithographed to simulate steel w/rivet detail; one-piece roof w/clerestory strip, all painted gray (some used up existing supply of two-piece roofs early on); baggage door at one end of windows, passenger door at other end above three double windows; type D-2 trucks; sides marked "The Ives Railway Lines," "No. 130," "Buffet," and "130." 72 145

130 Combination Car: 1925-1926, eight-wheel; green body lithographed to simulate steel w/rivet detail; one-piece roof w/clerestory strip, all painted gray (some used up existing supply of two-piece roofs early on); baggage door at one end of windows, passenger door at other end above three double windows; type D-3 trucks; sides marked "The Ives Railway Lines," "No. 130," "Buffet," and "130," also cataloged in orange in 1926. 70 140

130 Combination Car: 1927-1929, eight-wheel; orange steel lithographed body w/out rivet detail; brass journals on trucks; baggage door at one end of windows, passenger door at other end above three double windows; sides marked "The Ives Railway Lines," "130" and "Buffet." 60 120

131 Baggage Car: 1904-1909, eight-wheel; yellow body lithographed to simulate wood; black and red striped roof w/painted or lithographed clerestory strip; inboard trucks; two baggage doors per side, mail window to left of first one; sides marked "U.S. Mail," "Baggage Car," "Chicago," and "Limited Vestibule Express." 250 500

131 Baggage Car: 1910-1912, eight-wheel; green body lithographed to simulate wood; dark green frame T-trucks and flat truss rods; gray roof w/separate red or green clerestory; passenger door at each side end w/two sliding baggage doors between them; sides marked "Limited Vestibule Express," "No. 131" and "Baggage Express." 98 195

131 Baggage Car: 1913-1917, eight-wheel; green body lithographed to simulate wood; dark green frame Marklin trucks and rounded truss rods; gray roof w/separate red or green clerestory; passenger door at each side end w/two sliding baggage doors between them; sides marked "Limited Vestibule Express," "No. 131" and "Baggage Express." 85 170

131 Baggage Car: 1924-1926, eight-wheel; green body lithographed to simulate steel; gray one-piece roof w/clerestory strip; passenger door at end and baggage door; sides marked "The Ives Railway Lines," "No. 131," "Baggage Express" and "U.S. Mail," also cataloged in orange in 1926. 32 65

131 Baggage Car: 1927-1929, eight-wheel; orange steel body lithographed w/out rivet detail; one passenger door at each end, two baggage doors in middle; marked "Ives Railway Lines," "No. 131," "Baggage Express," and "U.S. Mail." 30 55

131 Baggage Car: 1930, eight-wheel; orange steel body lithographed w/out rivet detail; trucks w/brass journals; one passenger door at each end, two baggage doors in middle; sides marked "Ives Railway Lines," "No. 131," "Baggage Express," and "U.S. Mail." 30 55

C6   C8

132 Observation Car: 1926-1929, eight-wheel; one version was made from the 129 Saratoga car in 1926. Also cataloged w/orange lithographed body version; one-piece roof w/clerestory strip w/brass observation platform railing, four double windows and one door lithographed on each side; sides marked "The Ives Railway Lines," "No. 132" and "Observation." $32 $65

132 Observation Car: 1930, eight-wheel; orange lithographed body version; trucks w/ brass journals; one-piece roof w/clerestory strip and brass observation platform railing; four double windows and one door lithographed on each side; sides marked "The Ives Railway Lines," "No. 132" and "Observation."   32   65

133 Parlor Car: 1928-1930, eight-wheel; painted body and roof w/brass window inserts, brass plates and D-3 trucks; sides marked "133 Parlor Car 133," cataloged in various colors, but generally came in either orange or red; same body as 135 w/less trim; not cataloged w/lights but some cars had them.   53   105

134 Observation Car: 1928-1930, eight-wheel; orange or red painted body and roof w/brass window inserts, observation platform, brass plates and D-3 trucks; sides marked "134 Observation 134," same car as 136, but less trim; not cataloged w/lights, but some cars had them.   53   105

135 Parlor Car: 1926-1930, eight-wheel; painted body and roof; interior lights; brass window inserts and brass plates; brass journals on type D-four trucks; four celluloid windows; sides marked "Pullman," "Parlor Car," 1926–tan body; 1927–blue body; 1928–orange body; 1929–red body w/black roof and brass vestibules; 1930–orange body w/black roof, red body w/black roof, or blue body w/red roof.   88   175

136 Observation Car: 1926-1930, eight-wheel; painted body and roof; interior and platform lights; four celluloid windows w/brass window inserts and observation railing; brass journals on D-4 trucks; brass plates; sides marked "Pullman," "136 Observation 136," 1926–tan body; 1927–blue body; 1928–orange body; 1929–red body, black roof, brass vestibules; 1930–orange body w/black roof, or red body w/black roof, or blue body w/red roof.   88   175

137 Parlor Car: 1928, eight-wheel; black painted roof w/red body; another version of the 135 car; D-3 trucks; brass window inserts, celluloid windows; w/out lights or journals; brass plates read "137 Parlor Car 137."   45   90

138 Observation Car: 1928, eight-wheel; black painted roof w/red body; another version of the 136 car; brass window inserts w/celluloid windows; no lights or brass journals; D-3 trucks; brass observation platform; brass plate marked "138 Observation 138."   45   90

140 Automatic Crossing Gates: 1906-1920, lithographed or painted base w/ lithographed building and crossing gate tripped by oncoming train; for mechanical trains; 20-1/2 in. long.   35   70

140-3 Automatic Crossing Gates: 1910-1920, lithographed or painted base w/ lithographed building and crossing gate tripped by oncoming train; for electrical trains; 20-1/2 in. long.   35   70

141 Parlor Car: 1926-1930, eight-wheel; longer than the No. 135, painted gray, orange or black body and roof; brass journals; five double windows w/brass window inserts and two doors on each side; some have vestibules, and brass plate; w/lights; "Pullman," "Parlor Car," "141," and "Made In The Ives Shops."   80   160

142 Observation Car: 1926-1930, eight-wheel; body generally painted gray, orange or black, painted roof; longer than the No. 136; brass journals; five double windows w/ brass window inserts; lights; observation platform and vestibules; marked "Pullman," "Observation," "142," and "Made In The Ives Shops."   80   160

145 Turntable: 1910-1930, four-track outside, w/inside table rotated by clockwork mechanism; brake and signal on turning table portion; painted base and table; for mechanical trains.   50   100

146 Turntable: 1906-1919, automatic; four-truck outside; inside table rotated by clockwork mechanism; brake and signal on turning table portion; painted base and table; mechanical trains.   75   150

257 Locomotive

550 Baggage Car

	C6	C8

176 Locomotive: 1930, 0-4-0; black cast-iron body w/clockwork engine and hand brake; marked "Ives No. 176" beneath cab windows; 1930 version of the No. 17 locomotive; w/No. 17 tender w/decal. $110 $220

215 Crossing Gate: 1923-1930, lithographed base simulating earth; two fences w/pole gate between them; manually operated.   22   45

257 Locomotive: 1931, 2-4-0; Lionel No. 257, w/No. 257T four-wheel tender; black paint locomotive w/orange and brass trim; No reverse unit; nickel journals on tender; brass plates read "Ives Lines" and "Ives No. 257."   200   400

258 Locomotive: 1931-1932, 2-4-0 w/No. 1663 Tender; black painted locomotive w/ orange and copper trim, hand reverse unit w/brass plate that reads "Ives Lines" and "Ives No. 258," eight-wheel black tender w/brass journals.   230   460

339-0 Track Bumper: 1928-1930, Lionel bumper w/red light on top.   12   25

340-0 Spring Bumper: 1929-1930, sheet-steel w/spring cross bar; Lionel.
                                                                          10   20

550 Baggage Car: 1913-1915, four-wheel; painted one-piece roof, lithographed body simulating wood detail; red, rose or white body; passenger door at each end of side, leaf springs on frame; marked "The Ives Railway Lines" center door and "Baggage No. 550" to left of door, and "Express Mail" to right.   58   115

550 Baggage Car: 1916-1926, four-wheel; green lithographed body simulates steel, painted roof; flat springs on frame; passenger door at each end of side, open doorway in center; marked "The Ives Railway Lines" above door, "Express Service Baggage 550" to left and "U.S. Mail 550" to right; sometimes 60 series cars were used for these.
                                                                          58   115

550 Baggage Car: 1927-1930, four-wheel; lithographed green steel body, flat spring frame; white body, red roof in 1927 for White Owl set, blue and buff body w/blue roof in 1930 for Blue Vagabond set, green and buff body w/blue roof in 1930 for Pequot set, also red body w/blue roof in 1930; open doorway in center of car, passenger door at each end of side; marked "The Ives Railway Lines" above doorway; "Express Service Baggage 550" to left of center door and "U.S. Mail 550" to the right.
                                                                          58   115

	C6	C8

551 Chair Car: 1913-1915, four-wheel; red, white or rose body lithographed to simulate wood sheathing; painted one-piece roof; leaf springs on frame; eight square windows and door at the end of each side "The Ives Railway Lines" lettered above eight square windows; marked "No. 61," "Yale" and "No. 61" below windows. $55 $110

551 Chair Car: 1916-1926, four-wheel; green body lithographed to simulate steel; painted one-piece roof; flat springs on frame; eight windows and passenger door at the end of each side; "The Ives Railway Lines" above eight windows, "551," "Chair Car," and "551" below window level; 60 series cars were sometimes used.   55   110

551 Chair Car: 1927-1930, four-wheel; green body lithographed to simulate steel; white w/red roof in 1927 for White Owl set, blue and buff w/blue roof in 1930 for Blue Vagabond, green and buff in 1930 for Pequot, also came w/red body and blue roof in 1930; painted one-piece roof, eight windows and passenger doors at the end of each side; marked "The Ives Railway Lines" above windows and "551," "Chair Car," and "551" below window.   55   110

552 Parlor Car: 1913-1915, four-wheel; red, white or rose body lithographed to simulate wood; one-piece painted roof; leaf springs on frame; five wide windows and passenger door at the end of each side; marked "The Ives Railway Lines" windows, and "No. 62," "Harvard," and "No. 62" below windows.   55   110

552 Parlor Car: 1916-1926, four-wheel; one-piece painted roof; green body lithographed to simulate steel; flat springs on frame; five wide windows and passenger door at the end of each side; marked "The Ives Railway Lines" above windows, and "552," "Parlor Car," and "552" below.   55   110

552 Parlor Car: 1927-1930, four-wheel; green body lithographed to simulate steel; white w/red roof in 1927 for White Owl set, blue and buff w/blue roof in 1930 for Blue Vagabond set, green and buff in 1930 for Pequot set, also red body w/blue roof in 1930; painted one-piece roof; flat springs on frame; five wide windows and passenger door at the end of each side; marked "The Ives Railway Lines" above windows and "552," "Parlor Car" and "552" below.   55   110

558 Observation Car: 1927-1930, four-wheel; green body lithographed to simulate steel; painted one-piece roof; white in 1927 for White Owl set, blue and buff in 1930 for Blue Vagabond set, also red w/blue roof in 1930; flat springs on frame; five wide windows and passenger door at the front of each side; brass observation railing; marked "The Ives Railway Lines" above windows and "558," "Observation" and "558."   55   110

562 Caboose: 1930, four-wheel; red Lionel No. 807 body w/brass window inserts and green cupola roof; flat springs on trucks.   68   135

563 Gravel Car: 1913-1930, four-wheel; gray or green body lithographed to simulate steel.   35   70

564 Merchandise Car: 1913-1930, four-wheel; this series utilized the No. 64 boxcar series detailed in the 60 series section and in general notes.   125   250

565 Livestock Car: 1913-1930, four-wheel; red orange body lithographed to simulate wood (some examples had yellow body similar to No. 65 stock car); painted one-piece roof w/catwalk; some versions had sliding door; early examples marked w/"Livestock Transportation."   45   90

566 Tank Car: 1913-1929, four-wheel; painted body frame; follows evolution of No. 66 tank car, see this car's description for more detail; ends marked "566," sides read "Standard Oil."   45   90

566 Tank Car: 1930, Lionel No. 804 tank car w/brass domes; orange body; brass handrail and ladders; brass plates read "Ives" and "No. 566."   60   120

567 Caboose: 1913-1930, four-wheel; lithographed body w/painted roof and cupola; see caboose No. 67 for details.   45   90

569 Lumber Car: 1913-1930, four-wheel; body and stakes painted tan, maroon, brown, green or black; two chain supports hold carried lumber load; supported load.   40   80

600 Electric Arc Light: 1915-1922, single arm street light w/various shapes and lamp.   30   60

1125 Locomotive

	C6	C8

601 Electric Arc Light: 1915-1922, double arm streetlight w/various shapes and lamps.
$40　　$80

610 Pullman Car: 1931-1932, eight-wheel; Lionel car; green body and roof; air tanks beneath car; Lionel latch couplers; eight windows and passenger doors at each end of side; decal above windows reads "The Ives Lines," marked "610," "Pullman" and "610" below windows.　　70　　140

612 Observation Car: 1931-1932, eight-wheel; Lionel car; green body and roof; Lionel latch couplers; air tanks beneath car; observation platform of brass on rear; eight windows and passenger doors at the front of each side; decal above windows reads "The Ives Lines," marked "612," "Observation" and "612" below windows.　　70　　140

800 Trolley: 1910-1913, four-wheel; mechanical works w/trolley pole on roof; tin wheels and hinged pilots; four windows and passenger door at each end of side; marked "Local and Suburban Service" above windows and "Trolley" below; 6-1/2 in. long.　　800　　1,600

801 Trolley: 1910-1913, four-wheel; mechanical works w/spring pole on roof; lithographed body; tin wheels; four windows and two doors on each side; marked "Limited Vestibule Express" above windows "Buffalo" below; can also be marked "Pennsylvania Lines" "Newark" and "Washington," five in. long.　　600　　1,200

805 Trolley Car Trailer: 1913-1915, four-wheel; lithographed body w/cast pilot; roof w/separate clerestory; no trolley pole; cast-iron spoke wheels; five windows and one open and one blocked passenger door each on side; unpowered.　　175　　350

809 Streetcar: 1913-1915, four-wheel; lithographed body w/cast pilot; roof w/separate clerestory; no trolley pole; cast-iron spoke wheels; five windows and one open and one blocked passenger door each on side; marked "Suburban" below windows and "Ives No. 809" on side; 7-3/4 in. long.　　500　　1,000

810 Trolley: 1910-1912, four-wheel; same general configuration as No. 809; roof w/separate clerestory; 10 caternary poles; trolley pole on roof collected current for motor; tin wheels; sides lithographed "Suburban" and "Ives No. 810" on side; 7-1/2 in. long.　　500　　1,000

1100 Locomotive: 1910-1912, 2-2-0; cast black body; dummy headlight, two tin boiler bands, painted stack and bell; tin front wheels; cast drivers; no drive rods w/F.E. No. 1 tender; brass plates below rectangular window reads "Ives No. 1100."　　155　　310

1100 Locomotive: 1913-1914, 0-4-0; similar to 1912 version w/slightly different casting to accommodate front drive wheels; dummy headlight, two tin boiler bands, painted stack and bell; seven-spoke wheels; w/L.V.E. No. 11 tender; lithographed plate beneath cab roof reads "Ives No. 1100."　　140　　280

	C6	C8

1100 Locomotive: 1915-1916, 0-4-0; cast-iron black body; straight boiler w/dummy headlight on boiler top; two tin boiler bands; rectangular cab window; drive rods; seven- or twelve-spoke cast-iron wheels; stamped "Ives No. 1100" stamped below window; w/tender marked "Ives No. 11." $125 $250

1100 Locomotive: 1917-1922, 0-4-0; cast-iron black body; one tin boiler band and dummy headlight in boiler front; cast-iron wheels; rectangular cab window; drive rods; w/No. 11 tender; at some point during production (probably around 1920) 1100s were made from 1116 castings w/operating headlight in boiler front.   95   190

1116 Locomotive: 1917-1922, 0-4-0; same casting as No. 1100, but w/operating headlight in boiler front center; straight drive rods, No. 11 tender; see 1100 for more details.   150   300

1117 Locomotive: 1910-1914, 0-4-0; black cast-iron boiler, cast-iron wheels w/ angled drive rods; body extension over armature end in 1910; two tin boiler bands and dummy headlight on top of boiler; two cab windows; w/L.V.E. No. 11 tender; lithographed plates beneath windows read "Ives No. 1117."   150   300

1117 Locomotive: 1915-1916, 0-4-0; same boiler casting; cast-iron body and wheels w/angled drive rods; two tin boiler bands; w/Ives No. 11 tender; w/rubber stamped "Ives No. 1117" beneath windows.   140   280

1118 Locomotive: 1910-1914, 0-4-0; same boiler No. 1117, w/operative headlight on boiler top; body covers armature in 1910 version; two tin boiler bands; cast-iron body and wheels w/angled drive rods; two cab windows; lithographed plate below windows reads "Ives No. 1118," w/Ives No. 11 tender.   150   300

1118 Locomotive: 1915-1916, 0-4-0; same as previous version but w/rubber stamped lettering beneath cab windows instead of lithographed plate.   140   280

1118 Locomotive: 1917-1925, 0-4-0; larger w/higher body casting; cast-iron body, cast-iron wheels w/straight drive rods; headlight in center of boiler; one casting has extra sheeting below cab w/large rivet detail; w/Ives No. 17 tender; two rectangular windows; stamped "Ives No. 1118" below window.   110   220

1120 Locomotive: 1916, 0-4-0; same as No. 1118; cast-iron body and wheels w/drive rods; generally stamped "Ives No. 1120" below windows, although at least one version has lithograph plates; see 1118 for more details.   388   775

1120 Locomotive: 1928, 4-4-0; cast-iron body w/arched cab windows; die-cast wheels w/straight drive rods; separate grab rails and braces from boiler to pilot; w/No. 25 tender w/coal load; marked "Ives NYC & HR," boiler stamped "Ives No. 1120" below windows.   475   950

1122 Locomotive: 1929-1930, 4-4-2; die-cast body, headlight in boiler center and bell on boiler front; brass handrails, copper tubing and die-cast drive rods; die-cast wheels; drivers w/nickel tires; No. 25 die-cast tender; brass plate below cab windows reads "The Ives Railway Lines" and brass plate below boiler front reads "Made In The Ives Shops," tender marked "The Ives Railway Lines" on brass plate.   300   600

1125 Locomotive: 1910-1913, 4-4-0; tin pony wheels; cast-iron spoked drivers w/ angled rods; operating headlight on boiler top; separate handrails; two cab windows; plates below windows lithographed "Ives No. 1125," w/eight-wheel tender w/sides lithographed "Limited Vestibule Express."   250   500

1125 Locomotive: 1914-1917, 4-4-2; cast-iron spoked pony wheels and drivers w/ angled drive rods; separate grab rails, operating headlight on top of boiler; Marklin trucks; plates beneath cab windows lithographed "Ives No. 25," w/eight-wheel No. 25 tender marked "NYC & HR" or "Ives No. 25" on sides.   250   500

1125 Locomotive: 1930, 0-4-0; chunky-looking cast-iron body w/one separate boiler band; brass bell on boiler, operational headlight operates on boiler front; black or blue body; gold decal beneath cab windows reads "Ives RR Lines," "1125" cast on cab sides; w/No. 17 tender w/round Ives decal on sides and coal load.   225   450

1501 Locomotive: 1931-1932, 0-4-0; mechanized red tin body, die-cast wheels w/out drive rod; speed governed; w/bell activated during running; hand brake; no marks on engine; sides of tender marked "1502 Ives R.R. Lines 1502" on yellow simulated letterboard.   125   250

1651 Locomotive

1690 Pullman

1691 Observation Car

	C6	C8

1504 Pullman Car: 1931-1932, four-wheel; one-piece red lithographed tin body w/blue roof and yellow trim; tin wheels; five double windows; sides marked "1504 Pullman 1504" below windows. **$45 $90**

1506 Locomotive: 1931-1932, mechanical; larger than No. 1502; tin body painted black w/die-cast wheels and straight drive rods; bell and handbrake; black No. 1507 tender w/red lithographed rectangle marked "1507 Ives R.R. Lines 1507." **125 250**

1512 Gondola: 1931-1932, four-wheel; blue tin body. **40 80**

1513 Cattle Car: 1931-1932, four-wheel; green lithographed body w/sliding doors. **40 80**

1514 Boxcar: 1931-1932, four-wheel; yellow tin body w/blue roof and sliding doors; "Erie" logo on sides. **40 80**

1515 Tank Car: 1931-1932, four-wheel; silver body w/brass and copper trim; "Sunoco" logo on sides. **40 80**

1517 Caboose: 1931-1932, four-wheel; red lithographed tin body w/red-brown roof; "NYC" logo on sides. **40 80**

1550 Switch: 1931-1932, left and right; for clockwork trains. **8 16**

1555 Crossing: 1931-1932, 90 degrees for clockwork trains. **6 12**

1558 Accessory Bumper: 1931-1932, for clockwork track. **10 20**

1559 Crossing gate: 1931-1932, w/striped lithographed arm. **10 20**

1560 Station: 1931-1932, lithographed body and roof; housed either transformer or whistle. **40 80**

1561 Tunnel: 1931-1932, papier-máché, eight in. long. **10 20**

1564 Bridge: 1931-1932, same as No. 91, for clockwork track. **30 60**

1562 Water Tower: 1931-1932, green and maroon, w/hinged spout. **25 50**

1563 Telegraph Pole: 1931-1932. **3 6**

1565 Semaphore: 1931-1932, same as No. 107-S; single arm. **10 20**

1566 Semaphore: 1931-1932, same as No. 107-D; double arm. **10 20**

	C6	C8

1567 Crossing Sign: 1931-1932, same as No. 111. — $4 / $8

1568 Clock: 1931-1932, tin base; lithographed face w/movable hands; diamond shaped. 4 / 8

1569 Accessory Set: 1932, four telegraph poles, one clock, one crossing sign and one semaphore; w/box; seven pieces. 40 / 80

1570 Gift Set: 1932, includes No. 1572, No. 1514, No. 1515 and No. 1517; w/box. 175 / 350

1571 Telegraph Post: 1932, red and white. 3 / 6

1572 Semaphore: 1932. 6 / 12

1573 Warning signal: 1932, square post; diamond-shaped sign. 6 / 12

1574 Clock: 1932, square post; diamond-shaped face w/movable hands. 4 / 8

1575 Crossing Gate: 1932, lithographed gate, painted base. Manual. 8 / 16

1651 Locomotive: 1932, 0-4-0; electric-type box cab; lithographed steel in either red w/maroon roof or yellow w/blue roof; die-cast wheels; brass trim and journals; marked "Ives R.R. Lines" below roof line; also marked "1651" beneath windows. 150 / 300

1661 Locomotive: 1932, 2-4-0; black tin body w/red trim; die-cast wheels; some versions have drive rods and a hand reverse unit; copper and brass trim; No. 1661 tender marked "Ives R.R. Lines." 100 / 200

1663 Locomotive: 1931-1932, 2-4-2; Lionel engine w/Ives plates; die-cast body and wheels; nickel-plated drive rods; die-cast eight-wheel tender No. 1663; both painted black cast-iron. 213 / 525

1677 Gondola: 1931-1932, eight-wheel; blue body lithographed to simulate steel; brass journals; ovals on each side read "Ives R.R. Lines" and "1677." 31 / 62

1678 Cattle Car: 1931-1932, eight-wheel; green body lithographed to simulate wood w/sliding door and brass journals. 31 / 62

1679 Boxcar: 1931-1932, eight-wheel; yellow lithographed sides and blue roof; brass journals; marked "Ives R.R. Lines" and "1679" on sides. 31 / 62

1680 Tank Car: 1931-1932, eight-wheel; painted silver body w/brass and copper trim; brass journals; marked "Ives Tank Lines," "Fuel Oil" and "1680" on sides. 31 / 62

1682 Caboose: 1931-1932, eight-wheel; red lithographed body w/red-brown roof; brass journals; sides marked "Ives R.R. Lines" in oval and "1682" in rectangle. 31 / 62

1690 Pullman: 1931-1932, eight-wheel; red lithographed body w/maroon roof and cream trim or yellow body w/blue roof and orange trim; brass handrails and journals; six double windows and door at each end of side; "1690," "Ives R.R. Lines" and "1690" beneath windows. 35 / 70

1691 Observation Car: 1931-1932, eight-wheel; red lithographed body w/maroon roof and cream trim or yellow body w/blue roof and orange trim; brass handrails, journals and railing; w/door at front of each end and windows on both sides; marked "Ives R.R. Lines" and "1691" below windows. 35 / 70

1694 Locomotive: 1932, 4-4-4; New Haven-style electric box cab; puff painted sides w/maroon roof and brass trim; headlights at each end; die-cast wheels w/nickel-plated drive rods; punched ventilators on sides; brass plates read "1694," "Ives Lines" and "1694." 500 / 1,000

1695 Pullman Car: 1932, 12-wheel; buff painted body w/maroon roof; copper journals. Six double windows; decals below windows read "1695," "The Ives Lines" and "1695." 175 / 350

1696 Baggage Car: 1932, 12-wheel; buff painted body w/maroon roof; copper journals; baggage and mail doors on each side, w/three windows near each. "1696," "The Ives Lines" and "1696" decals on each side. 175 / 350

1697 Observation Car: 1932, 12-wheel; buff body w/maroon roof; brass observation platform and copper journals; passenger door at front and six double windows on each side; decal below windows read "1697," "The Ives Lines" and "1697." 175 / 350

1709 Boxcar, 1712 Caboose, 1707 Gondola

1871 Suburban Station

	C6	C8

1707 Gondola: 1932, eight-wheel; body lithographed to simulate wood w/cross braces; brass journals; "Ives" logo in oval on side. $45 $90

1708 Cattle Car: 1932, eight-wheel; green body lithographed to simulate boards w/ spaces between them; ovals on sides lithographed "1708" and "Ives." 135 270

1709 Boxcar: 1932, eight-wheel; lithographed blue body w/painted roof; yellow sliding doors and brass journals; ovals on sides read "1709" and "Ives." 45 90

1712 Caboose: 1932, eight-wheel; red lithographed body w/maroon roof; brass journals; ovals on sides read "1712" and "Ives." 45 90

1810 Locomotive: 1931-1932, 0-4-0; electric-style box cab; green body, red roof w/ yellow trim; brass pantograph and dummy headlight; sides marked "Ives R.R. Lines" above windows and ventilators and "1810" near each end. 95 190

1811 Pullman Car: 1931-1932, four-wheel; green body, red roof w/yellow trim; door at each end of sides; marked "Ives R.R. Lines" above four double windows and "1811," "Pullman" and "1811" below. 40 80

1812 Observation Car: 1931-1932, four-wheel; green body, red roof w/yellow trim; door at front, observation platform at rear; marked "Ives R.R. Lines" above five double windows; "1812," "Observation" and "1812" below. 40 80

1813 Baggage Car: 1931-1932, four-wheel; green body, red roof w/yellow trim; marked "Ives R.R. Lines" between two doors and "1813," "Baggage" and "1813" at lower level of car. 40 80

1815 Locomotive: 1931-1932, 0-4-0; black tin body w/red trim; die-cast wheels and nickel drive rods; dummy headlight; no reverse; w/black No. 1815 tender marked "Ives R.R. Lines." 95 190

1851 Crossing: 1931-1932, 90 degrees. 4 8

1853 Crossing: 1931-1932, 45 degrees. 4 8

1855 Bumper: 1931-1932, sprung bar type. 10 20

1857 Bumper: 1931-1932, sprung bar type w/illumination. 10 20

1859 Tunnel: 1931-1932, papier-mâché, 11 in. long. 15 30

1860 Tunnel: 1931-1932, papier-mâché, 16 in. long. 15 30

1863 Bridge Approach Signal: 1931-1932, die-cast base; painted round post w/arm and chairs; formerly Ives No. 338. 45 90

1866 Flag Pole: 1931-1932, American flag; raised and lowered on string. 40 80

1867 Signal Tower: 1931-1932, Lionel No. 438 tower w/switches on back "Ives" plates. 150 300

1868 Villa: 1931-1932, Lionel No. 191, red and green, illuminated; "Ives" stamped on bottom. 75 150

1869 Colonial House: 1931-1932, white Lionel No. 189, illuminated; "Ives" stamped on bottom. 80 160

1870 Cottage: 1931-1932, tan and green Lionel No. 184, illuminated; w/"Ives" stamped on bottom. 75 150

1871 Suburban Station: 1931-1932, red and green Lionel No. 126; two windows and door; dormer on roof; marked "Ives Town" above window. 125 250

1872 Station: 1931-1932, ivory and red Lionel No. 127 w/green and yellow windows, marked "Ives Town" plate above middle doors. 100 200

1873 City Station: 1931-1932, terracotta Lionel No. 122 w/green roof, yellow trim and swinging doors; plate above center window reads "Ives Town." 150 300

1874 City Station: 1931-1932, same as 1873 but w/exterior illumination. 150 300

1875 Freight Shed: 1931-1932, terracotta roof, maroon base and green piers; Lionel No. 155 w/illumination. 180 360

1876 Power House: 1931-1932, buff, terracotta and green Lionel No. 435 three windows on front door on each end; w/smokestack; "Ives" stamped on bottom. 145 290

3217 Locomotive

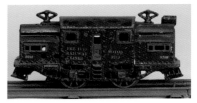

3218 Locomotive

3252 Locomotive

3253 Locomotive

3257 Locomotive

3258 Locomotive

	C6	C8
1877 Circuit Breaker: 1931-1932, same as Lionel No. 81 but illuminated.	$30	$60
1878 Crossing Gate: 1931-1932, automatically operated, lithographed arm, illuminated Lionel No. 077.	30	60
1879 Crossing Gate: 1931-1932, Standard-Ga., automatic operation, lithographed arm, illuminated; Lionel No. 77.	30	60
1880 Warning Signal: 1931-1932, Standard-Ga., white Lionel No. 79, illuminated; brass sign face.	65	130
1881 Signal Traffic Light: 1931-1932, blinking type; Lionel No. 83; yellow w/red base.	60	120
1882 Lamppost: 1931-1932, electric, boulevard type; green upright die-cast base w/ signal bulb.	45	90
1884 Bell Signal: 1931-1932, automatic; green base, brass diamond warning sign and bells on back.	60	120
1886 Target Signal: 1931-1932, automatic; green base, brass diamond warning sign and bells on back.	65	130
1887-1891 Transformers: 1931-1932.	10	20
1893 D.C. Reducer: 1931-1932, for houses w/direct current to run transformers.	10	20
1894 Rheostat: 1931-1932, used to control train speeds.	10	20
1895 Switches: 1931-1932, manual, illuminated.	15	30
1897 Switches: 1931-1932, electrically operated, illuminated.	20	40
1904 Semaphore: 1932, single blade, automatic; same as 1903.	75	150

		C6	C8

1905 Lamppost: 1932, gooseneck-style, double arm; same as No. 307. $50 $100

1906 Freight Station Set: boxed, 1932, includes two land trucks, a dump truck and a baggage truck; Lionel No. 163.   75   150

1907 Train Control: 1932, automatic, stops and starts train; Lionel No. 078.   75   150

1926 Light Bulb: 1931-1932, 6-volt, round.   —   1

1927 Light Bulb: 1931-1932, 12-volt, round.   —   1

1928 Light Bulb: 1931-1932, 18-volt, round.   —   1

1939 Light Bulb: 1931-1932, 12-volt, pear shaped.   —   1

1940 Light Bulb: 1931-1932, 18-volt, pear shaped.   —   1

3200 Locomotive: 1910, 0-4-0; cast-iron S-1 type electric body; painted gold pantograph and dummy headlight on each hood; no air tanks; steps beneath door in cab center; tin wheels held on w/nuts; separate pilots; raised lettering beneath windows reads "Ives" and "3200."   400   800

3200 Locomotive: 1911, 0-4-0; cast-iron S-1 type electric center cab; green or black body; gold painted pantograph and dummy headlight on each hood; separate pilots; cast-iron six-spoke wheels; center door flanked by two windows; steps below; air tanks; raised lettering reads "Ives" and "3200" below windows.   250   500

3200 Locomotive: 1912-1913, 0-4-0; cast-iron S-1 type center cab electric; maroon or black body w/separate pilots; gold-painted pantograph and dummy headlight on each hood; cast-iron 10-spoke wheels; centered door on side w/steps below; air tanks; stamped "The Ives Railway Lines" below left window and "Motor 3200" beneath right window.   150   300

3200 Locomotive: 1914, 0-4-0; cast-iron S-2 type center cab electric; black-painted body w/separate pilots; gold painted pantograph and dummy headlight on each hood; centered 10-spoke wheels; centered door w/steps below and air tanks; stamped "The Ives Railway Lines" beneath left window and "Motor 3200" beneath right window.   150   300

3200 Locomotive: 1915-1916, 0-4-0; S-1 type cast-iron center cab electric; black body w/integral pilots; painted gold pantograph and dummy headlight on each hood; 10-spoke wheels; center door w/steps; marked "The Ives Railway Lines" beneath left window and "Motor 3200" beneath right window.   150   300

3216 Locomotive: 1917, 0-4-0; cast-iron S-1 type center cab electric, larger than 3200, shorter and smaller than 3218; squared hoods, dummy headlight on one, operating headlight on the other; cast-iron 10-spoke wheels; silver painted pantograph on each hood; center door w/steps below; stamped "The Ives Railway Lines" beneath left window and "Motor 3216" beneath right window.   175   350

3217 Locomotive: 1911, 0-4-0; cast-iron S-1 type center cab electric, larger than 3216; maroon or red body; dummy headlight and pantograph on painted gold hood; separate pilots; one door and two windows on side; six-spoke wheels; raised lettering reads "Ives 3217" on sides.   275   550

3217 Locomotive: 1912-1913, 0-4-0; cast-iron type S-1 center cab electric; maroon or red body; gold dummy headlight and pantograph on each hood; separate pilots; 10-spoke wheels; one door and two windows on cab side; raised lettering reads "Ives" and "3217."   250   500

3217 Locomotive: 1914, 0-4-0; cast-iron S-1 type center cab electric; black body; dummy headlight and pantograph at each end, painted silver or gold; separate pilots; cast-iron 10-spoke wheels; door and two windows on cab side, stamped lettering reads "The Ives Railway Lines" on left and "Motor 3217" to right.   150   300

3217 Locomotive: 1915-1916, 0-4-0; cast-iron S-1 type center cab electric; black body; dummy headlight and pantograph on each hood; cast-iron 10-spoke wheels; pilots cast integrally to body; center door flanked by two windows on cab side center, stamped "The Ives Railway Lines" beneath left window and "Motor 3217" beneath right window.   150   300

C6   C8

3218 Locomotive: 1911, 0-4-0; cast-iron electric S-1 type center cab; maroon or red body; gold painted pantograph on each hood w/operational headlight on one and dummy on other; cast-iron six-spoke windows; separate pilots; centered door flanked by window; raised lettering reads "Ives" and "3218." $500 $1,000

3218 Locomotive: 1912-1913, 0-4-0; cast-iron electric S-type center cab; maroon or red body; gold pantograph on each hood w/operating headlight on one and dummy on other; separate pilots; cast-iron 10-spoke wheels; door and window on side; raised lettering reads "Ives" and "3218." 450   900

3218 Locomotive: 1914, 0-4-0; cast-iron electric S-1 type center cab electric; black body; silver painted pantographs; w/both dummy and operating headlight; separate pilots; 10 cast-iron wheels; center door flanked by two windows; stamped "The Ives Railway Lines" to left of door and "Motor 3218" to right. 200   400

3218 Locomotive: 1915-1917, 0-4-0; cast-iron electric S-1 type center cab; gray or black body; silver pantographs; dummy headlight on one hood, operating one on the other; pilots cast integrally to body; window above each door; stamped "The Ives Railway Lines" to left of door and "Motor 3218" to right. 200   400

3220 Locomotive: 1916, 0-4-0; cast-iron electric S-1 type center cab; black body; silver pantographs, one dummy and one operating headlight; pilots separate from body; window above door; stamped "The Ives Railway Lines" to left of door and "Motor 3220." 375   750

3238 Locomotive: 1910-1912, 2-4-2; cast-iron electric S-1 type center cab; black body w/operating headlight on each hood; gold painted bell and whistle; manual reverse; tin pilot wheels w/10-spoke drive wheels; raised lettering reads "New York Central Lines" to left of door and "3238 NYC & HR" to right. 308   615

3250 Locomotive: 1918-1924, 0-4-0; electric center cab; generally green, brown or red-stamped metal body on cast-iron frame; cast-iron spoked wheels; bell and whistle on top, operating headlight late in production; no handrails; stamped "The Ives Railway Lines" to left of cab door and "Motor 3250" or "3250 N.Y.C. & H.R." to right of cab door. 108   215

3250 Locomotive: 1925, 0-4-0; electric center cab; generally green, brown or red-stamped metal body on cast-iron frame; cast-iron spoked wheels; bell and whistle on top, operating headlight; no handrails; die-cast wheels; stamped "The Ives Railway Lines" to left of cab door and "Motor 3250" or "3250 N.Y.C. & H.R." to right of cab door. 108   215

3251 Locomotive: 1918-1924, 0-4-0; center electric cab; green, red or brown body and frame the same as No. 3250 w/handrails on hoods; operating headlight and bell; cast-iron wheels; stamped "The Ives Railway Lines" and "Motor 3251" or "3251 N.Y.C. & H.R." on either side of doorway. 108   215

3251 Locomotive: 1925-1927, 0-4-0; center electric cab; green, red or brown tin body w/cast-iron frame; operating headlight; brass bell, brass plate to left of door; die-cast wheels w/nickel tires; marked "The Ives Railway Lines" and "Motor 3251" to right of door. 108   215

3252 Locomotive: 1918-1924, 0-4-0; center electric cab; brown, red, burgundy, or green body and frame the same as No. 3251; operating headlight; brass bell and handrails; cast-iron wheels; stamped "The Ives Railway Lines" to left of cab door and either "Motor 3252" or "3252 N.Y.C. & H.R." to right of cab door. 108   215

3252 Locomotive: 1925-1927, 0-4-0; center electric cab; red, green, orange, or brown body, same general characteristics as before except w/die-cast wheels w/or w/out nickel tires; brass plates to the left of cab door read "The Ives Railway Lines"; plate to the right reads "Motor 3252." 138   275

3253 Locomotive: 1918-1924, 0-4-0; center electric cab; red or green stamped steel body w/cast-iron frame; larger than No. 3252; one operating headlight; handrails and nickel or brass bell; cast-iron wheels; hand reverse; stamped "The Ives Railway Lines" to left of cab door and either "Motor 3253" or "3253 N.Y.C. & H.R." to right of cab door. 175   350

	C6	C8

3253 Locomotive: 1925-1927, 0-4-0; center electric cab; green, orange or light brown stamped-steel body w/cast-iron frame; operating headlight and brass bell; die-cast wheels w/or w/out nickel tires; hand reverse; brass plate to the left of cab door reads "The Ives Railway Lines" and plate to the right of door reads "Motor 3253."

$188 $375

3254 Locomotive: 1925-1927, 0-4-0; center electric cab stamped-metal body and cast-iron frame; die-cast wheels w/nickel tires; hand reverse; brass plates read "Motor 3255" to the right of cab door.

70 140

3255-R Locomotive: 1925-1930, 0-4-0; center electric cab stamped-metal body; orange w/black frame, black w/red frame or blue w/red stamped-metal frame; brass journals; two operating headlights; grab rails and brass whistle; automatic reverse; brass plates read "Motor 3255" to the right of cab door.

110 220

3255 Locomotive: 1928-1930, 0-4-0; center electric cab stamped-metal body; orange w/black frame, black w/red frame or blue w/red stamped-metal frame; brass journals; two operating headlights; grab rails and brass whistle; reverse lever in different position; brass plates read "Motor 3255" to the right of cab door.

125 250

3257-R Locomotive: 1926-1930, 0-4-0; sheet metal St. Paul-type locomotive on stamped steel frame w/journals; gray, orange or black body; two operating headlights; brass bell and whistle w/hand rails; die-cast wheels w/nickel tires; cast-iron or die-cast pilots; automatic reverse; brass plates to the left of cab door read "The Ives Railway Lines" and brass plate to the right of cab door reads "Motor 3257."

450 900

3257 Locomotive: 1926-1930, 0-4-0; sheet metal St. Paul-type locomotive on stamped steel frame w/journals; gray, orange or black body; two operating headlights; brass bell and whistle w/hand rails; die-cast wheels w/nickel tires; cast iron or die-cast pilots; hand reverse; brass plates to the left of cab door read "The Ives Railway Lines" and brass plate to the right of cab door reads "Motor 3257."

313 625

3258 Locomotive: 1926-1930, 0-4-0; New Haven-type body; lithographed yellow body w/green roof or green body w/red roof; stamped-steel frame; operating headlight w/ brass whistle; die-cast wheels w/nickel tires; two windows per side w/door on each end; lithographed plate marked "Made In The Ives Shops" and "3258."

100 200

3259 Locomotive: 1927, 0-4-0; New Haven-type body; lithographed yellow body w/green roof or green body w/red roof (w/white body and red roof for the White Owl set); stamped-steel frame; operating headlight w/brass whistle and journals; die-cast wheels w/nickel tires; two windows per side w/door on each end; lithographed plate marked "Made In The Ives Shops" and "3258."

225 450

3260 Locomotive: 1928-1929, 0-4-0; stamped-steel New Haven body w/inserted ventilator and plate pieces; blue green, black or cadet blue Lionel No. 248 body; die-cast or stamped steel frame; operating headlight, brass whistle and pantograph on top; brass doors and journals; die-cast wheels w/nickel tires; two plates on side read "Made In The Ives Shops," plate inserts stamped "Ives" and "3260."

120 240

3261 Locomotive: 1929-1930, 0-4-0; stamped-steel New Haven body w/inserted ventilator and plate pieces; black Lionel No. 248 body; die-cast or stamped steel orange or red frame; operating headlight, brass whistle and pantograph on top; brass doors and journals; die-cast wheels w/nickel tires; hand reverse; two plates on side read "Made In The Ives Shops," plate inserts stamped "Ives" and "3261."

120 240

KUSAN

The history of Kusan Model Trains is indelibly linked to those trains produced by Auburn Model Toys—and unfortunately often blurred by well-meaning enthusiasts hypothesizing about the company's history. In fact, Kusan's history is pretty straightforward.

The Kusan Corp. was founded, and presided over, by Bill McLain. Kusan—the name itself taken from a Native American tribe near Coos Bay, Ore., was a successful plastic injection-molding firm based in Nashville, Tenn. In addition to producing plastic items on contract for outside firms, including the automotive industry, the Kusan Corp. also made a number of plastic toys, including trucks, pistols and dolls. In 1953, there were few toy markets bigger than trains, and McLain felt that Kusan could capture part of that market. At that time, Kusan's engineers went to work creating what would become Kusan's K-series of trains.

Coincidentally, that same year, AMT had entered into its disastrous relationship with Bernie Paul. Early in 1954, Paul's General Hobbies Corp. began returning large numbers of unsold—and unpaid for—trains to the small Indiana manufacturer, which was staggered by having invested so much in the manufacture of this product, which it now appeared it would

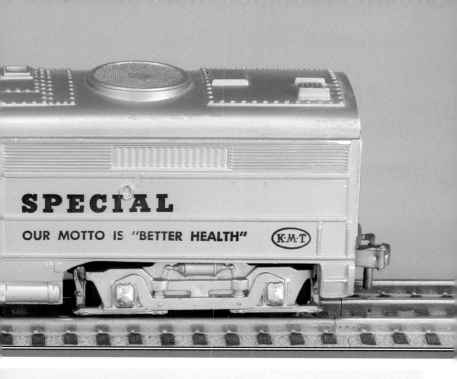

have to carry over for almost a full year.

Word of this situation reached Kusan's McLain, who saw this as an opportunity to enter the lucrative O-Gauge train market with an established product line. A purchase arrangement was made, and the inventory and tooling of AMT soon found their way to 2716 Franklin Rd., Nashville, Tenn. McLain stood one large step closer to achieving his goal. Compared to the K-series cars designed by Kusan's plastic-savvy engineers, the former AMT cars were complex, labor-intensive to produce and required outside sourcing for the die-cast components. Though they provided the company with a foothold in the market, it would take inexpensively produced trains, sold in sets, to gain the market position that McLain aspired to. With Kusan's established connections in the toy industry, these sets were aimed at the mass merchandisers, to whom low retail pricing was paramount.

Producing train sets required two key elements that AMT had not had—track and transformer. Kusan purchased power packs from an outside vendor, and had them labeled as their own product. Kusan's track was designed in-house, and was quite innovative. In addition to having 17 plastic crossties per section (compared to Lionel's standard of three metal ties), the center rail was removable. To utilize the track in its two-rail form, Kusan's locomotives had insulated wheels and a selector switch for two- or three-rail operation.

The firm introduced easy to assemble kits, essentially K-series cars that had not gone to final assembly, in 1957. Special retail displays were offered, promoting these cars, all of which sold for less than $2 each.

Kusan successfully struggled uphill in the train market until 1958. In that year, McLain negotiated a deal in which he would supply Sears, Roebuck and Co. stores with his trains on consignment. McLain was confident with his attractively packaged, economical trains prominently displayed in the nation's largest retailer and he was poised to move his train division from the red ink to black.

Unfortunately for McLain, history tends to repeat itself. In many stores, his products were displayed poorly, in others, not at all, and after Christmas the unsold trains began to arrive at the Nashville plant en masse—a haunting reminder of AMT's fate five years previously.

Kusan's other product lines however allowed the company to weather this storm, but McLain's spirit was broken. The remaining inventory of trains, with little new production, was sold through 1961. The firm continued to make other plastic toys, and its custom molding operation prospered.

Kusan's train production was dead, but the tooling wasn't. In 1967, Kusan sold the former AMT tooling to Andrew Kriswalus of Endicott, N.Y. Over the next several years, Kriswalus purchased the remaining dies, including those for the K-series cars, from Kusan as well. Building on the first syllable of his name, and the established KMT brand—Kris Model Trains was launched. Although he owned all the tooling, Kriswalus used only the former AMT freight car tooling.

In the early 1980s, the tooling was sold to Williams Electric Trains in Maryland, who unlike Kriswalus reactivated almost all of the tooling. But even this stop was not the end of the tooling travels. In 1985, Williams sold the former Kusan tooling to Maury D. Klein of K-Line trains. Williams retained the ex-AMT tooling. The former Kusan short diesel locomotive tooling has since been sold to Ready Made Toys.

That trains are still being produced from all this tooling is proof that the lack of success by AMT and KMT was not due inferior product.

Kusan initially offered trains identical to, or at least based on, those produced by Auburn. The next year, 1956, those of Kusan's own design, known as the K-series, joined them. Kusan's initial production, typified by the set at left, was high quality..

KMT F-7 Diesel Locomotives
Diesels

	C5	C7	C8

322 Santa Fe: F-7 A-unit, catalog number F2. Painted in Santa Fe's freight paint scheme of dark blue and yellow w/yellow lettering. Typically, Kusan production had better decorating than that of similar AMT items, and has improved screens on sides.

		C5	C7	C8
Powered		$120	$160	$200
Dummy		60	80	125

1733 New York Central: F7 A-unit, catalog number F3. These locos were painted in the two-tone gray "lightening stripe" scheme of the New York Central. The lettering was white.

	C5	C7	C8
Powered	120	160	200
Dummy	55	80	130

2019 Missouri, Kansas & Texas (The Texas Special): F7 A-unit, catalog number F1. Finished in the red, silver and black paint scheme worn by the "Texas Special" passenger train. Body is straighter than that of similar AMT unit, and has improved ventilation screens.

	C5	C7	C8
Powered	120	160	200
Dummy	75	125	175

5400 Chicago & Northwestern: F7 A-unit, catalog number F6. Finished in yellow and green paint scheme, including "400" markings near nose. Fuel tank skirts are black.

	C5	C7	C8
Powered	140	180	225
Dummy	80	140	200

6755 Southern: F7 A-unit, catalog number F5; green and gray paint; w/yellow lettering, green roof and black fuel tank skirts.

	C5	C7	C8
Powered	100	140	190
Dummy	70	110	160

8644 Pennsylvania: F7 A-unit, catalog number F4, body painted dark green.

	C5	C7	C8
Powered	—	120	150
Dummy	—	60	100

Baltimore & Ohio: F7 A-unit, catalog number F7. The elaborately painted body of this locomotive was painted dark blue and gray. The lettering was yellow.

	C5	C7	C8
Powered	180	300	400
Dummy	100	150	200

Southern Pacific: F7 A-unit: Loco finished black and red Southern Pacific "Black Widow" paint scheme.   **Too rarely traded to establish accurate pricing.**

322 Santa Fe

6755 Southern

	C5	C7	C8

KMT Rail Diesel Cars (RDCs)

The AMT Rail Diesel Cars had plastic bodies housing a seven-pole electric motor. Introduced in 1953, it continued to be offered after the Kusan takeover. All were numbered "3160" on their bodies.

	C5	C7	C8
New York Central: Catalog number 1-33.	$75	$110	$150
Pennsylvania: Catalog number 1-44.	60	90	125
Santa Fe: Catalog number 1-22.	80	110	140
Southern: Catalog number 1-55.	75	110	150

Extruded Aluminum Cars

Kusan continued to market the aluminum passenger cars originally created by AMT, at least until the existing stock–which was substantial–was exhausted.

The window glazing came most often in blue plastic, but some had two-piece acetate windows, the outer layer clear, the inner frosted. The vista domes too came in blue, which often warp, or white, which are frequently found cracked. Also, cars were available new with either smooth or fluted roofs. Originally, the fluted roof cars were lower cost, but today on the collector market they command a slight premium. The prices listed below are for the smooth-roof versions. Finally, catalog number, rather than the number on the side of the car lists the cars below.

"Texas Special" Set: Aluminum cars w/red painted trim wearing the markings of the Missouri-Kansas-Texas and Frisco jointly operated Texas Special passenger train.

	C5	C7	C8
1001 Mail Express: Number plate reads "3407."	75	125	200
1002 Roomette: "BOWIE."	75	125	200
1003 Diner: Number plate reads "DINER."	75	125	200
1004 Vista Dome: "CROCKETT."	75	125	200
1005 Observation: "SAM HOUSTON."	75	125	200
1006 Day Coach: Number plate reads "3160."	75	125	200
1007 Crew Combination: Number plate reads "5260."	75	125	200
1008 Baggage: Number plate reads "4170."	75	125	200

Santa Fe Set: Large letterboard reads "SANTA FE" w/smaller plates carrying numbers and car names.

	C5	C7	C8
2001 Mail Express: Number plate reads "3407."	40	75	125
2002 Roomette:			
(Type I) Number plate reads "INDIAN LAKE."	40	75	125
(Type II) Number plate reads "INDIAN SCOUT."	40	75	125
2003 Diner: "DINER."	40	75	125

2019 Missouri, Kansas & Texas (The Texas Special)

Chicago & North Western Set

34922 Santa Fe

	C5	C7	C8
2004 Vista Dome: "BUENA VISTA."	$40	$75	$125
2005 Observation: "INDIAN ARROW."	40	75	125
2006 Day Coach: Number plate reads "3160."	40	75	125
2007 Crew Combination: Number plate reads "5264."	40	75	125
2008 Baggage: Number plate reads "4170."	40	75	125
New York Central Set: Large letterboard reads "NEW YORK CENTRAL." w/smaller plates carrying numbers and car names.			
3001 Mail Express: Number plate reads "3407."	40	75	125
3002 Roomette:			
(Type I) "CITY OF DETROIT."	40	75	125
(Type II) "CITY OF ERIE."	40	75	125
(Type III) "CITY OF UTICA."	40	75	125
3003 Diner: "DINER."	40	75	125
3004 Vista Dome: "BUENA VISTA."	40	75	125
3005 Observation: "SENECA FALLS."	40	75	125
3006 Day Coach: Number plate reads "3160."	40	75	125
3007 Crew Combination: Number plate reads "5260."	40	75	125

	C5	C7	C8
3008 Baggage: Number plate reads "4170."	$40	$75	$125

Pennsylvania Set: Large letterboard reads "PENNSYLVANIA" w/smaller plates carrying numbers and car names.

	C5	C7	C8
4001 Mail Express: Number plate reads "3407."	40	75	125
4002 Roomette:			
(Type I) "CITY OF PITTSBURGH."	40	75	125
(Type II) "FORT WAYNE."	40	75	125
4003 Diner: "DINER."	40	75	125
4004 Vista Dome: "CITY OF NEW YORK."	40	75	125
4005 Observation: "CITY OF CHICAGO."	40	75	125
4006 Day Coach: Number plate reads "3160."	40	75	125
4007 Crew Combination: Number plate reads "5260."	40	75	125
4008 Baggage: Number plate reads "4170."	40	75	125

Southern Set: All cars bear a large plate on each side reading "SOUTHERN" and small plates w/additional lettering.

	C5	C7	C8
5001 Mail Express: Number plate reads "3407."	75	125	200
5002 Roomette:			
(Type I) "CATAWBA RIVER."	75	125	200
(Type II) "POTOMAC RIVER."	75	125	200
(Type III) "DAN RIVER."	75	125	200
5003 Diner: "DINER."	75	125	200
5004 Vista Dome: "GEORGIA."	75	125	200
5005 Observation: "CRESCENT CITY."	75	125	200
5006 Day Coach: Number plate reads "3160."	75	125	200
5007 Crew Combination: Number plate reads "5260."	75	125	200
5008 Baggage: Number plate reads "4170."	75	125	200

Chicago & North Western Set: These cars were attractively painted in the yellow and green scheme of the CNW. The "CHICAGO & NORTHW ESTERN" nameplates on these cars are significantly larger than the nameplates on the other cars. Once again, smaller plates were used for names and numbers.

	C5	C7	C8
6001 Mail Express: Number plate reads "3407."	80	150	250
6002 Roomette: "NORTHERN PINES."	80	150	250
6003 Diner: "DINER."	80	150	250
6004 Vista Dome: "NORTHERN STREAMS."	80	150	250
6005 Observation: "NORTHERN STATES."	80	150	250

6006 Day Coach: Number plate reads "3160."

Too rarely traded to establish accurate pricing.

6007 Crew Combination: Number plate reads "5260."

	C5	C7	C8
	80	150	250
6008 Baggage: Number plate reads "4170."	80	150	250

Baltimore & Ohio Set: Large letterboard is marked "BALTIMORE & OHIO" and small plates have additional lettering.

7001 Mail Express: Number plate reads "3407."

Too rarely traded to establish accurate pricing.

7002 Roomette: "YOUNGSTOWN." Too rarely traded to establish accurate pricing.

7003 Diner: "DINER." Too rarely traded to establish accurate pricing.

7004 Vista Dome: "CAPITOL CITY." Too rarely traded to establish accurate pricing.

7005 Observation: "WAWASEE." Too rarely traded to establish accurate pricing.

7006 Day Coach: Number plate reads "3160."

Too rarely traded to establish accurate pricing.

7007 Crew Combination: Number plate reads "5260."

Too rarely traded to establish accurate pricing.

7008 Baggage: Number plate reads "4170."

Too rarely traded to establish accurate pricing.

32066 Chicago, Burlington & Quincy

	C5	C7	C8

Boxcars

Kusan offered the series of scale-detailed boxcars Auburn had introduced in 1951, albeit with changes in some cases.

100 Rutland: Catalog number 9007, dark green and yellow. — $15, $30, $45

2710 Chicago & Eastern Illinois: Tuscan, catalog number 8102. — 25, 45, 65

4382 Minneapolis & St. Louis: Cataloged as number 9004, this car had yellow lettering on green body paint. Its doors were green as well. — 15, 30, 45

5124 Minneapolis & St. Louis: Cataloged as number 9004, this car had yellow lettering on green body paint. Its doors were green as well. — 15, 30, 45

5753 Central of Georgia: Black and silver, catalog number 9009. — 40, 60, 120

7698 Chicago & North Western: Tuscan, catalog number 8014. — 40, 60, 120

18841 Western Pacific: Tuscan w/orange feather, catalog number 8016. — 40, 60, 120

19509 Great Northern: Cataloged as number 8002, these cars wore tuscan paint, w/white lettering. Black doors were installed. — 15, 25, 40

25439 Erie: Assigned catalog number 8003, this car was painted tuscan and decorated w/black and white markings.
(Type I) Lettered "CU FT 3769," black doors. — 10, 20, 35
(Type II) Lettered "CU FT 3730," black doors. — 20, 40, 60
(Type III) Lettered "CU FT 3770," black doors. — 25, 45, 65
(Type IV) Reporting marks printed in two columns, fitted w/tuscan doors. — 30, 50, 75

30565 New York, New Haven & Hartford: Cataloged as number 8005, black doors and white lettering highlighted this otherwise tuscan boxcar. — 15, 25, 40

34922 Santa Fe: Assigned catalog number 8004, this tuscan boxcar w/black doors was lettered in white. — 10, 20, 30

36406 New Haven:
(Type I) Orange. Catalog number 9005. — 40, 60, 120
(Type II) Black. Catalog number 9011. — 40, 60, 120

45396 Soo Line: Tuscan, catalog 8015. — 40, 60, 120

54652 Minneapolis & St. Louis: Red, catalog number 9008. — 40, 60, 120

77066 Boston and Maine: Blue w/blue doors, catalog number 9006. — 40, 60, 120

120119 Missouri Pacific: Blue, gray and yellow, number catalog 9010. — 15, 25, 40

	C5	C7	C8

121834 Southern Pacific: Silver, catalog number 9012. $40 $60 $120

150231 Union Pacific: Tuscan w/yellow lettering, catalog number 8013.
    40   60   120

153902 Southern: The doors of this car, like the body, were painted tuscan. It was cataloged as item 8001.   15   25   40

180190 New York Central: Tuscan w/white lettering, catalog number 8011.
    40   60   120

465002 Baltimore & Ohio: Tuscan w/white lettering, catalog number 8010.
    40   60   120

466096 Baltimore & Ohio "Sentinel": The decal used on the Kusan-era cars were slightly smaller than that used by AMT on catalog number 9003.   20   30   45

677209 Pennsylvania: Cataloged as number 8009, this tuscan boxcar was decorated w/white lettering.   25   40   55

    Kusan also continued to sell freight cars of other body types pioneered by Auburn.

Depressed-Center Flatcars

412 Monon: Cataloged as number 7351, this was painted gray w/red lettering.
    20   45   75

Gondolas

51297 Louisville & Nashville: This dull black car w/white lettering was given catalog number 7651.   15   35   60

Refrigerator Cars

1008 Gerber's: Cataloged as number 7251, this multi-colored car had sides painted blue and white, its roof and ends were tuscan, and the lettering blue.   20   40   70

9241 Santa Fe: Cataloged w/number 7252, this car had dark yellow sides and tuscan roof and ends. The lettering was black.   20   35   65

Stock Cars

32066 Chicago, Burlington & Quincy: This tuscan-sided car w/black and white markings was given catalog number 7151.   15   25   35

47150 Missouri, Kansas & Texas: Assigned catalog number 7150 was this yellow-sided car w/tuscan roof and white lettering.   20   30   45

140449 Atlantic Coast Line: This tuscan car was given catalog number 7152; It had white lettering.   15   25   35

The K-Series Locomotives

    The locomotive for Kusan's equivalent to Lionel's 027-line was a replica of an Alco FA diesel. Originally developed as an un-powered floor toy by Kusan, it was good looking and easily adapted for use as a powered unit. The molded-in number board of each locomotive bore the number 2716, not coincidentally the address of the company on Franklin Road in Nashville, Tenn.

Bexel Special: Silver w/black lettering, produced as a promotion of the Bexel drug company. Powered.   35   55   75

Bexel Special: Blue w/black lettering, produced as a promotion of the Bexel drug company. Powered.   60   80   100

Burlington: Silver w/black numbers, cataloged as item number 3.
    Powered   20   30   50
    Dummy   10   20   30

Frisco: Black and yellow, w/yellow lettering. Cataloged w/stock numbers 2 and 14.
    Powered   10   20   30
    Dummy   5   10   20

K-M-T Lines: Gray and red, catalog number 11.
    Too rarely traded to establish accurate values.

Kusan Kannon Ball: Silver and black. Dummy.   5   10   20

Bexel Special

Burlington

Frisco

Kusan Kannon Ball

Missouri-Kansas-Texas

Silver Star

U.S. 135

	C5	C7	C8
Missouri–Kansas–Texas: Red and silver, catalog number 1.			
Powered	$10	$20	$30
Dummy	5	10	20
Missouri Pacific: Blue and white, blue lettering, catalog number 4.			
Powered	20	30	50
Dummy	10	20	30
Missouri Pacific: White lettering, catalog number 6.			
Powered	20	30	50
Dummy	10	20	30
Nacionales De Mexico: Silver w/black lettering "EL AZTECA."			
Powered	20	40	60
Dummy	10	25	50
Nacionales De Mexico: Yellow and gray w/red lettering "EL INTERNACIONAL."			
Powered	20	40	60
Dummy	10	25	50

	C5	C7	C8
New Haven: Black and red "McGinnis" paint scheme, catalog number 7.			
Powered	$20	$30	$50
Dummy	10	20	30
Silver Star: Silver and red w/black lettering.			
Powered	30	60	90
Southern: Gray and green w/yellow lettering. Catalog number 5.			
Powered	10	20	30
Dummy	5	10	20
Southern Pacific: Black, red, orange and silver. Cataloged as item 20.			
Too rarely, if ever, traded to establish accurate values.			
Union Pacific: Listed in catalogs w/both the stock numbers 18 and 28, these yellow locomotives had gray roofs and red lettering. They wore the number 1500 on their flanks.			
Powered	20	40	60
Dummy	10	25	50
U.S. 135: Yellow, gray and black w/black lettering, including number 21935, catalog number 19S.			
Powered	20	40	60
U.S. 135: Yellow and blue w/red lettering, including number 21938, catalog number 39.			
Powered	30	60	90
U.S. Army Atomic: Olive drab w/white lettering, including the atomic symbol. An aircraft-type machine gun turret replaced the "fan" area of the locomotive. The unit was assigned catalog number 10.			
Powered	10	25	50
U.S. Army Atomic: Black w/white lettering. An aircraft-type machine gun turret replaced the "fan" area of the locomotive. The unit was assigned catalog number 12.			
Powered	10	25	50
U.S. Navy: Two-tone gray w/black lettering. Catalog number 12.			
Powered	10	25	50

The "Beep"

The other locomotive originating from Kusan's ownership was this grossly foreshortened GP-7. Riding on only a single truck with four wheels, the DC powered locomotive was intended to power the Nashville firm's least expensive sets. The diminutive little locomotive soldiers on today, having survived at least two changes in tooling ownership.

As most of these units have a prominently displayed road number painted on their shell, they are listed here according to that number. The number "3206" is cast into all the numberboards, regardless of road name or painted number.

127 Minneapolis & St. Louis: Red w/white lettering, catalog number KF33, available w/ and w/out handrails.	20	40	60
248 Louisville and Nashville: Black, catalog number 23.			
Too rarely traded to establish accurate value.			
501 Chesapeake and Ohio: Blue body w/yellow lettering.			
(Type I) Catalog number KF25, features yellow "safety stripes" along frame edge.	20	40	60
(Type II) Catalog number KF35, no yellow "safety stripes" along frame edge.	15	35	50
612: This black locomotive, assigned catalog number B021, had no road name printed on it.			
Too rarely traded to establish accurate value.			
890 General Motors: Silver w/black lettering, this locomotive was given catalog number 37.			
(Type I) Features "safety stripes" and handrails along frame edge.	20	40	60
(Type II) No "safety stripes" or handrails.	15	35	50

U.S. Army Atomic

No-number Kusan

3206 Kusan

20065 Rock Island

29048 Pennsylvania

34005 New Haven

85023 Missouri-Kansas-Texas

499087 Union Pacific

Unnumbered Bexel Capsules

123 USAX

	C5	C7	C8
3206 Louisville and Nashville: Black w/white lettering.	$15	$35	$50
6800: This black locomotive had no road name printed on it, only the white "6800" number.	15	35	50
8900 USAF: Black, w/yellow lettering, catalog number B022.	15	25	35
9000 U.S. Army: Olive drab w/white markings. Assigned catalog number KF24.	15	35	50
No-number Gravy Train: White, unmarked, part of promotional set.	15	25	35
No-number Kusan: Red, catalog number B031.	15	25	35
No-number Kusan: Green, w/white lettering, catalog number B032.	15	25	35
No-number Nacionales de Mexico: Silver w/black lettering.	15	35	50

K-Series Freight Cars

This series of attractive but economical cars was offered in both ready-to-run, fully assembled form, as well as in kits. These kits were notably easy to assemble, and were well merchandised. Because the kit cars were fully decorated at the factory, they are difficult if not impossible to distinguish from factory-assembled cars in the absence of their boxes. Boxcars were furnished with a man who could be placed in the doorway. Cars are listed by type, and then by road number, where applicable.

Boxcars

	C5	C7	C8
3206 Kusan: Cataloged w/stock number 208, this car was offered in two types:			
(Type I) Yellow w/red lettering.	5	10	15
(Type II) Red w/white lettering.	5	10	15
5124 Minneapolis & St. Louis: This dark green car w/yellow lettering was assigned catalog number 203.	10	15	20
7989 Louisville & Nashville: Given stock number 211, this blue car w/yellow lettering was one of Kusan's more attractive offerings.	25	35	45
20065 Rock Island: Though this car was assigned only one stock number, 205, it was produced in at least five different variations.			
(Type I) Silver w/black lettering.	10	15	20
(Type II) White w/black lettering.	15	20	25
(Type III) Yellow w/red lettering.	Too rarely traded to establish values.		
(Type IV) Red w/white lettering.	Too rarely traded to establish values.		
(Type V) Red w/black lettering.	Too rarely traded to establish values.		
29048 Pennsylvania: Tuscan w/white lettering, this car was given catalog number 202.			
(Type I) Includes "Don't Stand Me Still" logo.	10	15	20
(Type II) W/out logo.	20	25	30
34005 New Haven: Orange w/black and white lettering, this car was listed as stock number 206.	10	15	20
55001 New Haven: Black w/red and white lettering, the catalog number 207 was assigned to this car.	20	30	40
62904 Burlington: Catalog number 209 was given to this red car w/white lettering.	15	25	35
66096 Western Pacific: Tuscan w/yellow lettering, this car was cataloged as stock number 212.	20	30	40
70203 Kusan Railroad:			
(Type I) Yellow w/red lettering.	5	10	15
(Type II) Yellow w/black lettering.	5	10	15
(Type III) Red w/white lettering.	5	10	15
85023 Missouri–Kansas–Texas: This yellow Katy boxcar had black lettering. It was given catalog number 201.			
(Type I) Bright yellow.	10	15	20
(Type II) Darker yellow.	10	15	20

123 USAX

24560 Louisville & Nashville

30100 U.S. Army Atomic Reactor

42010 U.S. Army Cannon

46250 Frisco

109840 U.S. Army Radar Scanner

5066 Reading

310794 Baltimore & Ohio

71908 Nickel Plate

401098 USA Searchlight

569028 Pittsburgh & Lake Erie

Unnumbered "Bexel"

	C5	C7	C8
499087 Union Pacific: Yellow and black w/black lettering.	$10	$15	$20
1089547 U.S. Army Boxcar: Olive drab w/olive drab trucks.	15	25	45
Unnumbered Bexel Capsules: Yellow and black.	10	15	20

Flatcars

123 USAX Dynamic Injection Compressortron:

(Type I) This yellow and dark gray flatcar was given catalog number K901. It carried a red and gray plastic mechanism housing decorated w/red, white and black-lettered decals.   25   50   75

(Type II) Catalog number K902 was assigned to this yellow flatcar w/a red and gray plastic mechanism housing w/black lettering.   25   50   75

(Type III) Red cars w/gray plastic housings and black lettering were variously assigned catalog numbers K903 through 906.   25   50   75

578 Navy Radar Scanner: Gray plastic flatcars w/gray mechanism housings supporting red radar antennas were given catalog number K805.   25   50   75

1389 USAF Missile Flat:

(Type I) Olive drab flatcar w/white lettering, w/red, white and blue rocket. Catalog number K803.   25   50   75

(Type II) Black plastic flatcar w/yellow lettering w/red rocket. Catalog number K803B.   25   50   75

(Type III) Unlettered black plastic flatcar w/white rocket. Assigned catalog number K803C.   25   50   75

(Type IV) Olive drab flatcar w/white lettering, w/red rocket. Catalog number K803E.   25   50   75

13445 Missouri–Kansas–Texas: This black flatcar w/white lettering was cataloged variously as stock number 401 and 407.   5   10   15

13893 U.S. Navy Missile Flat: Gray plastic flatcar w/black lettering. Assigned catalog number K803A, it hauled a white plastic rocket.   25   50   75

24560 Louisville & Nashville: This black flatcar w/white lettering was cataloged as stock number 403.   5   10   15

30100 U.S. Army Atomic Reactor: This car was decorated w/the nuclear symbol and "Danger Radiation" stamped in white.

(Type I) The olive drab version of the flatcar w/red housings was assigned catalog number K801A.   20   35   50

(Type II) Catalog number K801B was assigned to an olive drab flatcar w/white plastic housings.   25   40   55

(Type III) A black plastic flatcar w/white plastic housings was given catalog number K801C.   25   40   55

30100 U.S. Army Searchlight: Olive drab flatcar w/olive drab superstructure and lamp housing. Assigned catalog number K806.   30   50   75

40916 U.S. Army Radar Scanner: Olive drab flatcar w/olive drab radar assembly. White lettering decorated this car, which was given catalog number K805C.   30   50   75

42010 U.S. Army Cannon:

(Type I) This olive drab flatcar, catalog number K802, mounted a large olive drab cannon. White lettering decorated the car.   20   40   60

(Type II) A version of the car w/an unpainted gray plastic body and black plastic cannon was given catalog number K802A. **Too rarely traded to establish values.**

42010 U.S. Army Dynamic Injection Compressortron: An olive drab flatcar w/white lettering formed the base for this car. Assigned catalog number K904, its gray plastic Compressortron housing lettered in black.

Too rarely traded to establish values.

46250 Frisco: This car was of the depressed-center design and was given catalog number 460.   25   40   60

83756 Gulf, Mobile and Ohio: This black flatcar w/white lettering was cataloged as stock number 402.   5   10   15

18019 New York Central Hopper

97786 Chicago & Eastern Illinois Hopper

610 Dow Tank

2544 Cities Service Tank

Dupont Tank

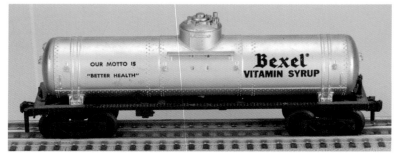

Unnumbered

	C5	C7	C8

109840 U.S. Army Radar Scanner: This yellow and gray plastic flatcar w/white lettering was equipped w/a red and gray superstructure and a red radar array. It was given catalog number K805A. $20 $50 $75

310794 Baltimore & Ohio: This tuscan flatcar w/white lettering was cataloged as stock number 404. 5 10 15

401098 USA Searchlight:

(Type I) Yellow flatcar w/gray superstructure and red lamp housing. Decorated w/ black lettering and crewed by a white plastic man, this car was given catalog number K806A. **Too rarely traded to establish values.**

(Type II) A second version, cataloged as stock number K806B, was based on a gray and yellow flatcar w/black lettering. A gray and red plastic superstructure w/white lettering w/red searchlight was mounted on the car. 25 40 65

968101 KMT Searchlight: A black flatcar w/yellow lettering was given catalog number K806C. Its superstructure was made of gray plastic parts w/black lettering. **Too rarely traded to establish values.**

41089547-S USAX 123: Blue and yellow w/black and white lettering, this depressed center car was assigned stock number 461. 25 35 55

Unnumbered Kusan: Red w/white lettering, catalog number 408. 5 10 15

Unnumbered Kusan: Yellow w/red pipe load, catalog number 409. 5 10 15

Unnumbered Kusan: Olive drab, catalog number 411. 5 10 15

Unnumbered Kusan: Black w/white lettering. 5 10 15

Unnumbered: Black, unlettered. 5 10 15

Gondolas

1776 U.S.: This silver gondola was laden w/18 "nuclear gas bottles"–which bore a startling resemblance to milk bottles–painted in three colors. Catalog number 310 was assigned to this car. **Too rarely traded to establish value.**

4190 U.S.: This dark gray gondola w/light gray interior carried four red plastic air activated cement containers w/the KMT logo. Assigned catalog number 308; its lettering, including the "#4190 SPACE RESEARCH" legend, was stamped in yellow. 10 15 20

5066 Reading: This black gondola w/white lettering was given catalog number 305. 5 10 15

7856 U.S. Army Gondola: This olive drab gondola w/white lettering, like most of Kusan's military-themed cars, rode on olive drab trucks. 20 40 60

54206 Western Maryland:

(Type I) Catalog number 303 was assigned to this tuscan gondola w/black lettering. 5 10 15

(Type II) Catalog number 303B was assigned to this black gondola w/white lettering. **Too rarely traded to establish value.**

71908 Nickel Plate: Painted black w/white lettering, this car was given catalog number 301. 5 10 15

99032 Norfolk & Western: Painted black w/white lettering, this car was given catalog number 302. 5 10 15

569028 Pittsburgh & Lake Erie: Painted black w/white lettering, this car was given catalog number 304. 5 10 15

Unnumbered Great Northern: A tuscan gondola w/white Great Northern lettering was cataloged as stock number 307. **Too rarely traded to establish value.**

Unnumbered Kusan: This plain-Jane car was given catalog number 309.

(Type I) Black w/white lettering. 5 10 15

(Type II) Red w/white lettering. 5 10 15

Unnumbered: All white, unlettered car was part of Gravy Train promotion. 15 20 25

Unnumbered Louisville & Nashville: Catalog number 306 was assigned to this black-painted, white-lettered gondola. 5 10 15

901 Missouri-Kansas-Texas

C528 New Haven

910 Missouri Pacific

2710 Kusan Line

X3239 Southern

20200 U.S. Army Master Control Center
Caboose

	C5	C7	C8

Unnumbered: An olive drab, but undecorated car was assigned catalog number 311.

Too rarely, if ever, traded to establish value.

Unnumbered "Bexel": This brown gondola was part of a promotional outfit.

	$5	$10	$20

Hoppers

316 G-E Hopper: This black open-top hopper car was given catalog number 603. It was decorated w/white lettering.

	25	40	60

800 Aluminum Ore Hopper: Assigned catalog number 604, this open-topped car was painted silver and decorated w/black lettering.

	30	60	90

18019 New York Central Hopper: A tuscan open-top hopper was decorated in New York Central markings and given catalog number 602.

	15	30	45

21640 Atlantic Coast Line Hopper: Dark gray ACL hoppers were cataloged in both open and covered versions w/stock number 611.

Too rarely, if ever, traded to establish values.

36180 Wabash Hopper: Catalog number 601; w/out cover; black paint, white lettering.

	10	25	35

97786 Chicago & Eastern Illinois Hopper:
(Type I) Cataloged as number 605 was this gray plastic, open-topped hopper w/red lettering.

	15	25	35

(Type II) A similar car was given catalog number 610. Though gray w/red lettering, this version was a replica of a covered hopper.

	15	25	35

Tank Cars

610 Dow Tank: Catalog number 701 was assigned to this tank car w/yellow "Dow" lettering. It was produced in both gloss and matte versions.

	15	25	40

X723 Radioactive Waste Tank: This silver-painted car w/red lettering was given catalog number 704.

	25	45	70

2544 Cities Service Tank: This attractive green tank car was assigned catalog number 703. The Cities Service lettering was applied in white.

	15	25	40

2544 Cities Service Tank: Some of the Cities Service cars were further enhanced by addition of a platform around the dome. Cars so equipped were given catalog number 710.

	30	40	60

2675 Dupont Tank: A silver-painted tank car w/black and red lettering used catalog number 702. It was offered in two versions.
(Type I) W/out platform.

	15	20	25

(Type II) W/platform.

	20	25	30

Unnumbered: Silver-painted car lettered "BEXEL VITAMIN SYRUP" in black for promotional outfit.

	10	20	30

Cabooses

C528 New Haven: This red caboose w/white lettering was assigned catalog number 507.

	10	15	25

763 General Motors: Silver lettering was applied to this red caboose, which was given catalog number 520.

	25	40	60

790 M-K-T (Missouri, Kansas & Texas): The black lettering of this caboose was stamped on a yellow base color. Catalog number 501 was assigned.

	15	25	40

790 KMT: White "KMT" lettering was applied to this red-painted caboose.

Too rarely traded to establish accurate values.

900 Minneapolis & St. Louis: Catalog number 518 was used for this red caboose w/white lettering.

	20	40	60

901 M-K-T (Missouri-Kansas-Texas): Catalog number 506 was assigned to this yellow and brown caboose w/black lettering.

	10	15	20

901 M-K-T (Missouri-Kansas-Texas): A similar, but red w/white lettering caboose was given catalog number 519.

	20	35	50

790 Missouri-Kansas-Texas

35443 U.S. Space Research

Unnumbered "Bexel Special"

126998 Frisco

	C5	C7	C8

910 Missouri Pacific: Red paint and white lettering adorned catalog number 504.
| | $10 | $20 | $30 |

2710 Kusan Line: This red-painted caboose, given catalog number 513, was produced in two versions.
| (Type I) Yellow lettering. | 10 | 15 | 25 |
| (Type II) White lettering. | 10 | 15 | 25 |

2710 Kusan Line: A similar, but yellow-painted caboose was given catalog number 517. It too came in two versions.
| (Type I) Black lettering. | 10 | 15 | 25 |
| (Type II) Red lettering. | 10 | 15 | 25 |

3206 Louisville & Nashville: This yellow caboose had black lettering.
| | 15 | 25 | 45 |

X3239 Southern: This red-painted caboose w/yellow lettering was given catalog number 505.
| | 10 | 20 | 30 |

3821 Union Pacific: Red paint and yellow lettering also decorated catalog number 508, a Union Pacific caboose.
| | 20 | 40 | 60 |

7989 Louisville & Nashville: L & N markings were also applied to this red caboose. White lettering was used on this car, which was given catalog number 515.
| | 20 | 30 | 45 |

13518 Chicago, Burlington & Quincy: Assigned catalog number 503, this car was produced in two variations.
| (Type I) Red paint w/white lettering. | 20 | 40 | 60 |
| (Type II) Yellow body w/brown roof and black lettering. | 10 | 15 | 25 |

20200 U.S. Army Master Control Center Caboose
| (Type I) Catalog number K804 was used for an olive drab w/white lettering. | 25 | 35 | 45 |
| (Type II) Catalog number K804A distinguished a gray plastic car w/black lettering. | 30 | 45 | 60 |

35443 U.S. Navy: A gray painted caboose w/radar dish and black lettering was given catalog number 510.
| | 25 | 40 | 60 |

35443 U.S. Space Research: Catalog number 512 was the reference assigned this yellow and gray caboose w/black lettering.
| | 20 | 35 | 55 |

35443 U.S. Air Force: Catalog number 514, a gray painted caboose w/yellow lettering, was produced in two variations.
| (Type I) W/radar dish in lieu of a smokejack. | 20 | 35 | 50 |
| (Type II) W/standard smokejack. | 15 | 30 | 45 |

35543 U.S. Space Research: This yellow and blue painted caboose w/red lettering was issued w/catalog number 521.
| | 20 | 30 | 40 |

37201 "KMT":
| (Type I) Yellow w/red lettering. | 5 | 10 | 15 |
| (Type II) Red w/yellow lettering. | 5 | 10 | 15 |

90079 Chesapeake & Ohio: Though only one catalog number, 516, was used for this car, it was produced in two distinct versions.
| (Type I) Red w/white lettering. | 15 | 30 | 45 |
| (Type II) Yellow w/red lettering. | 20 | 40 | 60 |

126998 Frisco: This red-painted car w/white lettering was given catalog number 502.
| | 10 | 15 | 20 |

Unnumbered Southern Pacific: Yet another red-painted caboose w/white lettering was given catalog number 509.
| | 10 | 15 | 20 |

Unnumbered: "Bexel Special" red caboose.
| | 10 | 15 | 25 |

LIONEL

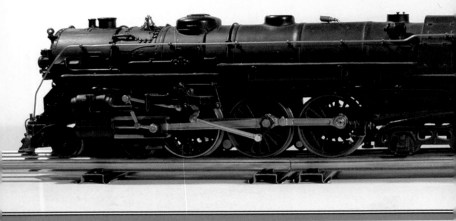

Few brand names have the instantaneous recognition that Lionel enjoys as it enters its second century. Young or old, male or female, it seems almost everyone identifies that name with toy trains. In fact, to many people the two are synonymous.

The firm bares the middle name of its founder, Joshua Lionel Cohen, the son of immigrants, born Aug. 25, 1877. Young Cohen, a clever inventor and shameless self-promoter with a clear head for business, formed the firm with Harry Grant on Sept. 5, 1900. Their first business was with the U.S. Navy, producing fuses for mines.

With the Navy work completed, Cohen began tinkering, trying to find a product to keep him and his partner busy and his new firm afloat. A motor he developed for a less-than-successful fan was installed under a gondola car. The car was placed on a circle of steel rails connected to dry cell batteries, and in 1900 the age of Lionel Electric Trains began.

As originally conceived, the "train," still only a motorized gondola car, was to be an animated window display for shopkeepers to use for promoting other products. Immediately though, it was apparent that there was more interest in the displays than the goods they held, and the transition from merchandising aid to retail product was made.

NEW YORK CENTRAL

In 1902, in addition to the gondola car, Lionel offered a miniature trolley, the first step towards realism. Like the gondola, the trolley ran on two-rail 2-7/8-in. gauge tracks. The first catalog was produced in 1900 and an American icon was born. Unfortunately, Cohen's partner Grant, though also a gifted inventor, was not a capable administrator. This lead to a man joining the payroll that was arguably as influential to the company and its trains as Cohen himself, an Italian immigrant named Mario Caruso. Hired at age 18 as a laborer, Caruso eventually rose to secretary-treasurer, managing the company's factories, first in New York, then New Haven, followed by Newark and ultimately the massive 15-acre Irvington plant, in a no-nonsense manner. Quality, production and cost-control were always of great concern and skillfully balanced by Caruso.

In 1906, Lionel began producing trains that rolled on "Standard-Gauge" track, and, in 1915, the smaller "O-Gauge" trains supplemented this. Though Lionel made forays into other sizes, namely OO in 1938, and, after World War II, three attempts at HO, it was to be O-Gauge where Lionel ultimately rose to notoriety. It is also the predominate size of trains produced after WWII and the size of trains featured in this volume.

In 1909, Lionel first used the slogan "Standard of the World," but it would be many years before the bold statement would become fact.

In 1910, for reasons unknown today, Cohen changed his last name to the one he is remembered by today, Cowen. A few years later, in 1918, the firm would change names as well, as the Lionel Manufacturing Co. became the Lionel Corp.

While toy train production continued in Lionel's plant during World War I, alongside were defense products, after all that is how the company was born—primarily signaling and navigational devices. This type of relationship would continue as long as the Lionel Corp. was in the manufacturing business, during both war and peacetime.

In 1923, Lionel revamped their Standard-Gauge offerings, replacing the somewhat realistic, but dingy colors used previously with a veritable kaleidoscope of blues, greens, yellows and oranges…all augmented with bright brass, copper and nickel trim. These later trains constitute what is considered the classic era of Standard-Gauge production.

The Depression was hard on Lionel, but harder on its competition. During the recession that preceded the Great Depression, Lionel, along with American Flyer, took over its bankrupt competitor, Ives. In 1930, Lionel became the sole owner of Ives. Thirty-six years later Lionel would take over American Flyer as well.

World War II would bring a halt to Lionel's toy production, with toy train production temporarily ceasing in June 1942. The Lionel plant, like countless others throughout the country, became totally devoted to manufacturing military products.

The complete cessation of train production for three years provided Lionel the opportunity to completely revamp their line. When production resumed in the fall of 1945, not only was Standard-Gauge not mentioned, but also the O-Gauge trains had totally new designed trucks and couplers, which were incompatible with the previous models and a newly designed plastic-bodied gondola car. Over the next few years, plastics would increasingly replace the previously used metals in Lionel's products.

Joshua Cowen resigned as Chairman of the Board at the end of 1958 and less than a year later sold his stock in the firm to a syndicate headed by his eccentric and controversial great-nephew, Roy Cohn.

Ultimately, in 1969 the Lionel Toy Corp. (as it had become known in 1965) exited the toy train business by licensing the name and selling the tooling to the Fundimensions Division of General Mills. Some production was moved immediately, and by the mid-1970s Lionel trains were no longer a presence in the huge Hillside plant.

With the exception of 1967, Lionel trains have been, and are still, in production every year since 1945, and trains were available even in the bleak 1967. Today's Lionel trains have elaborate paint schemes and sophisticated electronics undreamed of at the dawn of the last century. Despite these advances, they lack the mystique of the originals. Many of today's trains are manufactured as a collectable, to be displayed or operated, but rarely are they played with as Josh Cowen urged his young patrons. Perhaps it is memories of a small child remembering expectations of Christmases long ago or sneaking the new catalog to school hidden in a tablet, hoping to one day own that special item that fuels today's interest in yesterday's toys. Counter to what one may think by glancing at the prices in vintage catalogs, Lionel trains were always expensive, high-quality toys. They were built to last a lifetime and many have. Now that the baby boomers have reached adulthood, many of childhood's financial constraints are lifted—the toys of youthful dreams are at last within grasp.

4U Electric

154 Electric

226 or 226E Steam

227 Steam

232 Steam

233 Steam

248 Electric

251/251E Electric

250E Steam

	C5	C7	C8

4 Electric: 1928-32, 1-B-1, electric locomotive, painted orange or *gray*.

	$450-600	$650-900	$900-*1,300*

4U Electric: 1928-29, 1-B-1, electric locomotive. Kit of orange 4. To attain the values listed below, the kit must be unassembled and complete w/all packaging.

	1,200	2,000	4,000

150 Electric: 1917-25, 0-B-0, two different body styles. Dark green, dark olive, brown, maroon, *peacock*, *gray*, or *mojave*.

	50-*100*	75-200	110-300

152 Electric: 1917-29, 0-B-0, dark green, dark olive, dark gray, light gray, pea green, mojave, or *peacock*.

	50-*400*	75-550	110-700

153 Electric: 1924-25, 0-B-0, dark green, dark olive, gray, maroon, *mojave*, or peacock.

	80-*115*	110-*150*	150-200

154 Electric: 1917-23.

	80	110	150

156 Electric: 1917-23, 2-B-2, dark green, olive green, *gray*, maroon, or *mojave*.

	400-*750*	550-900	725-*1,100*

156X: 1923-24, less expensive 0-B-0 version of the 156, olive green, gray, maroon, mojave, or brown.

	350	425	550

158 Electric: 1919-23, 0-B-0, *dark green*, gray or *black*.

	80-*100*	125-140	175-200

201 Steam: 1940-42, 0-6-0 switcher, w/or w/out bell-ringing 2201 tender.

	350-*400*	500-550	700-*775*

203 Armored Locomotive: 1917-21.

	1,100	1,600	2,500

203 Steam: 1940-41, 0-6-0 switcher, w/or w/out bell-ringing 2203 tender.

	325-*400*	400-475	500-575

204 Steam: 1940-41, 2-4-2, *gunmetal* or black, w/1689T or 2689T tender.

	50-75	70-*110*	100-*150*

224 or 224E Steam: 1938-42, 2-6-2, black or *gunmetal* w/die-cast or plastic 2224 tender, 2689W sheet metal tender.

	125-*500*	165-*850*	225-*1,200*

225 or 225E Steam: 1938-42, 2-6-2, black or *gunmetal*, w/die-cast or plastic bodied 2235 tender, or 2225 or 2265 sheet metal tender.

	175-225	250-300	350-425

226 or 226E Steam: 1938-41, 2-6-4, w/2226W tender.

	350	475	650

227 Steam: 1939-42, 0-6-0, w/2227T or 2227B tender. Catalog number on boiler front, "8976" under cab window.

	550	750	975

228 Steam: 1939-42, 0-6-0, w/2228T or 2228B tender. Catalog number on boiler front, "8976" under cab window.

	550	750	975

229 or 229E Steam: 1939-42, 2-4-2, black or gunmetal w/2689T, 2689W, 2666T or 2666W tender.

	100-*125*	130-*175*	175-250

230 Steam: 1939, 0-6-0, w/2230T or 2230B tender. Catalog number on boiler front, "8976" under cab window.

	800	1,300	1,900

231 Steam: 1939, 0-6-0, w/2231T or 2231B tender. Catalog number on boiler front, "8976" under cab window.

	650	1,200	1,800

232 Steam: 1940-41, 0-6-0, w/2232B tender. Catalog number on boiler front, "8976" under cab window.

	650	1,200	1,800

233 Steam: 1940-42, 0-6-0, w/2233B tender. Catalog number on boiler front, "8976" under cab window.

	650	1,200	1,800

238/238E Steam: 1936-40, 4-4-2, gunmetal or black, w/265T, 265W, 2265W or 2225W.

	250	300	375

248 Electric: 1927-32, 0-B-0, dark green, peacock, *terracotta*, orange, peacock, or red.

	50-*150*	90-225	140-325

249/249E Steam: 1936-39, 2-4-2, gunmetal or black, w/265T or 265W tender.

	75	125	200

250 Electric: 1926, 1934, 0-B-0, dark green, peacock, terracotta, or orange.

	150	190	250

250E Steam: 1935-42, 4-4-2, gloss orange, black and gray. Came w/250W, 250WX, 250T, 2250W, or 2250T tender.

	600	1,000	1,600

252/252E Electric

254/254E Electric

256 Electric

262/262E Steam

259/259E Steam

261/261E Steam

263E Steam

	C5	C7	C8
251/251E Electric: 1925-32, 0-B-0, gray, red.	$275	$325	$400
252/252E Electric: 1926-35, 0-B-0, peacock, terracotta, yellow-orange, olive, or *maroon*.	75-300	110-450	150-650
253/253E Electric: 1924-36, 0-B-0, *maroon*, *gray*, mojave, dark green, peacock, terracotta, pea green, Stephen Girard green or red.	100-175	150-300	225-450
254/254E Electric: 1924-34, 0-B-0, dark green, mojave, olive green, orange, or **pea green**.	150-250	200-325	250-400
255E Steam: 1935-36, 2-4-2, w/263W.	500	700	1,000
256 Electric: 1924-30, 0-B+B-0, orange.	500	800	1,200
257 Steam: 1930-32, 2-4-0, w/257T or 259T tender.	125	200	300
258 Steam: 1930, 2-4-0 or 2-4-2, *black* or gunmetal w/257T or 1689T tender.	50-70	80-125	150-200
259/259E Steam: 1932-40, 2-4-2, black or gunmetal w/259T, 262T, 1588TX, 2689T, or 1689W.	50	80	125
260E Steam: 1930, black or *gunmetal*, w/260T, 263T or **263W**.	350-450	450-550	550-650
261/261E Steam: 1931, 1935, 2-4-2, black, w/257T or 261T.	125	175	225
262/262E Steam: 1931-36, 2-4-2, black, w/262T, 265T or 265W tender, 262 more desirable than 262E.	100-200	140-250	200-325
263E Steam: 1936-39, 2-4-2, gunmetal or *two-tone blue* w/263W or 2263W tender.	300-400	450-650	625-1,000
264E Steam: 1935-40, 2-4-2, *black* or red w/261T or 265T tender.	125-200	200-275	300-375
265E Steam: 1935-40, black, gunmetal or *blue* w/261TX, 2225T, 2225W, 265TX, or 265WX tender.	150-425	225-625	350-850
289E Steam: About 1936-37, black or gunmetal w/1588, 1688T, 1688W, 1689T, or 1689W.	100	200	325
450 Electric: 1928-31, 0-B-0 red or apple green.	400	750	1,125
529 Pullman: 1926-32, olive or terracotta.	20	30	40
530 Observation: 1926-32, olive or terracotta.	20	30	40
600 Pullman: 1915-1925, *four wheels*, 1933-42, eight wheels, *dark green*, brown, maroon, two-tone red, light blue and aluminum.	40-90	55-115	75-150
601 Pullman or Observation: 1915-1925, *four wheels*, 1933-42, *eight wheels*, dark green, brown, maroon, two-tone red, light blue and aluminum.	40-90	55-115	75-150
602 Baggage Car: 1915-1923, *four wheels*, 1933-37, eight wheels, dark green, yellow-orange, gray, two-tone red, light blue and aluminum.	25-80	40-100	60-135
603 Pullman: 1920-36, 6-1/2, 7 or 7-1/2 in. long, yellow-orange, red, *maroon*, green, and black.	25-75	35-100	50-140
604 Observation: 1920-25, 6-1/2 in. long, 1931-36, 7-1/2 in. long, yellow-orange, green, red, or *maroon*.	25-75	35-100	50-140
605 Pullman: 1925-32, gray, olive green, red, *orange Illinois Central*, Macy Special or Lionel Lines.	75-300	110-350	175-400
606 Observation: 1925-32, gray, olive green, red, *orange Illinois Central*, Macy Special or Lionel Lines.	75-300	110-350	175-400
607 Pullman: 1926-37, peacock, red, and Stephen Girard green.	75	85	100
608 Observation: 1926-37, peacock, red and Stephen Girard green.	75	85	100

264E Steam

529 Pullman

609 Pullman

611 Observation

613 Pullman

629 Pullman

651 Flatcar

656 Stock Car

700E Steam

700K Steam

	C5	C7	C8
609 Pullman: 1937-42, blue and silver.	$60	$75	$100
610 Pullman: 1915-42, dark green; mojave; maroon; olive green; terracotta body, maroon roof and cream trim; light red or blue w/aluminum roof; pea green; red lettered *Macy Special*.	45-200	55-300	70-400
611 Observation: 1937-42, blue and silver.	60	75	100
612 Observation: 1915-42, dark green; mojave; maroon; olive green; terracotta body, maroon roof and cream trim; light red or blue w/aluminum roof; pea green; red lettered *Macy Special*.	45-200	55-300	70-400
613 Pullman: 1931-40, terracotta, two-tone blue, *light red and aluminum*.	100-200	140-300	200-400
614 Observation: 1931-40, terracotta, two-tone blue, *light red and aluminum*.	100-200	140-300	200-400
615 Baggage: 1931-40, terracotta, two-tone blue, *light red and aluminum*.	100-200	140-300	200-400
616 Flying Yankee: 1935-41, the 616E or the similar whistle-equipped 616W headed replicas of the streamlined, articulated Boston and Maine "Flying Yankee." Chrome or painted aluminum, w/gunmetal, black, red or olive green trim. Complete train.	300	400	550
617 Coach: Matches 616, or blue.	50	60	75
618 Observation: Matches 617.	50	60	75
619 Combination: Matches 617.	100	140	200
620 Searchlight Car: 1937-38, red.	50	65	85
629 Pullman: 1924-32, dark green, peacock, orange or red.	25	32	40
630 Observation: 1924-32, dark green, peacock, orange or red.	25	32	40
636W UP City of Denver Power Unit: 1936-39, streamlined diesel painted yellow w/a brown roof. Came w/two 637 coaches and one 638 observation car from 1936 through 1939. Price for set.	500	650	1,100
651 Flatcar: 1935-38, green.	20	30	45
652 Gondola: 1915-42, yellow or orange.	25	35	50
653 Hopper: 1933-42, Stephen Girard Green.	30	50	75
654 Tank: 1933-42, aluminum, orange and gray, Sunoco or Shell.	25	35	50
655 Boxcar: 1933-41, cream or *tuscan* body.	30-45	40-60	55-80
656 Stock Car: 1935-42, light gray or *burnt orange*.	60-75	75-100	100-140
657 Caboose: 1933-42, red.	15	25	35
659 Ore Dump: 1935-42, dark green.	50	60	75
700 Electric: 1915-16, 0-B-0.	500	625	775
700E Steam: 1937-42, 4-6-4 Hudson, scale-detailed.	1,300	2,000	2,800
700EWX Steam: 4-6-4 Hudson. A number of customers liked the scale detailed appearance of Lionel's Hudson, but had extensive model railroad systems made of conventional tubular track. The 700EWX, available by special order, had blind (lacking flanges) center drivers, while the profile of the flanges of the other drivers was also slightly different.	1,500	2,250	3,000
700K Steam: 1938-42, 4-6-4, scale-detailed Hudson in kit form.			
Assembled:	1,000	2,500	4,000
Unassembled:	5,000	8,000	12,000
701 Electric: 1915-1916, 0-B-0.	400	500	625
701 Steam: 1939-42, 0-6-0 switcher w/701T tender, cab lettered "8976."	350	500	700

701 Steam

702 Baggage Car

710 Pullman

714 Boxcar

715 Tank Car

717 Caboose

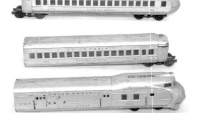

752 Union Pacific M10000

804 Tanker

805 Boxcar

806 Cattle Car

	C5	C7	C8
702 Baggage Car: 1917-21, unlettered gray, for armored train.			
	$125	$200	$300
703 Electric: 1915-16, 2-B-2, dark green.	1,100	1,700	2,500
706 Electric: 1915-1916, 0-B-0, dark green.	325	475	650
710 Pullman: 1924-34, olive green, "NEW YORK CENTRAL LINES," or orange "NEW YORK CENTRAL LINES," "ILLINOIS CENTRAL LINES" or "THE LIONEL LINES," *red or blue "THE LIONEL LINES,"* four- or *six-wheeled trucks*.			
	125-300	175-375	225-475
712 Observation: 1924-34, olive green, "NEW YORK CENTRAL LINES," or orange "NEW YORK CENTRAL LINES," "ILLINOIS CENTRAL LINES" or "THE LIONEL LINES," *red or blue "THE LIONEL LINES,"* four- or *six-wheeled trucks*.			
	125-300	175-375	225-475
714 Boxcar: 1940-42, scale replica Pennsylvania boxcar.			
	425	575	750
714K Boxcar: 1940-42, unpainted and unassembled scale boxcar.			
	600	1,000	1,500
Assembled:	300	400	550
715 Tank Car: 1940 Shell, 1941-42, *Sunoco* scale model tank car.			
	300-400	500-600	725-850
715K Tank Car: 1940-42, unpainted and unassembled scale tank car.			
	500	850	1,300
Assembled:	350	550	800
716 Hopper: 1940-42, black die-cast scale hopper.	300	450	625
716K Hopper: 1940-42, primered only, unassembled scale hopper car.			
	600	900	1,500
Assembled:	275	425	575
717 Caboose: 1940-42, scale caboose.	350	475	650
717K Caboose: 1940-42, unpainted and unassembled scale tank car.			
	600	1,000	1,500
Assembled:	300	400	550
728 Electric: 1916, 0-B-0, "Quaker."			
	Too infrequently traded to establish accurate values.		
732 Electric: 1916, 0-B-0, "Quaker."			
	Too infrequently traded to establish accurate values.		
752 Union Pacific M10000: 1935-41, yellow and brown or painted aluminum finish; three- or four-car sets. Price listed for three-car sets, additional cars add 100-200.			
Yellow and brown adds a similar premium.	600	1,000	1,400
763 Steam: 1937-40, semi scale Hudson. Black or gunmetal, w/263W, 2263W, 2226W or 2226WX tender.	1,100	1,800	2,750
782/783/784 Hiawatha Cars: 1935-41, orange sides, gray roof, and maroon frame. Part of streamlined articulated Hiawatha passenger set pulled by 250E locomotive.			
	600	1,200	1,800
792/793/794 Rail Chief Cars: 1937-41, red sides, maroon roof and maroon frame. Part of streamlined articulated Rail Chief passenger set pulled by 700E locomotive.			
Matches 793, 794, does not include vestibule.	800	2,500	3,800
800 Boxcar: 1915-27, orange, Wabash or Pennsylvania markings.			
	25	40	50
801 Caboose: 1915-26.	30	40	65
802 Stock Car: 1915-27, green.	25	40	55
803 Hopper: 1923-34, dark green or peacock.	25	35	50
804 Tanker: 1923-41, gray, terracotta, aluminum-painted or *yellow-orange*.			
	15-35	25-45	35-60
805 Boxcar: 1927-34, pea green, cream or orange.	20	35	50
806 Cattle Car: 1927-34, *pea green*, orange or maroon.			
	30-60	45-90	65-125

807 Caboose

810 Derrick

812 Gondola

813 Stock Car

815 Tank

816 Hopper

817 Caboose

1010 Electric

1015 Steam

1019 Observation

1020 Baggage

	C5	C7	C8
807 Caboose: 1927-42, peacock, red.	$20	$30	$40
809 Dump Car: 1930-32, orange or green dump bin.	60	70	85
810 Derrick: 1930-42, terracotta, cream cab or *yellow.*	125-175	150-210	225-250
811 Flatcar: 1926-42, maroon or *aluminum* colored body.	35-60	45-75	60-100
812 Gondola: 1926-42, mojave, dark green, 45N green, *Stephen Girard green* or *orange.*	25-60	35-75	45-100
813 Stock Car: 1926-42, orange, cream or *rubber-stamped tuscan.*	75-1,500	110-2,250	150-3,250
814 Boxcar: 1926-42, cream, yellow or orange.	60	90	125
814R: 1929-42, Ivory or white w/black frame, white w/aluminum frame, all w/blue roofs or *white w/brown roof.*	100-1,500	150-2,000	225-2,750
815 Tank: 1926-42, pea green, aluminum or *orange.*	50-200	75-300	110-550
816 Hopper: 1927-42, olive green, red or *black w/plates* or rubber-stamped black.	60-1,400	100-2,500	150-3,500
817 Caboose: 1926, peacock or red or *red w/brown roof.*	35-200	55-300	75-400
820 Searchlight Car: 1931-42, terracotta or green light base.	100	125	160
820 Boxcar: 1915-26, *dark olive A.T. & S.F.*, yellow-orange "ILLINOIS CENTRAL RAILROAD" or orange "UNION PACIFIC."	40-175	55-225	80-300
821 Stock Car: 1925-26, green.	50	65	90
831 Flatcar: 1927-42, black or dark, pale or 45N green.	20	30	40
900 Ammunition Boxcar: 1917-21, unlettered gray, included w/203-Armored Motorcar.	125	225	350
901 Gondola: 1917-27, brown, maroon, gray or green.	35	45	60
902 Gondola: 1927-31, dark green, peacock or Stephen Girard green.	20	30	40
1010 Electric: 1931-32, 0-B-0, orange.	75	110	150
1011 Pullman: 1931-32, light orange body w/green or olive roof.	50	60	75
1015 Steam: 1931-32, 0-4-0 w/1016 tender.	100	150	200
1019 Observation: 1931-32, orange body, w/green or olive roof.	50	60	75
1020 Baggage: 1931-32, light orange body, w/green or olive roof.	60	75	100
1035 Steam: 1931-32, 0-4-0 black w/copper trim.	75	100	125
1506 Steam: 1935, 0-4-0, clockwork, w/Mickey Mouse riding in its 1509 tender.	225	325	450
1506L Steam: 1933-34, 0-4-0, clockwork. No Mickey Mouse rode on this version.	80	100	125
1508 Steam: 1935, 0-4-0, clockwork, streamlined, painted red, w/Mickey Mouse riding in its 1509 tender.	325	450	600
1511 Steam: 1936-37, 0-4-0, clockwork, black or red, w/1516T oil-style tender.	100	125	150
1512 Gondola: 1931-37, blue or blue-green.	5	10	20
1514 Boxcar: 1931-37, light yellow, w/or w/out Baby Ruth logo.	15	20	30
1515 Tank Car: 1931-37, aluminum-colored, lithographed *Union Tank Lines*, *Fuel Oil* or Sunoco.	15-25	25-45	35-70

1512 Gondola

1514 Boxcar

1517 Caboose

1518, 1519 & 1520 Circus Set

1588 Steam

1630 Pullman

1651E Electric

1662 Steam

1663 Steam

1664/1664E Steam

	C5	C7	C8

1517 Caboose: 1931-37, no Lionel markings whatsoever. Red, orange "NEW YORK–CENTRAL–LINES" legend. $20 $30 $40

1518 Circus Dining Car: 1935, part of an uncataloged Mickey Mouse-themed circus outfit. 100 150 225

1519 Mickey Mouse Band: 1935, part of an uncataloged Mickey Mouse-themed circus outfit. 100 150 225

1520 Mickey Mouse Circus: 1935, part of an uncataloged Mickey Mouse-themed circus outfit. 100 150 225

1588 Steam: 1936-37, clockwork, black, w/1588T tender. 125 175 225

1630 Pullman: 1938-41, blue w/gray or aluminum-colored windows, roof and underframe. 30 45 65

1631 Observation: 1938-41, blue w/gray or aluminum-colored windows, roof and underframe. 30 45 65

1651E Electric: 1933, 0-B-0, red. 100 140 200

1661E Steam: 1933, 2-4-0, w/1661T tender. 70 100 150

1662 Steam: 1940-42, 0-4-0, w/2201T or 2203B tender. 225 300 400

1663 Steam: 1940-42, 0-4-0, w/2201T. 200 300 400

1664/1664E Steam: 1938-42, 2-4-2 black or gunmetal, w/1689T, 1689W or 2666W. 50 75 100

1666/1666E Steam: 1938-42, 2-6-2 black or gunmetal w/1689W, 2689T, 2689W, 2666T, or 2666W tender. 75 100 125

1668/1668E Steam: 1937-41, 2-4-2, Pennsylvania, streamlined, gunmetal or black, w/1689W tender. 75 100 125

1677 Gondola: 1933-38, blue, peacock or red. 20 30 40

1679 Boxcar: 1933-39, yellow "Baby Ruth"or "CURTISS BABY RUTH" on sides. 12 18 25

1679X Boxcar: 1936-42, the 1679X differed from the normal production by lacking journal boxes. 20 25 30

1680 Tank Car: 1931-42, lithographed orange, gray or aluminum-colored lithographed tank, lettered "Motor Oil," Sunoco, Shell or "PETROLEUM–PRODUCTS." 15 22 30

1680X Tank Car: 1936-42, orange, *gray* or aluminum-colored w/Sunoco, Shell or "Gas-Sunoco-Oils" markings. 15-30 22-40 30-55

1668/1668E Steam

1677 Gondola

1680 Tank Car

1681/1681E

1682 Caboose

1684 Steam

1685, 1686 & 1687 Passenger Cars

1689E Steam

1692 Pullman

1693 Observation

1717 Gondola

1719 Boxcar

	C5	C7	C8
1681/1681E: 1934, 2-4-0, black or *red*, w/1661T tender.	$50-75	$80-*100*	$110-*150*
1682 Caboose: 1933-41, vermilion, red or brown body.	20	30	40
1684 Steam: 1941-42, 2-4-2, die-cast, black or gunmetal.	40	55	75
1685 Passenger Car: 1933-37, gray, blue or red, four- or *six-wheel trucks*.	175-250	275-350	350-500
1686 Baggage Car: 1933-37, gray, blue or red, four- or *six-wheel trucks*.	175-250	275-350	350-500
1687 Observation Car: 1933-37, gray, blue or red, four- or *six-wheel trucks*.	175-250	275-350	350-500
1688/1688E Steam: 1936-40, 2-4-2, Pennsylvania streamlined boiler and cab, gunmetal or black, w/1689T or 1689W tender.	40	55	75
1689E Steam: 1936-37, 2-4-2, black or gunmetal Commodore Vanderbilt-style streamlined locomotive w/1689T, 1689W, 1688T or 1688W tender.	75	100	125
1690 Pullman: 1933-1940, dark red w/yellow windows, medium red and cream windows or orange-red.	30	40	55
1691 Observation: 1933-1940, dark red w/yellow windows, medium red and cream windows or orange-red.	30	40	55
1692 Pullman: 1939, lithographed blue.	40	50	65
1693 Observation: 1939, lithographed blue.	40	50	65
1700E Diesel: 1935-37, chrome finished, or painted yellow, orange or aluminum. Yellow too scarce to value.	150	200	250
1701 Coach: 1935-37, chrome finished, or painted red, yellow, orange or aluminum. Yellow too scarce to value.	25	35	50
1702 Observation: 1935-37, chrome finished, or painted red, yellow, orange or aluminum. Yellow too scarce to value.	25	35	50
1703 Front-End Car: 1935-37, chrome finished, or painted red, yellow, orange or aluminum. Yellow too scarce to value.	50	75	100
1717 Gondola: 1933-40, yellow.	15	25	35
1717X Gondola: 1940, yellow, equipped w/latch couplers.	30	45	60
1719 Boxcar: 1933-42, lithographed Stephen Girard or light green.	20	30	40
1719X Boxcar: 1942, lithographed light Stephen Girard green.	25	35	45
1722 Caboose: 1933-42, orange, light red or orange red.	20	30	40
1722X Caboose: 1939-1940, orange-red.	20	30	40
1811 Pullman: 1934-37, peacock, gray or red.	30	45	65
1812 Observation: 1934-37, peacock, gray or red.	30	45	65
1813 Baggage: 1934-37, peacock, gray or red.	30	45	65

1722 Caboose

1811 Pullman

1812 Observation

1813 Baggage

2600 Pullman

2623 Pullman

2630 Pullman

2631 Observation

2640 Pullman

2641 Observation

2643 Observation

2651 Flatcar

2653 Hopper

2654 Tank Car

2657 Caboose

2660 Crane

	C5	C7	C8
1816 Diesel: 1935, clockwork-powered, chrome finished, came w/a matching 1817 coach and 1818 observation w/orange vestibules and frames.	$100	$150	$200
1816W Diesel: 1936-37, clockwork-powered, chrome finished, came w/a matching 1817 coach and 1818 observation w/orange vestibules and frames.	110	160	225
1817 Coach: 1935-37, chrome finished, fluted body. Sold in sets w/matching 1816 or 1816W locomotive and 1818 observation.	20	35	50
1818 Observation: 1935-37, chrome finished, fluted body. Sold in sets w/matching 1816 or 1816W locomotive and 1818 observation.	20	35	50
2600 Pullman: 1938-40.	80	125	175
2601 Observation: 1938-40.	80	125	175
2602 Baggage: 1938-40.	80	125	175
2613 Pullman: 1938-42, blue body w/two-tone blue roof or *State green w/a two-tone State green and dark green roof.*	90-200	165-300	250-400
2614 Observation: 1938-42, blue body w/two-tone blue roof or *State green w/a two-tone State green and dark green roof.*	90-200	165-300	250-400
2615 Baggage: 1938-42, blue body w/two-tone blue roof or *State green w/a two-tone State green and dark green roof.*	90-200	165-300	250-400
2620 Searchlight Car: 1938-40, red.	50	80	120
2623 Pullman: 1941-42, "2623 IRVINGTON 2623."	200	300	425
2623 Pullman: 1941-42, "2623 MANHATTAN 2623."	125	200	300
2624 Pullman: "2624 MANHATTAN 2624."	800	1,500	3,000
2630 Pullman: 1938-42, blue w/aluminum or *gray roof.*	25-35	50-60	75-90
2631 Observation: 1938-42, blue w/aluminum or *gray roof.*	25-35	50-60	75-90
2640 Pullman: 1938-42, illuminated, blue or State green.	25	50	75
2641 Observation: 1938-42, illuminated, blue or State green.	25	50	75
2642 Pullman: 1941-42, tuscan w/gray windows.	40	60	85
2643 Observation: 1941-42, tuscan w/gray windows.	40	60	85
2651 Flatcar: 1938-40, green or *black.*	25-50	35-75	50-115
2652 Gondola: 1939-42, yellow or orange.	25	35	50
2653 Hopper: 1938-39, Stephen Girard green or *black.*	30-75	50-200	75-350
2654 Tank Car: 1938-42, aluminum-colored, orange or gray, Sunoco or Shell.	30	40	55
2655 Boxcar: 1938-41, yellow w/maroon or tuscan roof.	40	55	75
2656 Stock Car: 1938-40, light gray or *burnt orange.*	60-100	75-125	100-165
2657 Caboose: 1938-42, light red.	15	22	30
2657X: 1938-42, light red, equipped w/electrocouplers for use with switcher sets.	20	30	40
2659 Dump Car: 1938-42, w/dark green dump bin.	75	100	125
2660 Crane: 1938-42.	60	75	100
2672 Caboose: 1942, Pennsylvania, painted tuscan. No window frames, smokejack or steps.	20	30	40
2677 Gondola: 1940-42, dark red lithographed gondola.	35	50	70

2672 Caboose

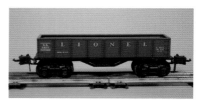

2677 Gondola

2679 Boxcar

2680 Tank

2682 Caboose

2719 Boxcar (Type II)

2755 Tank Car

2757 Caboose

2758 Automobile Boxcar

2810 Crane

2811 Flatcar

2812 Gondola

	C5	C7	C8
2679 Boxcar: 1938-42, yellow lithographed, "Baby Ruth" or a "Curtiss Baby Ruth Candy."	$15	$25	$40
2680 Tank: 1938-42, gray or aluminum-painted, Sunoco or orange w/Shell markings.	15	25	35
2682 Caboose: 1938-41, red Lionel Lines or tuscan New York Central.	15	22	30
2682X Caboose: 1940-41, caboose w/two automatic couplers.	20	30	40
2717 Gondola: 1938-42, lithographed, yellow.	20	30	40
2719 Boxcar: 1938-42, lithographed light peacock.	15	25	40
2719 Boxcar (Type II): In 1939, solenoid operated couplers were installed, but the rest of the car was unchanged. These cars were continued in 1940.	15	25	40
2722 Caboose: 1938-42, orange-red body.	20	30	45
2755 Tank Car: 1941-42, aluminum or *gray*.	50-100	80-150	125-225
2757 Caboose: 1941-1942, tuscan w/Pennsylvania markings, separately installed steps, smokejack and red window frames.	20	30	45
2757X: 1941-42, same as 2757, but w/automatic box couplers on both ends. Requires box for full value.	30	45	60
2758 Automobile Boxcar: 1941-42, tuscan double door.	40	50	65
2810 Crane: 1938-42, cream or yellow cab.	175	210	250
2811 Flatcar: 1938-42, aluminum-colored.	65	95	135
2812 Gondola: 1938-42, 45N orange or green gateman.	30	40	50
2812X Gondola: 1940-42, dark orange car.	40	50	70
2813 Stock Car: 1938-39, cream or tuscan.	150	225	350
2814 Boxcar: 1938-42, cream or *orange*.	75-750	150-1,500	250-2,500
2814R Refrigerator Car: 1938-40, white, blue or *brown roof*.	250-750	325-1,500	450-2,500

2812X Gondola

2813 Stock Car

2814 Boxcar

2814R Refrigerator Car

2815 Tank Car

2816 Hopper

2817 Caboose

2820 Searchlight Car

2954 Boxcar

2955 Tank Car

2956 Hopper

2957 Caboose

3652 Operating Gondola

3659 Operating Dump Car

3814 Merchandise Car

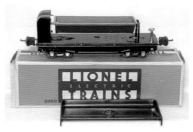

3859 Operating Dump Car

	C5	C7	C8
2815 Tank Car: 1938-42, aluminum-colored Sunoco or orange Shell.			
	$100	$150	$225
2816 Hopper: 1938-42, red or *black*.	125-150	175-250	250-425
2817 Caboose: 1938-42, red body, red or *brown roof*.			
	75-100	100-200	125-300
2820 Searchlight Car: 1938-42, light green, light base.			
	125	175	225
2954 Boxcar: 1940-42, semi scale tuscan Pennsylvania boxcar.			
	150	250	400
2955 Tank Car: 1940, black w/Shell markings, 1941-42, Sunoco markings.			
	200	350	525
2956 Hopper: 1940-42, semi scale hopper.	200	400	625
2957 Caboose: 1940-42, semi scale.	125	250	400
3651 Log Dump: 1939-40, black.	20	35	60
3652 Operating Gondola: 1939-41, yellow.	30	50	75
3659 Operating Dump Car: 1938-42, red dump bin.			
	30	50	75
3811 Log Dump Car: 1939-42, black.	35	50	80
3814 Merchandise Car: 1939-40, tuscan boxcar w/operating mechanism, includes cube-like plastic "boxes."	125	175	225
3859 Operating Dump Car: 1938-42, light red.	60	85	115

1 Bild-A-Motor

2 Bild-A-Motor

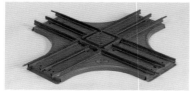

020 90-Degree Crossing

27 Lighting Set

41 Contactor

35 Boulevard Lamp

042 Pair of Manual Switches

43/043 Bild-A-Motor Gear Set

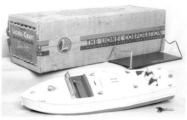

43 Lionel Craft Pleasure Boat

	C5	C7	C8
Accessories			
1 Bild-A-Motor: 1928-31, mounted on a red or black base.			
	$60	$90	$150
2 Bild-A-Motor: 1928-31.	100	125	225
011 Pair of Remote Control Switches: 1933-37.	20	30	40
011L Left Hand Remote Control Switch: 1933-37.			
	10	15	20
011R Right Hand Remote Control Switch: 1933-37.			
	10	15	20
012 Pair of Remote Control Switches: 1927-33.	25	30	40
012L Left Hand Remote Control Switch: 1927-33.			
	12	15	20
012R Right Hand Remote Control Switch: 1927-33.			
	12	15	20
013 Remote Control Switch Set: 1929-31.	100	140	200
020 90-Degree Crossing: 1915-61.	4	6	8
020X 45-Degree Crossing: 1915-59.	4	7	10
021 Pair of Manual Switches: 1915-27.	15	25	40
021L Left Hand Manual Switch: 1915-37.	7	12	20
021R Right Hand Manual Switch: 1915-37.	7	12	20
022 Pair of Manual Switches: 1915-26. Priced per pair.			
	25	40	65
022 Remote Control Switches: 1938-42, 1945-66.	60	75	90
022L Left Hand Remote Control Switch: 1938-42, 1950-61.			
	35	45	55
022R Right Hand Remote Control Switch: 1938-42, 1950-61.			
	35	45	55
023 Bumper: 1915-33, red or black.	15	25	35
025 Illuminated Bumper: 1928-42, cream or black.	15	20	25
27 Lighting Set: 1911-23.	15	30	45
32 Miniature Figures: 1909-18.	70	100	150
35 Boulevard Lamp: 1940-42, 1945-49. Painted aluminum color or gray.			
	20	35	55
41 Contactor: 1936-42.	1	5	8
042 Pair of Manual Switches: 1938-42, 1946-59.	40	50	60
042L Left Hand Manual Switch: 1938-42, 1946-59.	20	25	30
042R Right Hand Manual Switch: 1938-42, 1946-59.			
	20	25	30
43/043 Bild-A-Motor Gear Set: 1929.	40	60	90
43 Lionel Craft Pleasure Boat: 1933-36.	325	550	750
44 Lionel Craft Racing Boat: 1935-36.	500	800	1,250
45 Automatic Gateman, 045 Automatic Gateman, 45N Automatic Gateman: 1935-42, 1945.	30	45	60
46 Single Crossing Gate: 1939-42, roadway area painted ivory, the remainder of the accessory base was painted 45N green.	75	100	125
47 Double Crossing Gate: 1933-42, roadway area painted ivory, the remainder of the accessory base was painted 45N green.	60	100	150
48W Whistle Station: 1937-42.	30	45	60
49 Airport: 1937-39.	400	700	1,100
50 Remote Control Airplane: 1936.	425	650	850
50 Wartime Freight Train: 1943.	200	300	500
51 Airport: 1936, 1938.	200	300	500
52 Lamppost: 1933-41.	35	55	75

44 Lionel Craft Racing Boat

45 Automatic Gateman, 045 Automatic Gateman, 45N Automatic Gateman

46 Single Crossing Gate

47 Double Crossing Gate

48W Whistle Station

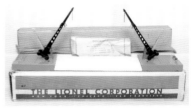

50 Wartime Freight Train

0051 Curved Track

51 Airport

Remote Control Airplane

54 Lamp-post

	C5	C7	C8
53 Lamppost: 1931-42, ivory, aluminum, light mojave, gray or white.			
	$25	$35	$45
0054 Curved Terminal Track: 1939-42.	12	18	25
54 Lamppost: 1929-35, maroon, pea green or State brown.			
	40	60	80
55 Remote Control Airplane: 1937-39.	325	550	750
56 Lamppost: 1924-42, 1946-49, *copper*, green, pea green, dark green, gray, dark gray or aluminum.	30-40	45-55	60-90
57 Lamppost: 1922-42, *orange*.	30-60	45-85	60-115
58 Lamppost: 1922-42, dark green, pea green, orange, cream, peacock or maroon.			
	30	40	60
59 Lamppost: 1920-36, dark green, olive green, light green, maroon, State brown or red.	35	55	75
060 Telegraph Post: 1929-42, orange, gray, green, aluminum or gray.			
	20	25	30
61 Lamppost: 1914-32, 1934-36, olive green, mojave, dark green, pea green, maroon, State brown and black.	40	50	60
62 Semaphore: 1920-32, bases painted dark green, olive green, apple green, pea green or *yellow*.	30-40	40-50	50-60
63 Semaphore: 1915-21, red and black.	25	40	55
63 Lamppost: 1933-42.	150	200	250
64 Highway Lamppost: 1940-49, green.	45	60	75
64 Semaphore: 1915-21.	30	45	65
65 Semaphore: 1915-26.	30	45	65
65 Whistle Controller: 1935.	3	5	7
66 Semaphore: 1915-26, upper arm red and black, lower arm green and black.			
	30	45	65
66 Whistle Controller: 1936-38.	3	5	7
67 Lamppost: 1915-32, dark or state green, rarely in peacock.			
	75	115	150
67 Whistle Controller: 1936-38.	3	5	7
68 Warning Signal: 1920-39, dark olive, orange, maroon, pea green, peacock or white.			
	5	10	15
068 Warning Signal: 1925-42, orange or pea green.	5	10	15
69 Electric Warning Bell Signal, 069 Electric Warning Bell Signal and 69N Electric Warning Bell Signal: 1921-35, olive, maroon, dark green, white, red, aluminum or 9E orange paint and black lettering.	30	45	60
70 Accessory Outfit: 1921-32.	75	125	175

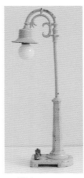

56 Lamppost   57 Lamppost   58 Lamppost   59 Lamppost

63
Lamppost

64 Highway Lamppost

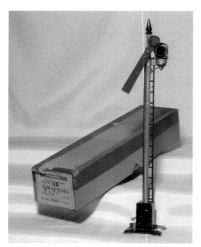

65 Semaphore

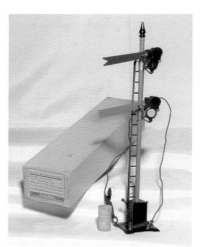

66 Semaphore

65 Whistle Controller

66 Whistle Controller

67 Whistle Controller

	C5	C7	C8
071 Telegraph Post Set: 1929-42, gray w/light red crossarms, green w/red crossarms or orange w/maroon crossarms.	$75	$125	$175
76 Block Signal, 076 Block Signal: 1923-28.	30	50	80
76 Warning Bell and Shack: 1939-42, brass or die-cast sign.	85	150	250
77 Automatic Crossing Gate, 077 Automatic Crossing Gate and 77N Automatic Crossing Gate: 1923-39.	30	40	50
78 Train Control Block Signal, 078 Train Control Block Signal: 1924-32, various colors.	40	70	100
79 Flashing Highway Signal: 1928-40, cream base and a pole painted either cream or mojave.	100	125	150
80 Semaphore, 080 Semaphore: 1926-35, various colors.	50	75	110

68 Warning Signal

068 Warning Signal

69 Electric Warning Bell Signal, 069 Electric Warning Bell Signal and 69N Electric Warning Bell Signal

071 Telegraph Post Set

76 Warning Bell and Shack

77 Automatic Crossing Gate, 077 Automatic
Crossing Gate and 77N Automatic Crossing
Gate

82N Semaphore

83 Traffic and
Crossing Signal

79 Flashing
Highway Signal

80 Semaphore, 080
Semaphore

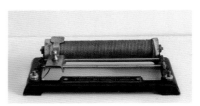

86 Telegraph Post Set

81 Rheostat

88 Direction Controller

85 Telegraph Post

87 Railroad
Crossing Signal

91 Circuit Breaker

	C5	C7	C8

80N Semaphore: 1936-42, light red base, aluminum-painted pole and black ladder.
| | $50 | $75 | $110 |

81 Rheostat: 1927-33.
| | 5 | 10 | 15 |

82 Train Control Semaphore, 082 Train Control Semaphore: 1927-35, peacock or 45N-green base.
| | 50 | 80 | 110 |

82N Semaphore: 1936-42, green base, aluminum-painted pole, black ladder and nickel finial.
| | 50 | 80 | 110 |

83 Traffic and Crossing Signal: 1927-42, *mojave* or red base.
| | 50-75 | 100-150 | 175-250 |

84 Semaphore, 084 Semaphore: 1927-32, dark green or maroon base, orange or cream pole.
| | 40 | 80 | 130 |

85 Telegraph Post: 1929-42, orange or *aluminum*-colored post.
| | 12-20 | 25-40 | 45-65 |

86 Telegraph Post Set: 1929-42, six orange or *aluminum*-colored posts, original box critical to value.
| | 100-125 | 200-250 | 400-500 |

87 Railroad Crossing Signal: 1927-42, orange, tan, mojave or *dark green base*.
| | 75-125 | 125-225 | 200-350 |

88 Battery Rheostat: 1915-27.
| | 5 | 10 | 15 |

88 Direction Controller: 1933-42.
| | 5 | 10 | 15 |

89 Flagpole: 1923-34.
| | 50 | 75 | 110 |

90 Flagpole: 1927-42, brass, nickel or black pedestal.
| | 75 | 110 | 150 |

91 Circuit Breaker: 1930-42, mojave or State brown, two or three terminals.
| | 25 | 35 | 45 |

092 Illuminated Signal Tower: 1923-27, terracotta or *white* walls.
| | 50-90 | 90-150 | 150-225 |

93 Water Tower: 1931-42, 1946-49, pea green, aluminum or gray tank.
| | 25 | 35 | 60 |

95 Rheostat: 1934-42, brass or nickel instruction plate.
| | 10 | 15 | 20 |

096 Telegraph Post: 1934-35.
| | 15 | 20 | 25 |

96 Coal Elevator: 1938-40.
| | 100 | 175 | 275 |

097 Telegraph Post and Signal Set: 1934-35.
| | 200 | 275 | 375 |

97 Motorized Coal Elevator: 1938-42, aluminum-painted supporting structure, except 1942 when *gray*.
| | 100-125 | 175-200 | 225-275 |

98 Coal Bunker: 1938-40, cream-colored house on aluminum structure.
| | 200 | 325 | 500 |

092 Illuminated Signal Tower

93 Water Tower

96 Coal Elevator

97 Motorized Coal Elevator

98 Coal Bunker

99/099 Train
Control Block
Signal

99N Train Control
Block Signal

112 Station

113 Station

114 Station

116 Station

	C5	C7	C8
99/099 Train Control Block Signal: 1932-35, black or red base w/cream, or mojave poles.	$40	$75	$125
99N Train Control Block Signal: 1936-42, red base and ladder w/aluminum-painted pole.	40	75	125
105 Bridge Approaches: 1920-31.	10	20	30
106 Bridge: 1920-31, cream, light mustard or pea green sides.	50	75	110
107 DC Reducer: 1911-38. Too infrequently traded to establish accurate value.			
108 Bridge: 1920-31, cream or light mustard sides.	75	100	150
109 Bridge: 1920-31, cream or light mustard sides.	100	150	200
110 Bridge Center Span: 1920-31, pea green.	20	30	40
111 Bulb Assortment: 1920-31, set of *wooden* or cardboard individual bulb containers w/bulbs.	250-500	500-1,000	1,000-2,000
112 Station: 1931-34, cream, beige or ivory walls.	150	250	375
113 Station: 1931-34.	200	400	600
114 Station: 1931-34, cream, beige or ivory walls.	500	1,000	1,600
115 Station: 1935-42, 1946-49, includes train-stop circuit.	250	350	500
116 Station: 1935-42, mojave or red base.	700	1,200	1,800
117 Station: 1935-42.	100	200	300
118 Tunnel: 1915-32.	20	35	50
118L Tunnel: 1927, illuminated version of the 118.	40	75	150
119 Tunnel: 1915-42.	20	35	50
119L Tunnel: 1927-33, illuminated version of the 119.	40	75	150
120 Tunnel: 1915-27, papier mache or steel.	35	75	125
120L Tunnel: 1927-42, illuminated version of 120.	50	100	200
121 Station: 1908-26, wooden or steel construction.	150	200	250
122 Station: 1920-31, gray or gray-speckled base.	75	150	225
123 Station: 1920-23.	150	225	350
123 Tunnel: 1933-42.	75	150	225
124 Station: 1920-30, 1933-36, terracotta walls, tan, dark gray or *pea green* base.	100-200	200-300	300-400
125 Station: 1923-25, red brick and a dark mojave base w/a pea green roof and white windows.	100	150	225
125 Track Template: 1938.	2	5	10
126 Station: 1923-36, lithographed walls, or red or *mustard-painted* walls.	75-200	125-275	200-375
127 Station: 1923-36, white, cream, *mustard* or ivory-colored walls.	75-100	110-150	150-225

119L Tunnel

123 Tunnel

124 Station

126 Station

127 Station

128 Station and Terrace

134 Station

136 Station

140L Tunnel

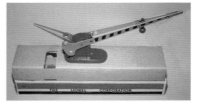

152 Automatic Crossing Gate

	C5	C7	C8
128 Station and Terrace: 1928-42, came w/124, 113 or 115 station.	$1,000-1,200	$1,500-1,800	$2,100-2,500
128 Tunnel: 1920.	Too rarely, if ever, traded to establish market pricing.		
129 Terrace: 1928-42, light mojave w/pea green decoration or *cream w/red trim*.	600-800	900-900	1,200-1,700
129 Tunnel: 1920.	Too rarely, if ever, traded to establish market pricing.		
130 Tunnel: 1920.	Too rarely, if ever, traded to establish market pricing.		
130 Tunnel: 1926.	200	400	1,000
130L Tunnel: 1927-33, 1927 edition was 1926 130 w/the addition of lighting, 1928 and up were smaller (18-1/2x14-1/2-in. base).	100-200	200-400	500-1,000
131 Corner Elevation: 1924-28.	125	250	500
132 Corner Grass Plot: 1924-28.	125	250	500
133 Heart-Shape Grass Plot: 1924-28.	125	250	500
134 Oval Grass Plot: 1924-28.	125	250	500
134 Station: 1937-42.	175	275	450
135 Small Circular Grass Plot: 1924-28.	100	200	400
136 Large Elevation: 1924-28.	125	250	500
136 Station: 1937-42, cream or *mustard* walls.	75-125	125-250	175-400
137 Station: 1937-42, ivory or white walls, vermilion roof, green or yellow door and window frames.	100	150	225
140L Tunnel: 1927-32.	600	1,200	2,000
152 Automatic Crossing Gate: 1940-42, aluminum or gray gate.	20	40	55
153 Automatic Block Signal and Control: 1940-42, 1945-59, *gray* or silver-colored post on a green die-cast base.	30-40	40-55	50-70
153C Contactor: 1940-42.	1	2	10
154 Automatic Highway Signal: 1940-69, black or *Hiawatha orange*.	30-50	40-75	50-100
155 Freight Shed: 1930-42, yellow base w/maroon roof or *white base and gray roof*.	175-225	250-325	350-450
156 Illuminated Station Platform: 1939-42, 1946-51, green base and red roof, silver or *gray posts*.	60-90	100-150	150-225
157 Hand Truck: 1930-32, 1942 red.	20	30	40
158 Station Set: 1940-42.	400	700	1,000

153 Automatic Block
Signal and Control

154 Automatic
Highway Signal

155 Freight Shed

156 Illuminated Station Platform

157 Hand Truck (left); 161 Baggage Truck (top, right); 162 Dump Truck (bottom, right)

163 Freight Accessory Set

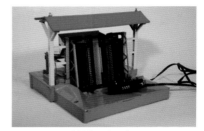

164 Log Loader

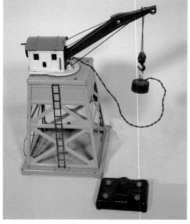

165 Magnetic Crane

170 DC Reducer

184 Bungalow

167 Whistle and Direction Controller

185 Bungalow

	C5	C7	C8
159C Block Control Contactor Set: 1940-42.	$10	$15	$25
160 Unloading Bin: 1938-42.	1	1	2
161 Baggage Truck: 1930-32, 1942.	30	40	55
162 Dump Truck: 1930-32, 1942, orange, terracotta or yellow hand truck w/dump bin, rare in red.	30	50	75
163 Freight Accessory Set: 1930-42.	175	250	350
164 Log Loader: 1940-42, 1946-50, aluminum or *gray*-painted supporting structures.	150-200	225-275	350-400
165 Magnetic Crane: 1940-42, aluminum or *gray*-painted supporting structure.	200-300	275-375	375-475
166 Whistle Controller: 1938-39.	5	7	10
167 Whistle and Direction Controller: 1939-42.	4	8	15
167X Whistle and Direction Controller: 1940-42.	10	20	30
168 Magic Electrol Controller: 1940-42, styled like 167 whistle control or 1019 controller.	10	20	30
169 Direction Controller: 1940-42.	10	20	30
170 DC Reducer: 1914-38.	10	20	30
171 DC to AC Inverter: 1936-42.	4	8	15
172 DC to AC Inverter: 1936-42.	4	8	15
184 Bungalow: 1923-42.	40	90	150
185 Bungalow: 1923-24.	50	100	175
186 Illuminated Bungalow Set: 1923-32.	400	1,000	1,800
186 Log Loader Outfit: 1940-41.	500	800	1,200
187 Bungalow Set: 1931-32.	400	1,000	1,800
188 Coal Elevator Outfit: 1938-41.	500	800	1,200
189 Villa: 1923-32.	150	250	375
191 Villa: 1923-32.	150	275	400
192 Illuminated Villa Set: 1923-32.	1,500	2,500	4,000
193 Automatic Accessory Set: 1927-29.	250	500	800
194 Automatic Accessory Set: 1927-29.	200	400	700
195 Illuminated Terrace: 1927-30.	400	800	1,600
196 Accessory Set: 1927.	250	500	800
206 Artificial Coal: 1938-42.	5	10	15
207 Sack of Coal: 1938-42.	5	10	15
208 Tool Set: 1928-42, miniature section gang tools in metal toolbox.	50	150	275
0209 Barrels: 1934-42, O-Ga. turned wooden representations of wooden or steel drums.	100	175	250
217 Lighting Set: 1914-23.	20	35	50
220 Pair of Manual Turnouts: 1926.	20	40	70

186 Illuminated Bungalow Set

186 Log Loader Outfit

188 Coal Elevator Outfit

189 Villa

191 Villa

192 Illuminated Villa Set

217 Lighting Set

313 Bascule Bridge

280 Bridge

314 Plate Girder Bridge (Type I)

315 Illuminated Trestle Bridge

	C5	C7	C8
222 Pair of Remote Control Turnouts: 1926-31.	$40	$60	$100
222L Left Hand Remote Control Turnout: 1926-31.	20	30	50
222R Right Hand Remote Control Turnout: 1926-31.	20	30	50
223 Pair of Remote Control Turnouts: 1932-42, pea green or black bases.	60	90	125
223L Left Hand Remote Control Turnout: 1932-42, pea green or black base.	30	45	60
223R Right Hand Remote Control Turnout: 1932-42, pea green or black base.	30	45	60
225 Remote Control Turnout Set: 1929-32.	125	250	400
270 Bridge: 1931-42, light red, maroon and vermilion.	25	35	50
270 Lighting Set: 1915-23, for DC current.	20	35	50
271 Lighting Set: 1915-23, for AC current.	20	35	50
271 Bridges: 1931-40, except 1934.	150	250	400
272 Bridges: 1931-40, except 1934.	250	450	750
280 Bridge: 1931-42, gray, red, pea or 45N green.	50	80	125
281 Bridges: 1931-40, except 1934.	150	250	400
282 Bridges: 1931-40, except 1934.	250	450	750
308 Railroad Sign Set: 1940-42, 1945-49, green base w/artificial grass, rectangular base painted white or round white bases.	35	50	75
310 Track: 1901-05.	75	125	200
313 Bascule Bridge: 1940-42, 1946-49, silver or *gray* superstructure of the bridge was painted silver.	300-400	525-625	675-775
314 Plate Girder Bridge (Type I): 1940-1941, silver, 1942 gray.	25	35	50
315 Illuminated Trestle Bridge: 1940-42, 1946-47, silver or *gray*.	75-100	100-125	125-150
316 Trestle Bridge: 1941, 1942 and 1949, aluminum or *gray*.	25-30	40-50	55-70
435 Power Station: 1926-38, *terracotta walls*, *gray base*, mustard walls, gray base; ivory walls, gray base; terracotta walls, gray base; cream walls, gray base, or cream walls, 45N green base.	125-300	250-600	400-1,000
436 Power Station: 1926-37, terracotta walls, light green windows, gray base; terracotta walls, orange windows, gray base; cream walls, orange windows, gray base; cream walls, white windows, 45N green base. Add 300 percent premium for "EDISON SERVICE" sign rather than "POWER STATION."	150	275	425

316 Trestle Bridge

435 Power Station

436 Power Station

437 Switch Signal Tower

438 Signal Tower

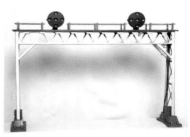

439 Panel Board

440 Signal Bridge/0440 Signal Bridge

440N Signal Bridge

442 Landscaped Diner

550 Miniature Railroad Figures

	C5	C7	C8

437 Switch Signal Tower: 1926-37, terracotta lower walls, mustard upper walls, pea green roof; terracotta lower walls, cream upper walls, peacock roof: burnt orange lower walls, mustard upper walls, pea green roof; burnt orange lower walls, light mustard upper walls, pea green roof or *yellow lower and upper walls, orange roof*.

$200-1,200 $350-1,800 $550-2,500

	C5	C7	C8

438 Signal Tower: 1927-39, pea green or *aluminum-painted* supports.
| | $200-300 | $325-475 | $500-700 |

439 Panel Board: 1928-42, black or *white* simulated marble backgrounds mounted on red or maroon supports.
| | 75-100 | 125-150 | 175-200 |

440 Signal Bridge/0440 Signal Bridge: 1932-35, supported by die-cast terracotta or *red* bases.
| | 175-200 | 250-325 | 350-450 |

440C Panel Board: 1932-42, light, glossy or flat red, includes switches to control 440 signal bridge in addition to knife switches.
| | 75 | 125 | 175 |

440N Signal Bridge: 1936-42, red die-cast bases w/silver or *gray* structure.
| | 175-250 | 225-450 | 275-650 |

442 Landscaped Diner: 1938-42, ivory or cream bodies w/pink or red foundations and steps.
| | 150 | 250 | 375 |

455 Electric Range: 1930, 1932-34, green and cream porcelain range.
| | 400 | 800 | 1,500 |

500 Pine Bushes: 1927-28. Too rarely traded to establish market pricing.
501 Small Pine Trees: 1927-28. Too rarely traded to establish market pricing.
502 Medium Pine Trees: 1927-28. Too rarely traded to establish market pricing.
503 Large Pine Trees: 1927-28. Too rarely traded to establish market pricing.
504 Rose Bushes: 1927-28. Too rarely traded to establish market pricing.
505 Oak Trees: 1927-28. Too rarely traded to establish market pricing.
506 Platform: 1924-28. Too rarely traded to establish market pricing.
507 Platform: 1924-28. Too rarely traded to establish market pricing.
508 Sky: 1924-28. Too rarely traded to establish market pricing.
509 Composition Board Mountains: 1924-28. Too rarely traded to establish market pricing.
510 Canna Bushes: 1927-28. Too rarely traded to establish market pricing.

550 Miniature Railroad Figures: 1932-36, original box significant portion of values listed.
| | 225 | 375 | 550 |

551 Engineer: 1932-36, medium or dark blue clothing.
| | 20 | 30 | 40 |

552 Conductor: 1932-36.
| | 20 | 30 | 40 |

553 Porter: 1932-36, came w/a removable yellow step box.
| | 20 | 30 | 40 |

554 Male Passenger: 1932-36, brown or mojave clothing.
| | 20 | 30 | 40 |

555 Female Passenger: 1932-36, variety of different colored clothing.
| | 20 | 30 | 40 |

556 Red Cap: 1932-36, dark blue clothing and a red cap.
| | 20 | 30 | 40 |

711 Pair of Remote Control Turnouts: 1935-42. 75 | 125 | 200

711L Left Hand Remote Control Turnout: 1935-42.
| | 40 | 60 | 100 |

711R Right Hand Remote Control Turnout: 1935-42.
| | 40 | 60 | 100 |

720 90-Degree Crossing: 1935-42. 25 | 35 | 45
721 Pair of Manual Turnouts: 1935-42. 50 | 75 | 125
721L Left Hand Manual Turnout: 1935-42. 25 | 40 | 60
721R Right Hand Manual Turnout: 1935-42. 25 | 40 | 60
730 90-Degree Crossing: 1935-42. 30 | 45 | 60
731 Pair of Remote Control Turnouts: 1935-42. 75 | 125 | 200

731L Left Hand Remote Control Turnout: 1935-42.
| | 40 | 60 | 100 |

731R Right Hand Remote Control Turnout: 1935-42.
| | 40 | 60 | 100 |

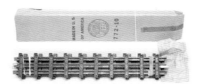

772 Straight Track

840 Industrial Power Station

910 Grove of Trees

911 Country Estate

912 Suburban Home

914 Park Landscape

913 Landscaped Bungalow

918 Scenic Hillside

916 Tunnel

920 Scenic Park

	C5	C7	C8
760 072 Track: 1954-58.	$50	$75	$120
761 Curved Track: 1934-42, 072.	1	2	3
762 Straight Track: 1934-42, 072.	1	2	3
762S Straight Track: 1934-42, 072 short straight.	1	2	3
771 Curved Track: 1935-42, "T-rail."	5	10	15
772 Straight Track: 1935-42, "T-rail."	10	15	20
772S Straight Track: 1935-42, "T-rail."	20	30	40
773 Fish Plate Set: 1935-42, "T-rail."	25	50	75
812T Tool Set: 1930-41.	50	100	150
840 Industrial Power Station: 1928-40, cream walls, orange roof or *white walls w/red roof.*	1,000-1,500	1,700-2,500	2,500-3,500
910 Grove of Trees: 1932-42.	100	250	500
911 Country Estate: 1932-42, variety of color combinations.	200	500	1,000
912 Suburban Home: 1932-42, variety of color combinations.	200	500	1,000
913 Landscaped Bungalow: 1932-42.	150	300	550
914 Park Landscape: 1932-36, cream colored plywood base and urn.	150	350	650
915 Tunnel: 1932-35, 60 or 65 in. long.	100-150	200-300	300-650
916 Tunnel: 1932-42, 29-1/4 or 37 in. long.	100-150	200-300	300-550
917 Scenic Hillside: 1932-36.	150	200	250
918 Scenic Hillside: 1932-36.	150	200	250
919 Artificial Grass: 1932-42.	7	7	25
920 Scenic Park: 1932-33.	1,000	2,000	3,000
921 Scenic Park: 1932-33.	2,000	3,200	4,500
921C Park Center Section: 1932-33.	750	1,500	2,250
922 Lamp Terrace: 1932-36, w/green, mojave, pea green or *copper*-colored lamppost.	100-200	150-350	200-550
923 Tunnel: 1933-42.	100	200	400
924 Tunnel: 1935-42.	100	200	400
924 Tunnel (Type I): 1935.	200	350	550
924 Tunnel (Type II): 1936.	100	200	400
925 Lubricant: 1935-42.	1	4	10
927 Ornamental Flag Plot: 1937-42, cream base.	100	200	400
1012 Winner Station: 1931-33, cream walls, orange roof, two or three binding posts. Transformer mounted internally.	40	55	75
1012K Winner Station: 1932-33, same as 1012, but sans transformer.	40	55	75
1013 Curved Track: 1933-42.	.25	.50	1
1017 Winner Station: 1932-33.	40	55	75
1018 Straight Track: 1933-42.	.25	.50	1
1019 Remote Control Track Set: 1938-42, 1946-50.	5	8	10

921 Scenic Park

923 Tunnel

927 Ornamental Flag Plot

1022 Tunnel

1025 Illuminated Bumper

1041 Transformer

1027 Lionel Junior Transformer Station

1045 Operating Watchman

1100 Handcar

1105 Handcar

1103 Handcar

	C5	C7	C8
1021 90-Degree Crossing: 1933-42, 1945-54.	$2	$4	$8
1022 Tunnel: 1935-42.	20	40	75
1023 Tunnel: 1934-42.	20	40	75
1024 Pair of Manual Turnouts: 1935-42, 1946-52.	10	15	25
1024L Left Hand Manual Turnout: 1934-42.	5	8	10
1024R Right Hand Manual Turnout: 1934-42.	5	8	10
1025 Illuminated Bumper: 1940-42, 1946-47.	10	15	20
1027 Lionel Junior Transformer Station: 1933-34, yellow.	40	60	85
1028 Lionel Junior Transformer Station: 1935.	40	60	85
1029 Lionel Junior Transformer Station: 1936.	40	60	85
1038 Transformer: 30-watt.	5	10	20
1039 Transformer: 1937-40, 35-watt.	5	10	20
1040 Transformer: 1937-39, 60-watt.	20	35	50
1041 Transformer: 1939-42, 60-watt.	20	35	50
1045 Operating Watchman: 1938-42, 1946-50, w/blue, dark blue, black or brown figure.	20	35	50
1100 Handcar: 1934-37, Mickey and Minnie Mouse, red, *orange*, green or maroon base.	350-500	600-900	1,100-1,600
1103 Handcar: 1935-37, Peter Rabbit Chick Mobile, metal-flanged wheels or *rubber wheels*.	300-400	600-675	900-1,250
1105 Handcar: 1935-36, Santa w/Mickey Mouse peering from sack, red or *green* base.	500-700	1,000-1,500	2,000-2,500
1106: Santa handcars were made w/out Mickey as well.			
Too rarely traded to establish pricing.			
1107 Rail Car: 1936-37, Donald Duck and Pluto, white or *orange doghouse*.	400-700	600-1,000	900-1,500
1121 Remote Control Turnouts: 1937-42, 1946-51.	20	35	45
1550 Pair of Manual Turnouts: 1933-37.	1	2	5
1555 90-Degree Crossing: 1933-37.	1	2	5
1560 Lionel Junior Station: 1933-37.	15	25	35
1569 Lionel Junior Accessory Set: 1933-37, included four telegraph poles, one each semaphore, warning signal, clock and crossing gate, mounted on red or black bases. Box critical to value.	100	200	400

1106 Santa Car

1107
Rail
Car

A Transformer

B Transformer

K Transformer

R Peerless Motor

UTC Lockon

V Transformer

	C5	C7	C8
1571 Telegraph Pole: 1933-37.	$5	$10	$15
1572 Semaphore: 1933-37, gray or pea green post mounted on black or red bases.			
	5	10	15
1575 Crossing Gate: 1933-37, pea green or gray post.	5	10	15
A Miniature Motor: 1904.	50	75	100
A Transformer: 1921-37, 40 or 60 watts.	5	10	15
B New Departure Motor: 1906-16.	75	110	150
B Transformer: 1916-38, 50 or 75 watts.	5	10	25

	C5	C7	C8
C New Departure Motor: 1906-16.	$100	$130	$175
C Transformer: 1922-31, 75 watts.	5	10	25
D New Departure Motor: 1906-16.	100	130	175
E New Departure Motor: 1906-16.	100	130	175
F New Departure Motor: 1906-16.	100	130	175
F Transformer: 1931-37, 40 watts.	5	10	25
G Fan Motor: 1909-14.	100	130	175
H Transformer: 1938-39, 75 watts.	5	10	25
K Sewing Machine Motor: 1904-06.	100	130	175
K Transformer: 1913-38, 150 or 200 watts.	20	40	60
L Sewing Machine Motor: 1905.	75	100	125
L Transformer: 1913-38, 50 or 75 watts.	10	15	20
M Peerless Motor: 1915-20.	50	75	100
MS Straight Track: 1933-38, two-rail 027-type track.	.50	1	2
MWC Curved Track: 1933-38, two-rail 027-type track.	.50	1	2
N Transformer: 1941-42, 50 watts.	5	10	15
OC Curved Track: 1915-61, O-Ga.	.25	.50	1
OCC Curved Track: 1915-22, O-Ga. terminal track.	.25	.50	1
OCS Curved Track: 1933-42, O-Ga. insulated.	.25	.50	1
OS Straight Track: 1915-61, O-Ga.	.50	1	2
OSC Straight Track: 1915-22, O-Ga. terminal.	.50	1	2
OSS Straight Track: 1933-42, O-Ga. insulated.	.50	1	2
OTC Lockon: 1923-36.	.25	.50	1
Q Transformer: 1914-42, 50 or 75 watts.	10	20	40
R Peerless Motor: 1915-20.	75	100	125
R Transformer: 1939-42, 1946, 100 or 110 watts.	50	75	100
RCS Remote Control Track: 1938-42, 1946-48, O-Ga.	5	10	15
S Transformer: 1914-17, 1938-42, 1947, 50 or 80 watts.	20	35	60
SMC Curved Track: 1935-36, two-rail, 027-style track to activate the Mickey Mouse stoker.	1	2	3
T Transformer (Type I): 1914-22, 75, 100, 110, or 150 watts.	10	15	25
U Transformer: 1932-33, 50 watts.	10	15	25
UTC Lockon: 1936-42.	.25	.50	1
V Transformer: 1938-1942, 1946-47, 150 watts.	100	125	150
W Transformer: 1933-42, 75 watts.	10	15	25
WX Transformer: 1933-42, 75 watts, 25-cycle.	10	15	25
Y Peerless Motor: 1915-20.	50	75	100
Z Transformer: 1938-42, 1945-47, 250 watts.	100	125	150

42 Picatinny Arsenal Switcher

45 U.S. Marines Mobile Missile Launcher

51 Navy Yard New York Switcher

53 Rio Grande Switcher

54 Ballast Tamper

56 M St. L Switcher

60 Lionelville Rapid Transit Trolley

69 Maintenance Car

209 New Haven Alco A-A

	C5	C7	C8

Postwar Locomotives and Rolling Stock

41 United States Army Switcher: 1955-57, **painted** or *unpainted* black body.
　　　　　　　　$125-200　　　$160-300　　　$200-400

42 Picatinny Arsenal Switcher: 1957, unpainted olive drab body.
　　　　　　　　200　　　　300　　　　400

44 U.S. Army Mobile Missile Launcher: 1959-62, painted blue body.
　　　　　　　　150　　　　225　　　　350

45 U.S. Marines Mobile Missile Launcher: 1960-62, painted olive drab.
　　　　　　　　175　　　　275　　　　425

50 Lionel Gang Car: 1954-64, gray (1954) or *blue* bumpers, **two-piece** (1954) or *one-piece* horn.　　40-375　　　60-500　　　75-675

51 Navy Yard New York Switcher: 1956-57, unpainted blue plastic body.
　　　　　　　　125　　　　175　　　　250

52 Fire Car: 1958-61, red-painted black plastic body. 125　　　200　　　300

53 Rio Grande Switcher: 1957-60, **"a" in Rio Grande printed normally** or *"a" in Rio Grande reversed* (prototypically correct).　225-425　　325-600　　450-900

54 Ballast Tamper: 1958-61, 1966-69, unpainted yellow plastic body.
　　　　　　　　150　　　　225　　　　325

55 Tie-Jector: 1957-61, early units had a solid wall behind engineer, a vent behind the engineer was added later.　　150　　　225　　　325

56 M St. L Switcher: 1958, body painted red, cab sides painted white.
　　　　　　　　300　　　　550　　　　800

57 AEC Switcher: 1959-60, unpainted white body, cab sides painted red.
　　　　　　　　450　　　　700　　　　1,200

58 Great Northern Switcher/Snowplow: 1959-1961, unpainted green plastic w/ white cab sides equipped w/a rotary snow blower.
　　　　　　　　300　　　　500　　　　800

59 U.S. Air Force Minuteman Switcher: 1961-63, unpainted white body.
　　　　　　　　300　　　　500　　　　750

60 Lionelville Rapid Transit Trolley: 1955-58, yellow body, red roof, **black lettering, no vents, metal motorman silhouettes**, or black lettering, no vents, no motorman silhouettes, or *blue lettering, no vents, no motormen*, or blue lettering, no motormen, w/vents.　　　　100-200　　　175-300　　　250-400

65 Handcar: 1962-66, molded light or *dark* yellow plastic body, final version has **improved body** molding.　175-225　　325-450　　500-650

68 Executive Inspection Car: 1958-61, gray plastic, painted red and cream.
　　　　　　　　175　　　　300　　　　425

69 Maintenance Car: 1960-62, dark gray brush plate, black body, both unpainted.
　　　　　　　　225　　　　350　　　　500

202 Union Pacific Alco A: 1957, painted orange.　75　　　100　　　150

204 Santa Fe Alco A-A: 1957, powered and dummy painted blue and yellow. Dummy has operating headlight.　　100　　　175　　　275

205 Missouri Pacific Alco A-A: 1957-58, solid blue-painted, made **w/or w/out** factory installed steel nose supports that are painted to match the unit.
　　　　　　　　75-100　　　150-175　　　250-275

208 Santa Fe Alco A-A: 1958-59, painted blue and yellow, no headlight in dummy.
　　　　　　　　75　　　　150　　　　250

209 New Haven Alco A-A: 1958 only, black, white and orange paint on molded black plastic body.　　　400　　　600　　　1,000

210 Texas Special Alco A-A: 1958 only, painted red and white body.
　　　　　　　　75　　　　150　　　　250

211 Texas Special Alco A-A: 1962-63, 1965-66, cosmetically almost identical to the 210.　　　　　　75　　　　150　　　　250

	C5	C7	C8

212 Santa Fe Alco A-A: 1964-66, painted red and silver. Some stamped "BLT/BY LIONEL." Others were stamped "BLT 8-57/BY LIONEL," but no difference in value or scarcity.
$100 $175 $275

212 United States Marine Corps Alco A: 1958-59, painted *dark* or medium blue.
100-150 175-225 250-325

212(T) United States Marine Corps Alco A Dummy: 1958, painted medium blue body.
450 675 1,100

213 Minneapolis & St. Louis Alco A-A: 1964, painted red.
125 225 325

215 Santa Fe Alco: 1965-66, painted red and silver. Sold as A-A w/212T or **A-B** w/218C.
100-110 150-175 250-275

216 Burlington Alco A: 1958, painted silver and red.
200 350 450

216 Minneapolis & St. Louis Alco A: 1965, painted red body, came as either *single* A-unit or w/213T as **A-A** combination.
100-175 150-225 200-350

217 B & M Alco A-B: 1959, unpainted blue plastic bodies w/the roof and A-unit nose painted black.
100 165 250

218 Santa Fe Alco: 1959-63, painted silver and red, came either as A-A or in 1961 as A-B combinations. From time to time A-A units were produced which had **solid yellow nose decals** that lacked the red areas inside the perimeter.
100-125 150-175 225-275

218C Santa Fe Alco B-Unit: 1961-63, painted silver.
50 75 115

219 Missouri Pacific Alco A-A: 1959 only, uncataloged, blue-painted pair.
100 175 290

220 Santa Fe Alco: 1960-61, painted silver and red, sold as an **A** *only* or w/a dummy as an **A-A** combination.
75-150 125-225 175-300

221 2-6-4 Steam: 1946-47, painted either **gray** or *black*, w/either **silver** or black *wheels* and furnished w/either 221T or 221W tender.
50-100 75-150 125-200

221 Rio Grande Alco A: 1963-64, unpainted yellow body.
50 70 90

221 Santa Fe Alco A: 1964, uncataloged, unpainted olive drab body, no E-unit, wired for forward-only travel.
250 500 750

221 United States Marine Corps Alco A: 1964, uncataloged, unpainted olive drab body.
225 375 550

211 Texas Special Alco A-A

216 Burlington Alco A

225 Chesapeake & Ohio Alco A

227 Canadian National Alco A

	C5	C7	C8

222 Rio Grande Alco A: 1962, painted yellow, wired to run forward only.

	$50	$75	$100

223 Santa Fe Alco A-B: 1963, painted silver and red.

	125	200	325

224 2-6-2 Steam: 1945-46, w/2466W or 2466WX tender, w/or **w/out** drawbar, *black* or silver railings, *squared* or rounded cab floor.

	60-75	100-125	150-200

224 United States Navy Alco A-B: 1960 only, painted blue.

	150	225	350

225 Chesapeake & Ohio Alco A: 1960 only, painted dark blue.

	75	125	175

226 B & M Alco A-B: 1960 only, B-unit unpainted blue plastic, A-unit also blue either *unpainted* or **painted**.

	100-150	175-225	275-325

227 Canadian National Alco A: 1960 only, molded gray body painted green.

	100	150	200

228 Canadian National Alco A: 1960 only, uncataloged, body painted green.

	100	150	200

229 Minneapolis & St. Louis Alco: 1961-62, sold as single A or in **A-B** combination.

	75-125	100-175	150-275

230 Chesapeake & Ohio Alco A: 1961 only, painted dark blue.

	75	125	175

231 Rock Island Alco A: 1961-63, painted black w/white heat-stamped lettering and a white roofline stripe, w/or **w/out** broad red stripe on sides.

	75-225	125-375	175-500

232 New Haven Alco A: 1962, painted overall orange w/two narrow black stripes.

	75	125	175

233 2-4-2 Steam: 1961-62, w/233W tender.

	50	75	125

235 2-4-2 Steam: 1961, supplied w/either the 1050T or 1130T tender.

	150	250	350

236 2-4-2 Steam: 1961-62, supplied w/either the 1050T or 1130T tender.

	20	35	50

237 2-4-2 Steam: 1963-66, paired variously w/a number of different tenders, including the 1061T and 1062T slope-back models, the 242T and 1060T small streamlined, or 234W square whistle tender. Thick or thin running boards.

	30-60	50-100	85-175

238 2-4-2 Steam: 1963-64, furnished w/the 234W whistle tender. Thick or thin running boards.

	100	150	250

229 Minneapolis & St. Louis Alco

230 Chesapeake & Ohio Alco A

231 Rock Island Alco A

233 2-4-2 Steam

236 2-4-2 Steam

237 2-4-2 Steam

238 2-4-2 Steam

240 2-4-2 Steam

239 2-4-2 Steam

241 2-4-2 Steam

242 2-4-2 Steam

244 2-4-2 Steam

245 2-4-2 Steam

246 2-4-2 Steam

	C5	C7	C8

239 2-4-2 Steam: 1965-66, cab number either *heat* or rubber stamped in white, and came w/either **234W** or 242T tender. | $30-80 | $45-125 | $70-175

240 2-4-2 Steam: 1964, uncataloged, came w/242T tender. | 150 | 225 | 375

241 2-4-2 Steam: 1965-66, uncataloged, w/234W tender. White running board applied by *painting* or rubber stamping. | 90-*100* | 150-*175* | 240-275

242 2-4-2 Steam: 1962-66, came w/242T, 1060T, 1061T or 1062T tender. | 10 | 20 | 40

243 2-4-2 Steam: 1960 only, came w/the 243W tender. | 70 | 100 | 200

244 2-4-2 Steam: 1960-61, came w/either 244T or 1130T tender. | 25 | 35 | 50

245 2-4-2 Steam: 1959, uncataloged, came w/1130T tender. | 40 | 70 | 90

246 2-4-2 Steam: 1959-61, came w/either the 1130T or the 244T tender. | 20 | 30 | 40

247 2-4-2 Steam: 1959 only, came w/247T tender, which had a blue stripe to match the locomotive. | 45 | 65 | 90

248 2-4-2 Steam: 1958, uncataloged, came w/1130T. | 60 | 70 | 85

249 2-4-2 Steam: 1958 only, came w/250T tender, which had matching red stripe. | 30 | 45 | 60

250 2-4-2 Steam: 1957 only, came w/250T tender, which had matching red stripe. | 30 | 40 | 50

251 2-4-2 Steam: 1966 only, came w/1062T tender. | 150 | 200 | 350

400 Baltimore and Ohio RDC-1: 1956-58. | 150 | 225 | 300

404 Baltimore and Ohio RDC-4: 1957-58. | 200 | 300 | 400

520 Lionel Lines 1-B-0 Electric: 1956-57, unpainted red plastic body w/*black* or copper-colored plastic pantograph mounted on top. | 75-100 | 120-150 | *175-200*

600 M K T NW-2: 1955, unpainted red plastic body mounted on **gray frame w/yellow platform railings and blued steel steps**, or on gray or black or *blued steel* frame wblued steel railings and steps. | *115-375* | *160-550* | *225-800*

247 2-4-2 Steam

400 Baltimore and Ohio RDC-1

250 2-4-2 Steam

600 M K T NW-2

617 Santa Fe NW-2

624 Chesapeake & Ohio NW-2

627 Lehigh Valley Center Cab

	C5	C7	C8
601 Seaboard NW-2: 1956, painted black and red.	$115	$150	$225
602 Seaboard NW-2: 1957-58, painted black and red.	125	175	250
610 Erie NW-2: 1955 only, body painted black w/yellow heat-stamped number. **Yellow**, black or *blued steel* frame.	100-425	150-650	225-1,100
611 Jersey Central NW-2: 1957-58, blue and orange body, blue can be unpainted light or dark shade, or *painted*.	150-400	225-600	350-900
613 Union Pacific NW-2: 1958 only, yellow and gray.	250	400	600
614 Alaska Railroad NW-2: 1959-60, "BUILT BY/LIONEL" either in *molded color* or outlined in yellow.	150-325	225-475	300-750
616 Santa Fe NW-2: 1961-62, painted black w/white safety stripes. Bodies came w/*open but unused E-unit and bell slots*, or plugged E-unit slot and open bell slot, or w/*both E-unit and bell slots plugged*.	125-200	175-325	250-450
617 Santa Fe NW-2: 1963, painted black w/white safety stripes. Came w/black ornamental bell, silver ornamental horn, head and marker light lenses and radio antenna. Early units had separately installed frame steps, steps on late units integral with frame.	150	250	375
621 Jersey Central NW-2: 1956-57, unpainted blue plastic body.	100	150	200
622 A.T. & S.F. NW-2: 1949-50, black, die-cast frame. **W**/or *w/out* "622" stamped on the nose of the locomotive.	150-200	200-325	350-500
623 A.T. & S.F. NW-2: 1952-54, black, die-cast frame. Hood-side handrail retained by 10 or *three* stations.	100-125	150-175	225-250
624 Chesapeake & Ohio NW-2: 1952-54, *medium* or *light* blue, die-cast frame. Hood-side handrail retained by **10** or *three* stations.	150-300	225-450	375-700
625 Lehigh Valley Center Cab: 1957-58, unpainted red body.	125	175	225
626 Baltimore and Ohio Center Cab: 1957 only, unpainted blue body.	250	400	625
627 Lehigh Valley Center Cab: 1956-57, unpainted red plastic body.	75	115	150
628 Northern Pacific Center Cab: 1956-57, unpainted black body.	100	150	225

	C5	C7	C8
629 Burlington Center Cab: 1956, silver painted body.	$250	$450	$800
633 Santa Fe NW-2: 1962, painted blue body w/yellow safety stripes.	125	200	300
634 Santa Fe NW-2: 1963, 1965-66, painted blue body, **yellow safety stripes** in 1963 only, *no stripes* 65-66.	75-125	125-175	200-250
635 Union Pacific NW-2: 1965 only, painted yellow body.	75	125	200
637 2-6-4 Steam: 1959-61, came w/2046W or 736W tenders. Number *rubber* or **heat** stamped.	75-120	125-175	200-300
638-2361 Stokely-Van Camp's Boxcar: 1962-64, uncataloged.	25	40	60
645 Union Pacific NW-2: 1969, unpainted yellow plastic body.	75	125	200
646 4-6-4 Steam: 1954-58, came w/2046W tenders, silver or white cab lettering.	175	250	350
665 4-6-4 Steam: 1954-56, 1966, furnished w/6026W, 2046W or 736W tender; Rubber or heat-stamped numbers on loco.	165	250	300
671 6-8-6 Steam: 1946-49, 1946, locos have bulb-type smoke units, heater units used thereafter, "6200" stamped in **white** on some boiler fronts, *decaled* on most, came w/671W or 2671W tenders, some of the latter having **backup lights**.	135-325	175-475	275-600
671R 6-8-6 Steam: 1946-49, "Electronic Control" **bulb** or *heater*-type smoke units used.	225-250	325-350	425-475
671 RR 6-8-6 Steam: 1952 only, came w/2046W-50 tender. Cabs *may* or may not have the "RR" suffix stamped on them.	185-225	275-350	350-450

646 4-6-4 Steam

665 4-6-4 Steam

671R 6-8-6 Steam

682 6-8-6 Steam

726 2-8-4 Steam

736 2-8-4 Steam   X1004 Baby Ruth Boxcar

746 4-8-4 Steam

773 4-6-4 Steam

1005 Sunoco Tank Car   1060 2-4-2 Steam

	C5	C7	C8

675 2-6-2 Steam: 1947-49, **white** "675" stamped on boiler front or *red keystone decal* applied. Came w/2466WX or 6466WX tender.

| | $95-125 | $145-175 | $225-250 |

675 2-6-4 Steam: 1952 only, w/2046W tender.
| | 95 | 145 | 225 |

681 6-8-6 Steam: 1950-51, 1953, came w/267IW or 2046W-50 tender, number stamped in *silver* or white.
| | 165-175 | 250-275 | 350-375 |

682 6-8-6 Steam: 1954-55, came w/a 2046W-50 tender.
| | 275 | 425 | 600 |

685 4-6-4 Steam: 1953 only, came w/6026W tender, **rubber**- or *heat*-stamped numbers on loco.
| | 200-250 | 300-350 | 400-500 |

726 2-8-4 Steam: 1946-49, 1946, locos have **bulb-type smoke units**, *heater* units used thereafter. Came w/2426W tender.
| | 225-300 | 350-475 | 475-600 |

726RR 2-8-4 Steam: 1952 only, came w/2046W tender. Cabs *may* or may not have the "RR" suffix stamped on them.
| | 225-300 | 375-425 | 475-600 |

736 2-8-4 Steam: 1950-51, 1953-68, came w/**2671WX**, 2046W or 736W tender.
| | 200-300 | 300-425 | 400-575 |

746 4-8-4 Steam: 1957-60, came w/*long-striped* tender stamped 746W or short-striped 746W w/out number stamping.
| | 650-700 | 850-900 | 1,200-1,500 |

773 4-6-4 Steam: 1950 w/**2426W tender**, 1964-66, 736W or 773W tender 64-66.
| | 600-950 | 850-1,200 | 1,100-1,800 |

1001 2-4-2 Steam: 1948 only, **die-cast** or *plastic*, plastic w/*white* or silver numbers, all w/1001T tender.
| | 25-225 | 40-325 | 60-450 |

1002 Lionel Gondola: 1948-52, *black*, blue, **red**, silver, and **yellow**.
| | 7-225 | 10-375 | 15-500 |

X1004 Baby Ruth Boxcar: 1948-52, outline or solid lettering.
| | 6 | 10 | 14 |

1005 Sunoco Tank Car: 1948-50, gray tank w/medium or dark blue lettering.
| | 5 | 7 | 12 |

1007 Lionel Lines Caboose: 1948-52, *red* or **tuscan** body.
| | 2-75 | 4-200 | 6-300 |

1050 0-4-0 Steam: 1959 only, came w/a 1050T slope-back tender.
| | 150 | 200 | 350 |

1055 Texas Special Alco A: 1959-60, painted red w/white lettering.
| | 40 | 60 | 90 |

1060 2-4-2 Steam: 1960-62, came w/1050T or 1060T tender, long or short rain shield over loco headlight.
| | 10 | 25 | 50 |

1061 0-4-0 or 2-4-2 Steam: 1963-64, 1969, used 1061T, 1062T, 1060T or 242T tenders. Numbers white *heat stamped*, omitted or applied to **paper label**.
| | 10-150 | 25-225 | 45-300 |

1062 0-4-0 or 2-4-2 Steam: 1963-64, used 1061T, 1062T, 1060T or 242T tenders. Streamlined tender sometimes lettered "*Southern Pacific.*"
| | 10-95 | 20-125 | 35-175 |

1065 Union Pacific Alco A: 1961 only, body painted yellow.
| | 45 | 65 | 100 |

1061 0-4-0 Steam

1062 0-4-0 Steam

1065 Union Pacific Alco A

1130 2-4-2 Steam

1625 0-4-0 Steam

1666 2-6-2 Steam

1872 4-4-0 Steam

1875W Western & Atlantic Coach w/Whistle

1876 Western & Atlantic Mail-Baggage

1877 Flatcar

1885 Western & Atlantic Coach

	C5	C7	C8
1066 Union Pacific Alco A: 1964, uncataloged unpainted yellow body.	$45	$65	$100
1101 2-4-2 Steam: 1948 only, w/1001T tender.	15	35	55
1110 2-4-2 Steam: 1949, 1951-52, w/1001T tender. **Baldwin disc** or *spoke* drive wheels.	10-25	20-40	35-60
1120 2-4-2 Steam: 1950 only, w/1001T tender.	15	30	50
1130 2-4-2 Steam: 1953-54, **die-cast** or *plastic*, plastic w/white or *silver* numbers, w/6066T or 1130T tender.	10-225	25-350	40-450
1615 0-4-0 Steam: 1955-57, w/1615T tender.	125	175	275
1625 0-4-0 Steam: 1958 only, w/1625T tender.	175	275	400
1654 2-4-2 Steam: 1946-47, w/1654T or *1654W* tender.	30-35	50-60	70-95
1655 2-4-2 Steam: 1948-49, w/6654W tender.	40	70	95
1656 0-4-0 Steam: 1948-49, w/6403B tender w/**separate Bakelite coal pile** or *integral die-cast coal pile.*	200-225	300-350	425-475
1665 0-4-0 Steam: 1946 only, w/*heat* or **rubber**-stamped 2403B tender.	200-250	325-375	450-500
1666 2-6-2 Steam: 1946-47, black or *silver* handrails, *moveable* or **rigid** bell.	75-100	100-150	175-250
1862 4-4-0 Steam: 1959-62, w/1862T tender.	125	200	300
1865 Western & Atlantic Coach: 1959-62, body painted yellow w/brown roof.	20	30	40
1866 Western & Atlantic Mail-Baggage: 1959-62, body painted yellow w/brown roof.	20	30	40
1872 4-4-0 Steam: 1959-62, w/1872T tender.	150	250	350
1875 Western & Atlantic Coach: 1959-62, body painted yellow w/brown roof.	125	200	275
1875W Western & Atlantic Coach w/Whistle: 1959-62, body painted yellow w/ brown roof.	60	100	140
1876 Western & Atlantic Mail-Baggage: 1959-62, body painted yellow w/brown roof.	40	65	90
1877 Flatcar: 1959-62, unpainted brown plastic, came w/a load of two white, two tan and brown, and two black horses made by Bachmann Bros. (hence the "BB" logo on the horses' bellies), and a 10-section maroon fence.	35	75	110
1882 4-4-0 Steam: 1960 only, came w/1882T tender.	425	550	800
1885 Western & Atlantic Coach: 1960, painted blue w/brown roof.	175	250	350
1887 Flatcar: 1960 only, unpainted brown plastic, came w/a load of two white, two tan and brown and two black horses made by Bachmann Bros. (hence the "BB" logo on the horses' bellies), and a 10-section fence.	140	200	275

1882 4-4-0 Steam

2016 2-6-4 Steam

2018 2-6-4 Steam

2025 2-6-2 Steam

2026 2-6-2 Steam

2029 2-6-4 Steam

2037 2-6-4 Steam

2037-500 2-6-4 Steam

2055 4-6-4 Steam

	C5	C7	C8
2016 2-6-4 Steam: 1955-56, w/6026W tender. Number *heat* or **rubber stamped** in white.	$75-150	$100-250	$175-350
2018 2-6-4 Steam: 1956-59, came w/**6026W**, 6026T or 1130T tenders.	50-65	65-100	100-150
2020 6-8-6 Steam: 1946-49, 1946 locos have **bulb**-type smoke units, *heater* units used thereafter, "6200" stamped in **white** on some boiler fronts, *decaled* on most, came w/2020W or 6020W tender.	150-175	200-250	275-350
2023 Union Pacific Alco A-A: 1950-51, came in **yellow w/gray roof and nose**, yellow w/gray roof and *silver w/gray roof*.	175-2,000	300-2,800	450-3,800
2024 Chesapeake & Ohio Alco A: 1969 only, unpainted dark blue body.	40	60	90
2025 2-6-2 Steam: 1947-49, **white** "2025" stamped on boiler front or *red keystone decal* applied. Came w/2466WX or 6466WX tender.	70-125	100-175	175-250
2025 2-6-4 Steam: 1952 only, w/6466W tender.	85	125	200
2026 2-6-2 Steam: 1948-49, **Baldwin disc** or *spoke* wheels, w/6466WX tender.	50-75	75-100	100-150
2026 2-6-4 Steam: 1951-53, w/6066T, 6466T or **6466W** tender, loco numbers rubber-stamped in *silver* or heat-stamped in **white**.	40-90	60-125	100-185
2028 Pennsylvania GP-7: 1955, **gold** or yellow rubber-stamped lettering, *gold* or **tan** frame.	225-350	350-600	500-900
2029 2-6-4 Steam: 1964-69, came w/*1060T, 234T* or 234W "Lionel Lines" or **234W** "**Pennsylvania**" tender, the latter carries a $200 premium above listed prices.	35-55	50-75	80-125
2031 Rock Island Alco A-A: 1952-54, painted black w/broad red stripe.	250	375	550
2032 Erie Alco A-A: 1952-54, painted black w/narrow yellow striping.	150	225	350
2033 Union Pacific Alco A-A: 1952-54, painted silver w/silver roof.	175	275	450
2034 2-4-2 Steam: 1952 only, came w/a 6066T tender.	15	35	60
2035 2-6-4 Steam: 1950-51, came w/the 6466W tender.	85	125	200
2036 2-6-4 Steam: 1950 only, w/6466W tender.	100	150	225
2037 2-6-4 Steam: 1953-55, 1957-63, came w/6026W, 233W or 234W whistle tender or non-whistling 6066T, 6026T or 1130T tender. Reduce the values listed 1/3 for non-whistle tender.	75	120	175
2037-500 2-6-4 Steam: 1957-58, pink, w/1130T-500 pink tender.	500	700	950
2041 Rock Island Alco A-A: 1969, unpainted black plastic bodies w/wide red stripe.	75	115	170
2046 4-6-4 Steam: 1950-51, 1953, came w/2046W tender, silver numbers w/die-cast trailing truck or white numbers w/plastic and sheet metal trailing truck.	140	200	275
2055 4-6-4 Steam: 1953-55, came w/6026W or 2046W tender.	140	200	275
2056 4-6-4 Steam: 1952 only, came w/2046W tender.	175	250	350
2065 4-6-4 Steam: 1954-56, came w/6026W or 2046W tender.	175	250	325

2240 Wabash F-3 A-B

2242 New Haven F-3 A-B

2245 The Texas Special F-3 A-B

2321 Lackawanna FM

2329 Virginian El-C Rectifier

2330 Pennsylvania GG1

2331 Virginian FM

2332 Pennsylvania GG1

2338 The Milwaukee Road GP-7

2339
Wabash
GP-7

	C5	C7	C8

2240 Wabash F-3 A-B: 1956 only, molded in medium blue, painted blue w/the roof and upper body painted gray, the white band was silk-screened on. The final segment of the B-unit's white stripe near "Built by Lionel" is 1/2 in. long.

	$500	$750	$1,150

2242 New Haven F-3 A-B: 1958-59, heat-stamped white "NH" on the nose door.

	750	1,250	2,000

2243 Santa Fe F-3 A-B: 1955-57, *high profile* or flush molded cab door ladder.

	300-350	450-500	675-750

2243C Santa Fe F-3 B-Unit: 1955-57, not originally sold separately, but often sold individually on the collector market.

	150	225	300

2245 The Texas Special F-3 A-B: 1954-55, painted glossy red w/white silk-screened lower panels. The red lettering on the sides of the units was actually the red paint, which had been masked off. Horizontal motors in 1954, vertical in 1955, late 1955 B-units have *closed porthole* openings.

	400-750	550-*1,000*	800-*1,400*

2257 Lionel-SP Caboose: 1947, *red no stack, red-orange no stack,* red-orange w/ matching stack, **tuscan w/matching stack,** *heat-* or rubber-stamped markings.

	3-300	5-500	*10-775*

2321 Lackawanna FM: 1954-56, **maroon** or *gray* roof.

	375-550	500-800	750-1,200

2322 Virginian FM: 1965-66, *unpainted blue* plastic w/painted-on yellow trim, or both blue and yellow **painted** on.

	400-500	600-750	800-960

2328 Burlington GP-7: 1955-56, painted silver body, red frame.

	300	450	750

2329 Virginian El-C Rectifier: 1958-59, blue-painted body w/yellow frame.

	500	800	1,200

2330 Pennsylvania GG1: 1950, painted green.

	800	1,400	2,200

2331 Virginian FM: 1955-58, **molded gray body painted yellow and blue**, or molded gray body painted black and yellow or *molded blue* body w/yellow painted on.

	600-1,000	800-1,350	1,100-2,000

2332 Pennsylvania GG1: 1947-49, *green,* or *very* dark, almost **black** green.

	300-600	450-1,000	750-2,000

2333 Santa Fe F-3 A-A: 1948-49, **clear, unpainted body,** or *silver and red painted body.*

	300-3,000	600-5,000	1,200-9,000

2334 New York Central F-3 A-A: 1948-49, **rubber-stamped** or *heat-stamped lettering.*

	300-350	600-650	1,200-1,250

2337 Wabash GP-7: 1958, unpainted blue plastic body.

	250	350	525

2338 The Milwaukee Road GP-7: 1955-56, translucent orange plastic body w/**orange stripe on cab**, or translucent orange plastic body w/no cab stripe or *opaque* orange plastic bodies w/*no cab stripe.*

	175-1,000	275-1,500	400-2,200

2339 Wabash GP-7: 1957, unpainted blue plastic body.

	200	300	450

2340 Pennsylvania GG1: 1955, painted *green* or tuscan **red**.

	800-1,000	1,250-1,500	2,100-2,500

2341 Jersey Central FM: 1956 only, molded blue plastic body w/**gloss** or *matte* orange paint applied.

	1,250-1,500	2,000-2,350	2,800-3,500

2343 Santa Fe F-3 A-A: 1950-52, painted red and silver.

	300	500	1,200

2343C Santa Fe F-3 B-Unit: 1950-55, screen-type (50-51) or molded louver roof vents.

	150	250	450

2344 New York Central F-3 A-A: 1950-52.

	350	600	1,100

2344C New York Central F-3 B-Unit: 1950-55, screen-type (50-51) or molded louver roof vents.

	175	300	450

2343 Santa Fe F-3 A-A

2344 New York Central F-3 A-A

2344C New York Central F-3 B-Unit

2346 Boston and Maine GP-9

2347 Chesapeake & Ohio GP-7

2348 Minneapolis & St. Louis GP-9

2354 New York Central F-3 A-A

2355 Western Pacific F-3 A-A

2356 Southern F-3 A-A

	C5	C7	C8

2345 Western Pacific F-3 A-A: 1952, painted silver and orange.

	$1,250	$2,100	$3,000

2346 Boston and Maine GP-9: 1965-66, black plastic body painted blue.

		200	300	425

2347 Chesapeake & Ohio GP-7: 1965 only, body painted blue w/yellow heat-stamped markings.

	1,500	2,500	3,500

2348 Minneapolis & St. Louis GP-9: 1958-59, painted red w/a white stripe painted on the middle of each side, the cab roof was painted blue and red and white lettering was heat-stamped on.

	250	350	500

2349 Northern Pacific GP-9: 1959-60, painted black brilliant gold-painted ends and side stripes.

	300	450	600

2350 New Haven EP-5: 1956-58, **orange "N," a black "H," painted nose**; or orange "N," a black "H," decal nose; or white "N," orange "H," painted nose; or *white "N," orange "H," decal nose.*

	300-1,000	400-1,600	550-2,400

2351 Milwaukee Road EP-5: 1957-58, yellow-painted body w/a maroon-painted stripe in the middle and a black-painted upper quarter and roof, heat-stamped yellow lettering.

	350	500	750

2352 Pennsylvania EP-5: 1957-58, tuscan-painted body.

	350	500	750

2353 Santa Fe F-3 A-A: 1953-55, painted silver and red.

	350	650	1,100

2354 New York Central F-3 A-A: 1953-55.

	300	550	950

2355 Western Pacific F-3 A-A: 1953, silver and orange paint.

	1,100	1,800	2,800

2356 Southern F-3 A-A: 1954-56, green-painted body had its lower side panels and nose painted gray w/rubber-stamped yellow stripes and lettering.

	800	1,250	2,000

2356C Southern F-3 B-Unit: 1954-56, decorated to match the 2356 A-A units.

	275	400	550

2357 Lionel-SP Caboose: 1947-48, *tuscan body and stack*, or red body no stack or **red body and stack**.

	18-250	25-450	30-750

2358 Great Northern EP-5: 1959-60 "Great Northern" heat-stamped on sides in yellow, end markings, number and "BLT BY LIONEL" were a large decal.

	700	1,100	1,800

2359 Boston and Maine GP-9: 1961-62, black plastic body painted blue, cab painted black, white heat-stamped lettering.

	200	300	450

2360 Pennsylvania GG1: 1956-58, green w/five stripes, **tuscan w/five stripes** or tuscan w/single applied by rubber-stamping, *painting or decal.*

	750-900	1,100-1,500	1,750-2,500

2363 Illinois Central F-3 A-B: 1955-56, unpainted or painted orange stripe.

	400	800	1,500

2365 Chesapeake and Ohio GP-7: 1962-63, painted blue w/yellow heat-stamped markings.

	200	325	475

2367 Wabash F-3 A-B: 1955 only, molded in royal blue plastic, A-unit painted, B-unit unpainted. The final segment of white stripe on B-unit, near the "Built by Lionel" marking is 1/8-in. long, **rubber-stamped** or *heat-stamped* B-unit lettering.

	725-1,200	1,150-1,900	1,700-3,000

2356C Southern F-3 B-Unit

2358 Great Northern EP-5

2363 Illinois Central F-3 A-B

2365 Chesapeake and Ohio GP-7

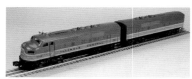

2378 Milwaukee Road F-3 A-B

2379 Rio Grande F-3 A-B

2400 Maplewood Pullman

2408 Santa Fe Vista Dome

2411 Flatcar

2412 Santa Fe Vista Dome

2419 D.L. & W. Wrecking Car

2420 D.L. & W. Wrecking Car

2421 Maplewood Pullman

2422 Chatham Pullman

2423 Hillside Observation

2430 Pullman

	C5	C7	C8
2368 Baltimore and Ohio F-3 A-B: 1956 only, *unpainted* blue plastic or **blue-painted** gray plastic body.	*$1,600*-2,000	*$2,400*-2,800	*$3,400*-4,000
2373 Canadian Pacific F-3 A-A: 1957, painted gray and brown w/yellow heat-stamped stripes and lettering.	1,200	1,800	2,800
2378 Milwaukee Road F-3 A-B: 1956 only, unpainted gray bodies, painted-on red stripe and yellow heat-stamped delineating stripes. Each unit w/or w/out a thin yellow roofline stripe, matched combinations are preferred.	1,500	2,400	3,300
2379 Rio Grande F-3 A-B: 1957-58, painted yellow, black horizontal stripes and side lettering was heat-stamped.	1,100	1,600	2,300
2383 Santa Fe F-3 A-A: 1958-66, silver and red, or silver and orange-red.	300	450	700
2400 Maplewood Pullman: 1948-49, painted green w/yellow stripes and window outlines, dark gray roof.	90	140	200
2401 Hillside Observation: 1948-49, matches 2400.	85	125	175
2402 Chatham Pullman: 1948-49, matches 2400.	90	140	200
2404 Santa Fe Vista Dome: 1964-65, no lights or silhouetted window strips.	35	70	100
2405 Santa Fe Pullman: 1964-65, matches 2404.	35	70	100
2406 Santa Fe Observation: 1964-65, matches 2404.	30	60	90
2408 Santa Fe Vista Dome: 1966 only, has lights and silhouetted window strips.	40	70	100
2409 Santa Fe Pullman: 1966 only, matches 2408.	40	70	100
2410 Santa Fe Observation: 1966 only, matches 2408.	35	60	90
2411 Flatcar: 1946-48, loaded w/**steel pipe** w/groove inside or three seven-inch long 3/8-in. diameter *wooden dowels*.	20-75	30-100	42-140
2412 Santa Fe Vista Dome: 1959-63, blue stripe, illuminated, w/silhouetted window strips.	30	60	90
2414 Santa Fe Pullman: 1959-63, matches 2412.	30	60	90
2416 Santa Fe Observation: 1959-63, matches 2412.	25	55	80
2419 D.L. & W. Wrecking Car: 1946-47.	25	35	50
2420 D.L. & W. Wrecking Car: 1946-47, dark gray cab on **light** or dark gray die-cast frame; *Heat-stamped serif* or rubber-stamped sans-serif lettering.	*60*-150	*100*-200	*150*-300
2421 Maplewood Pullman: 1950-51, *gray roof*, 1952-53 silver roof.	50-*60*	75-*90*	100-*125*
2422 Chatham Pullman: 1950-53, matches 2421.	50-*60*	75-*90*	100-*125*
2423 Hillside Observation: 1950-53, matches 2421.	50-*60*	70-*80*	90-*100*
2429 Livingston Pullman: 1952-53, matches 2421.	90-*100*	125-*150*	180-225
2430 Pullman: 1946-47, sheet metal w/blue body w/silver roof.	20	50	80
2431 Observation: 1946-47, matches 2430.	20	50	80
2432 Clifton Vista Dome: 1954-58, silver, illuminated, w/silhouetted window strips and red lettering.	25	50	75
2434 Newark Pullman: 1954-58, matches 2432.	25	50	75
2435 Elizabeth Pullman: 1954-58, matches 2432.	40	75	125
2436 Summit Observation: 1954-56, matches 2432.	35	60	100
2436 Mooseheart Observation: 1957-58, matches 2432.	35	60	100

2442 Pullman

2442 Clifton Vista Dome

2446 Summit Pullman

2460 Bucyrus Erie Crane

2465 Sunoco Tanker

2481 Plainfield Pullman

Presidential Series

2530 Lionel Lines/Railway Express Agency

2531 Lionel Lines/Silver Dawn Observation

	C5	C7	C8
2440 Pullman: 1946-47, two-tone green sheet metal, silver rubber-stamped white heat-stamped lettering.	$25	$50	$75
2441 Observation: 1946-47, two-tone green sheet metal, silver rubber-stamped white heat-stamped lettering.	25	50	75
2442 Pullman: 1946-48, brown sheet metal; silver rubber-stamped or white heat-stamped lettering.	25	50	75
2442 Clifton Vista Dome: 1956, red stripe illuminated w/silhouetted window strips.	75	125	175
2443 Observation: 1946-48, brown sheet metal; silver rubber-stamped or *white heat-stamped lettering.*	25	45-55	70-90
2444 Newark Pullman: 1956, matches 2442.	75	125	175

	C5	C7	C8
2445 Elizabeth Pullman: 1956, matches 2442.	$100	$175	$225
2446 Summit Pullman: 1956, matches 2442.	75	125	175
2452 Pennsylvania Gondola: 1945-47.	12	20	40
2452X Pennsylvania Gondola: 1946-47.	12	20	40
X2454 Baby Ruth Boxcar: 1946-47.	15	25	35
X2454 Pennsylvania: 1946 only, **orange** or *brown* doors.	80-125	150-175	225-250
2456 Lehigh Valley Hopper: 1948 only, black painted body.	15	25	35
2457 Pennsylvania Caboose: 1945-47, "477618" on side, **brown** or *red* body, **red** or *black* window frames. Has illumination and glazed windows.	20-60	30-100	40-150
X2458 Pennsylvania Boxcar: 1946-48, brown 9-1/4 in. double-door automobile car.	20	45	65
2460 Bucyrus Erie Crane: 1946-50, dark or light **gray**, or *black cab.*	60-125	80-200	100-275
2461 Transformer Car: 1947-48, **red** or *black* transformer load.	40-60	75-100	100-150
2465 Sunoco Tanker: 1946-48, "SUNOCO" logo decal **centered** or *offset.*	5-100	8-150	12-250
2472 Pennsylvania Caboose: 1946-47, numbered "477618" on sides, red, no illumination or window glazing.	15	25	35
2481 Plainfield Pullman: 1950, yellow, red markings, gray roof.	150	225	375
2482 Westfield Pullman: 1950, matches 2481.	150	225	375
2483 Livingston Observation: 1950, matches 2481.	125	200	325
2521 Observation/President McKinley: 1962-66, extruded aluminum.	75	110	150
2522 Vista Dome/President Harrison: 1962-66, matches 2521.	75	110	150
2523 Pullman/President Garfield: 1962-66, matches 2521.	75	110	150
2530 Lionel Lines/Railway Express Agency: 1954-60, extruded aluminum baggage car w/**large** or *small* doors.	75-250	125-400	175-550
2531 Lionel Lines/Silver Dawn Observation: 1952-60, extruded aluminum, *w/or w/out* fluted channels above and below the windows.	60-125	75-160	100-200
2532 Lionel Lines/Silver Range Dome: 1952-60, matches 2531.	60-125	100-160	125-200
2533 Lionel Lines/Silver Cloud Pullman: 1952-60, matches 2531.	60-125	100-160	125-200
2534 Lionel Lines/Silver Bluff Pullman: 1952-60, matches 2531.	60-125	110-200	150-275
2541 Pennsylvania/Alexander Hamilton Observation: 1955-56, extruded aluminum Congressional.	125	200	275
2542 Pennsylvania/Betsy Ross Dome: 1955-56, matches 2541.	125	200	275

2532 Lionel Lines/Silver Range Dome

2533 Lionel Lines/Silver Cloud Pullman

2534 Lionel Lines/Silver Bluff Pullman

Congressional Series

2555 Sunoco Tanker

2563 Santa Fe/Indian Falls Pullman

2625 Irvington Pullman

2628 Manhattan Pullman

2855 Sunoco Tanker

3359 Lionel Lines Dump Car

	C5	C7	C8
2543 Pennsylvania/William Penn Pullman: 1955-56, matches 2541.			
	$125	$200	$275
2544 Pennsylvania/Molly Pitcher Pullman: 1955-56, matches 2541.			
	125	200	275
2550 Baltimore and Ohio RDC-4: 1957-58.	350	550	700
2551 Canadian Pacific/Banff Park Observation: 1957, extruded aluminum.			
	150	225	325
2552 Canadian Pacific/Skyline 500 Dome: 1957, matches 2551.			
	150	250	325
2553 Canadian Pacific/Blair Manor Pullman: 1957, matches 2551.			
	225	350	500
2554 Canadian Pacific/Craig Manor Pullman: 1957, matches 2551.			
	225	350	500

	C5	C7	C8
2555 Sunoco Tanker: 1946-48, w/or w/out "GAS" and "OILS" in SUNOCO logo, "2555" on *side* or bottom of the car.	$25-35	$40-45	$55-60
2559 Baltimore and Ohio RDC-9: 1957-58, non-powered.	200	300	400
2560 Lionel Lines Crane: 1946-47, similar to prewar 2660 crane, green, brown or black two-piece boom.	45	65	110
2561 Santa Fe/Vista Valley Pullman: 1959-61, extruded aluminum.	175	225	325
2562 Santa Fe/Regal Pass Dome: 1959-61, matches 2561.	200	250	375
2563 Santa Fe/Indian Falls Pullman: 1959-61, matches 2561.	200	250	375
2625 Irvington Pullman: 1946-50, *plain* or **silhouetted** windows (1950 only).	125-150	225-275	350-400
2625 Madison Pullman: 1947, plain windows.	175	300	425
2625 Manhattan Pullman: 1947, plain windows.	175	300	425
2627 Madison Pullman: 1948-50, *plain* or **silhouetted** windows (1950 only).	125-150	250-300	325-400
2628 Manhattan Pullman: 1948-50, *plain* or **silhouetted** windows (1950 only).	125-150	250-300	325-400
2755 Sunoco Tanker: 1945 only, silver.	70	100	185
X2758 Pennsylvania Boxcar: 1945-46, brown 9-1/4-in. double-door automobile car.	25	50	75
2855 Sunoco Tanker: 1946-47, **black** or *gray*, w/or w/out "GAS" and "OILS" in SUNOCO logo.	100-145	175-225	225-350
3309 Turbo Missile Launching Car: 1962-64, *light* or **cherry** red, non-operating couplers.	20-45	35-70	55-100
3330 Flatcar w/Operating Submarine Kit: 1960-62, submarines lettered 3830; those lettered 3330 are forgeries.	100	150	200
3349 Turbo Missile Firing Car: 1962-65, unpainted red plastic, two operating couplers.	30	50	65
3349-100 Turbo Missile Launching Car: 1963-64, *red* or **olive drab**, one operating coupler.	20-200	35-350	55-500
3356 Santa Fe Horse Car with Corral: 1956-60, 1964-66, bar-end *metal* or AAR-**plastic** trucks. Reduce value by 50 percent if corral is missing.	100-125	150-175	180-250
3357 Hydraulic Platform Maintenance Car: 1962-64, w/overhead "bridge," trip and police and hobo figures.	35	65	100
3359 Lionel Lines Dump Car: 1955-58.	40	60	80
3360 Burro Crane: 1956-57, w/actuator, yellow, **painted** or *unpainted*.	175-425	275-650	400-850
3361 Log Dump Car: 1955-59, serif or sans-serif lettering, "336155" either to right or left of "LIONEL LINES."	30	42	55
3362 Helium Tank Unloading Car: 1961-63, unpainted dark green plastic, white rubber-stamped "LIONEL LINES 3362," three "helium tanks" AAR trucks w/ operating couplers.	15	20	45
3362/3364 Operating Unloading Car: 1969, unpainted dark green plastic, no markings, two "helium tanks," non-operating couplers.	15	35	75
3364 Operating Log Unloading Car: 1965-66, 1968, identical to the 3362 and rubber-stamped "3362," came 3-5/8 x 6-in. wooden dowels stained brown.	15	30	70
3366 Circus Car: 1959-61 unpainted white body and doors, red-painted roofwalk. Reduce value 50 percent if matching corral and nine white horses are missing.	150	250	350

3360 Burro Crane

3361 Log Dump Car

3376 Bronx Zoo

3435 Traveling Aquarium

3444 Erie Operating Gondola

3451 Operating Lumber Car

3454 Automatic Merchandise Boxcar

3456 N & W Hopper

	C5	C7	C8

3370 Wells Fargo Sheriff and Outlaw: 1961-64. Action simulates gunfight.

| | $25 | $50 | $75 |

3376 Bronx Zoo: 1960-66, 1969, giraffe "ducks" to avoid obstacle. Includes telltale and operating plate assembly. *White* or **yellow** (1969) lettering on blue body.

| | 40-175 | 65-300 | 90-450 |

3376-160 Bronx Zoo: green body w/yellow lettering.

| | 85 | 110 | 150 |

3386 Bronx Zoo: 1960 only, blue w/white markings, arch-bar trucks and non-operating couplers.

| | 60 | 80 | 115 |

3409 Operating Helicopter Launching Car: 1960-62, came w/an operating single rotor helicopter w/a gray body heat-stamped "NAVY."

| | 100 | 150 | 225 |

	C5	C7	C8

3410 Helicopter Launching Car: 1961-63, and carried a gray-bodied single rotor helicopter w/heat-stamped "NAVY" w/separate pale yellow tail rotor or solid yellow helicopter w/integral tail. $65 $100 $150

3413 Mercury Capsule Launching Car: 1962-64, unpainted red plastic chassis w/ gray plastic superstructure. Came w/parachute-equipped rocket.
100 160 225

3413-150 Mercury Capsule Launching Car: 1963, equipped w/one operating and one non-operating coupler. 100 160 225

3419 Operating Helicopter Launching Car: 1959-65, its body was made of blue plastic, which ranged from medium blue to a dark, almost-purple shade. In 1959 the launch spindle was two inches in diameter, in subsequent years a 1-3/8-in. spindle was used. Black or plated operating mechanism, single- or two blade gray "Navy" helicopter or all-*yellow helicopter*. 60-80 90-120 150-180

3424 Wabash Boxcar w/Brakeman: 1956-58, w/two contactor/pole-support assemblies and two telltale poles. The brakeman figures came in two colors: blue and white, and the car bodies came molded in both medium and dark blue, but there is no difference in value associated w/either variation. 50 75 125

3428 United States Mail Operating Boxcar: 1959-60, red, white and blue boxcar. Rubber figure of a blue or gray mailman ejects rubber "bag" of mail.
50 85 125

3429 U.S.M.C. Operating Helicopter Launching Car: 1960, painted olive drab and white heat-stamped "BUILT BY/LIONEL U. S. M. C. 3429." Came w/single rotor operating helicopter w/a gray body heat-stamped "USMC" on the tail boom.
350 425 650

3434 Operating Poultry Dispatch: 1959-60, 1964-66, bar-end **metal trucks** early, AAR *plastic trucks*, 64-66. 65-75 100-110 *150-175*

3435 Traveling Aquarium: 1959-62, gold circle around "L" logo and gold "TANK No. 1" and "TANK No. 2" markings; or gold markings w/out "TANK No. 1" and "TANK No. 2" or circle, or *yellow* markings. 125-650 200-1,100 275-1,650

3444 Erie Operating Gondola: 1957-1959. 50 75 110

3451 Operating Lumber Car: 1946-48, **rubber-stamped** and *heat-stamped* lettering.
25-30 35-40 50-60

3454 Automatic Merchandise Boxcar: 1946-47, painted silver, *blue* or **red** lettering.
80-600 110-1,000 160-1,600

3456 N & W Hopper: 1950-55, operating doors. 25 45 65

3459 Lionel Lines Dump Car: 1946-48, **aluminum**, green or *black* colored dump bin.
30-150 50-225 80-375

3460 Flatcar w/Trailers: 1955-1957, unpainted green plastic trailers w/removable roofs, die-cast landing gear and metal side signs reading "LIONEL TRAINS."
40 70 100

3461 Operating Lumber Car: 1949-55, *black* or **green** frame.
25-30 35-45 50-50

3462 Automatic Refrigerated Milk Car: 1947-48, **gloss cream**, matte cream or matte cream or *white* painted body. If platform and milk cans are absent, the values should be reduced by 50 percent. 30-75 45-125 60-200

X3464 A.T. & S.F. Boxcar: 1949-52, 9-1/4 in. long, *orange* or **tan** body.
12-275 20-400 30-650

X3464 NYC Boxcar: 1949-52, 9-1/4 in., tan. 12 20 30

3469 Lionel Lines: 1949-55, black. 30 40 60

3470 Aerial Target Launching Car: 1962-64, dark blue flatcar.
50 75 100

3470-100 Aerial Target Launching Car: 1963, powder blue.
200 325 450

3461 Operating Lumber Car

3469 Dump Car

3470 Aerial Target Launching Car

3472 Automatic Refrigerated Milk Car

3494-275 State of Maine Operating Boxcar

3530 Electro Mobile Power Generator Car

3562-25 A.T. & S.F. Operating Barrel Car

3562-50 A.T. & S.F. Operating Barrel Car

3650 Lionel Lines

	C5	C7	C8

3472 Automatic Refrigerated Milk Car: 1949-53, painted cream or unpainted white w/aluminum doors or unpainted white w/plastic doors. If platform and milk cans are absent, the values should be reduced by 50 percent.

	$30	$45	$60

3474 Western Pacific Boxcar: 1952-53, silver 9-1/4 in. long.

	35	55	80

3482 Automatic Refrigerated Milk Car: 1954-55, 9-1/4 in. long unpainted white milk car. Right of door stamped **RT3472** or *RT3482*. If platform and milk cans are absent, the values should be reduced by 50 percent.

	40-75	60-100	85-150

3484 Pennsylvania Operating Boxcar: 1953, 10-5/8 in. long.

	30	50	80

3484-25 A.T. & S.F. Operating Boxcar: 1954, 1956, 10-5/8 in. long, orange body w/**black** or *white* lettering.

	50-700	80-900	125-1,400

3494-1 Pacemaker Operating Boxcar: 1955 10-5/8 in. long.

	75	110	165

3494-150 Missouri Pacific Lines Operating Boxcar: 1956 10-5/8 in. long.

	60	100	160

3494-275 State of Maine Operating Boxcar: 1956-58, 10-5/8 in. long. W/or *w/out* "3494275" stamped to the left of the door.

	60-*100*	80-*175*	125-250

3494-550 Monon Operating Boxcar: 1957-58 10-5/8 in. long.

	200	325	500

3494-625 Soo Line Operating Boxcar: 1957-58 10-5/8 in. long.

	200	325	525

3509 Satellite Launching Car: 1961, unpainted dark green, gray and yellow.

	40	65	100

3510 Satellite Launching Car: 1962, bright red, no number on car.

	100	150	225

3512 Operating Fireman and Ladder Car: 1959-61, *black* or **silver** extension ladder.

	75-100	125-160	*180-225*

3519 Operating Satellite Launching Car: 1961-64, dark green unpainted plastic.

	35	55	80

3520 Lionel Lines Searchlight Car: 1952-53, **serif** or *sans-serif* lettering.

	35-75	55-125	75-180

3530 Electro Mobile Power Generator Car: 1956-58, white stripe stops at ladder or extends through the molded-in ladder on the right-hand end of the car.

	60	100	150

3535 Operating Security Car w/Rotating Searchlight: 1960-61.

	75	115	175

3540 Operating Radar Car: 1959-62.

	100	175	250

3545 Operating TV Monitor Car: 1961-62.

	125	200	275

3559 Coal Dump: 1946-48, black or brown Bakelite mechanism housing.

	20	35	50

3562-1 A.T. & S.F. Operating Barrel Car: 1954, *black* w/black or yellow trough or gray w/**red** lettering.

	110-800	*175-1,200*	*250-1,700*

3562-25 A.T. & S.F. Operating Barrel Car: 1954 only, gray painted body marked 356225 on car side, w/**red** or *blue* heat-stamped markings.

	40-250	65-400	85-625

3562-50 A.T. & S.F. Operating Barrel Car: 1955-56, marked "356250" on car side, yellow **painted** or *unpainted* body.

	45-60	70-95	85-150

3562-75 A.T. & S.F. Operating Barrel Car: orange unpainted body marked "356275."

	60	90	150

3619 Helicopter Reconnaissance Car: 1962-64, spring-loaded mechanism launches a red HO-Gauge helicopter through the roof of this boxcar. *Light* or **dark** yellow unpainted plastic.

	60-100	100-175	*150-250*

3662 Automatic Refrigerated Milk Car

3927 Lionel Lines Track Cleaning Car

4452 Pennsylvania Gondola

X4454 Baby Ruth Boxcar

5459 Lionel Lines Dump Car

6015 Sunoco Tanker

	C5	C7	C8

3620 Lionel Lines: 1954-56, *gray* or **orange** searchlight housing.
$30-100 | $40-140 | $60-200

3650 Lionel Lines: 1956-59, came w/*light gray*, dark gray or **olive gray** frame.
40-125 | 60-175 | 80-250

3656 Lionel Lines Operating Cattle Car: 1949-55, reduce value 50 percent if matching corral and cattle are missing. Heat-stamped **black lettering**, adhesive "Armour" logo, heat-stamped white lettering, adhesive "Armour" logo, heat-stamped white lettering, *no* "Armour" logo.
50-150 | 75-225 | 110-300

3662 Automatic Refrigerated Milk Car: 1955-60 and 1964-66, if platform and milk cans are absent, the values should be reduced by 50 percent. **Painted** or *unpainted* white.
45-50 | 70-75 | 100-115

3665 Minuteman: 1961-64, unpainted white body w/red and white rocket w/blue rubber nose cone **light** or *dark* (almost purple) blue roof.
60-150 | 90-200 | 125-325

3666 Minuteman: unpainted white body housing, large olive drab cannon w/four wooden artillery shells.
350 | 550 | 800

3672 Corn Products Co.-Bosco: 1959-60, if platform and milk cans are absent, the values should be reduced by 50 percent.
225 | 350 | 500

3820 U.S.M.C. Operating Submarine Car: 1960-62, painted olive drab body carrying factory-assembled gray "U.S. NAVY 3830" submarine. Be aware that in addition to reproduction 3830 submarines, forgeries stamped "U.S.M.C. 3820" also exist.
150 | 225 | 350

3830 Submarine Car: 1960-63, unpainted blue carrying submarine lettered "U.S. NAVY 3830."
90 | 115 | 150

3854 Automatic Merchandise Car: 1946-47, w/six plastic "crates" (actually cubes) engraved "BABY RUTH."
375 | 600 | 850

3927 Lionel Lines Track Cleaning Car: 1956-60.
40 | 65 | 90

4357 Lionel-SP Caboose: 1948-49, tuscan-painted plastic body.
85 | 150 | 250

	C5	C7	C8
4452 Pennsylvania Gondola: 1946-49.	$75	$115	$150
X4454 Baby Ruth Boxcar: 1946-49.	100	175	300
4457 Pennsylvania Caboose: 1946-47, steel-bodied caboose painted red.			
	75	150	250
5459 Lionel Lines Dump Car: 1946-49.	100	175	275
6002 New York Central Gondola: 1950 only, it was not supplied with a load.			
	12	20	30
X6004 Baby Ruth Boxcar: 1950 only, unpainted orange.			
	5	7	10
6007 Lionel Lines Caboose: 1950 only, unpainted red plastic.			
	5	10	15
6012 Lionel Gondola: 1951-56, unpainted black plastic body.			
	5	8	15
6014 Airex Boxcar: 1959 only.	35	50	75
X6014 Baby Ruth Boxcar: 1951-56, these cars had metal trucks, **red** or *white* body.			
	4-7	8-12	10-16
6014 Bosco Boxcar: 1958, AAR-type trucks, unpainted red, *white* or orange body.			
	6-30	9-50	12-75
6014 Chun King Boxcar: 1956.	100	150	250
6014 Frisco Boxcar: 1957, 1963-69, red, white or *orange* body.			
	4-40	6-60	10-80
6014 Wix Filters Boxcar: 1959 only.	100	150	250
6015 Sunoco Tanker: 1954-55, *painted* or unpainted yellow tank.			
	5-65	8-100	10-150
6017 Lionel Lines Caboose: 1951-62, red body, tuscan, semi-gloss tuscan, gloss tuscan, maroon, tile red, *brown*.	2-75	4-125	6-200
6017 Lionel Caboose: 1956 only, often mistaken for the common 6017 Lionel Lines.			
	35	60	90
6017-50 United States Marine Corps Caboose: 1958 only, dark blue.			
	35	60	90
6017 Lionel Lines Caboose: 1958 only, painted light gray.			
	15	30	45
6017 Boston and Maine Caboose: 1959, 1962 and 1965-66, light, medium or *dark* blue.	20-275	35-425	60-650
6017 A.T. & S.F. Caboose: 1959-60, painted light gray.			
	20	30	45
6017-200 United States Navy Caboose: 1960 only.			
	50	75	110
6017-235 A.T. & S.F. Caboose: 1962 only, painted red.			
	30	50	75
6024 RCA Whirlpool Boxcar: 1957 only.	35	60	80
6024 Shredded Wheat Boxcar: 1957 only.	12	20	30
6025 Gulf Tank Car: 1956-58, black, gray or *orange* tank.			
	5-16	10-25	15-40
6027 Alaska Railroad Caboose: 1949 only, painted dark blue, heat stamped in yellow.	40	65	95
6032 Lionel Gondola: 1952-54, unpainted black plastic.			
	5	8	15
X6034 Baby Ruth Boxcar: 1953-54, unpainted orange.			
	7	10	14
6035 Sunoco Tank Car: 1952-53, unpainted gray body.			
	3	8	15
6037 Lionel Lines Caboose: 1952-54, unpainted *tuscan* or **red** bodies.			
	3-25	5-40	7-65
6042 Lionel Gondola: 1959-64, equipped w/archbar or AAR trucks, w/or w/out operating couplers, black or blue.	5	8	12

6025 Gulf Tank Car

6032 Lionel Gondola

6037 Lionel Lines Caboose

6045 Lionel Lines Tank Car

6045 Cities Service Tank Car

6058 Chesapeake and Ohio Caboose

6059 M & St. L Caboose

6112 Lionel Gondola

6111/6121 Flatcar

6119 D.L. & W. Work Caboose

6119-25 D.L. & W. Work Caboose

	C5	C7	C8

6044 Airex Boxcar: 1959-61, *medium*, teal or very dark (approaching purple) blue.
| | $10-175 | $18-275 | $25-400 |

6044-1X McCall's-Nestle's Boxcar: produced in the early 1960s, unpainted blue body was decorated by pasting a miniature McCall's-Nestle's billboard on each side.
| | 700 | 1,000 | 1,500 |

6045 Lionel Lines Tank Car: 1959-64, unpainted gray, beige or *orange* tank.
| | 15-20 | 30-50 | 45-75 |

6045 Cities Service Tank Car: 1960-61, green.
| | 20 | 50 | 75 |

6047 Lionel Lines Caboose: 1959-62, unpainted medium *red* or coral-pink.
| | 3-20 | 5-40 | 10-65 |

6050 Libby's Tomato Juice Boxcar: 1963, unpainted white body w/red and blue lettering and a red, blue and green tomato juice logo.
| | 20 | 35 | 60 |

6050 Lionel Savings Bank Boxcar: 1961, "BUILT BY LIONEL." **spelled** out or *abbreviated* as "BLT."
| | 20-50 | 30-75 | 45-100 |

6050 Swift Boxcar: 1962-63, unpainted red w/white heat-stamped lettering.
| | 12 | 20 | 30 |

6057 Lionel Lines Caboose: 1959-62, 1969, **painted** or *unpainted* red or coral pink body.
| | 6-35 | 10-60 | 15-90 |

6057-50 Lionel Lines Caboose: 1962, unpainted orange.
| | 15 | 25 | 40 |

6058 Chesapeake and Ohio Caboose: 1961, painted dark yellow.
| | 20 | 35 | 60 |

6059 M & St. L Caboose: 1961-69, **painted** or *unpainted* red or unpainted maroon.
| | 4-15 | 8-20 | 12-30 |

6059-50 M & St. L: 1963-64, unpainted red body w/white heat-stamped markings.
| | 12 | 18 | 25 |

6062 New York Central Gondola: 1959-1962, 1969, black, **w/or** *w/out* metal underframe.
| | 15-25 | 20-40 | 28-60 |

6067 Caboose: 1961-62, unlettered, *red*, yellow or **brown** plastic.
| | 2-20 | 4-35 | 7-50 |

6076 A.T.S.F. Hopper: unpainted gray, black heat-stamped lettering.
| | 15 | 30 | 40 |

6076 Lehigh Valley Hopper: black, red or gray unpainted or *painted pale yellow body*.
| | 10-400 | 14-800 | 18-1,100 |

6110 2-4-2 Steam: 1950 only, w/a 6001T tender.
| | 25 | 40 | 55 |

6111/6121 Flatcar: 1955-58, assorted colors.
| | 10 | 15 | 20 |

6112 Lionel Gondola: 1956-58, *black*, blue or **white** body.
| | 5-15 | 8-30 | 12-50 |

6119 D.L. & W. Work Caboose: 1955-56, unpainted red open tool compartment and unpainted red plastic cab.
| | 12 | 25 | 40 |

6119-25 D.L. & W. Work Caboose: 1956 only, overall orange work caboose.
| | 20 | 35 | 55 |

6119-50 D.L. & W. Work Caboose: 1956 only, all-brown 6119.
| | 25 | 45 | 75 |

6119-75 D.L. & W. Work Caboose: 1957, **serif** or *sans-serif* frame lettering.
| | 12-125 | 25-225 | 45-350 |

6119-100 D.L. & W. Work Caboose: 1957-66, unpainted gray tool compartment and an *unpainted* or **painted** red cab.
| | 8-60 | 15-100 | 25-150 |

6119-125 Rescue Caboose: 1964 only, cab and tool compartment unpainted olive drab plastic.
| | 100 | 175 | 250 |

6120 Undecorated Caboose: unpainted yellow tool compartment and cab.
| | 20 | 30 | 40 |

6130 A.T.S.F. Caboose: 1961-65, 1969, red tool compartment and a red cab.
| | 16 | 25 | 40 |

6119-50 D.L. & W. Work Caboose

6119-100 D.L. & W. Work Caboose

6142 Lionel Gondola

6162 New York Central Gondola

6167-85 Union Pacific Caboose

6176 Lehigh Valley Hopper

6219 C & O Work Caboose

6250 Seaboard NW-2

6264 Lumber Car

(6346) Alcoa Covered Hopper

6352 Pacific Fruit Express Boxcar

6356 NYC Stock Car

	C5	C7	C8
6142 Lionel Gondola: 1963-66, 1969, black, green, blue or *olive drab* body.	$5-75	$8-110	$12-165
6151 Flatcar w/Range Patrol Truck: 1958 only.	65	110	160
6162 New York Central Gondola: 1959-68, blue, teal or *red* body.	10-85	12-125	15-200
6162-60 Alaska Railroad Gondola: 1959.	40	55	80
6167 Lionel Lines Caboose: 1963-64, *unpainted* or **painted** red.	4-60	7-100	10-175
6167 Undecorated Caboose: unpainted olive drab.	200	375	550
6167-25 Undecorated Caboose: 1963-64, red.	5	7	10
6167-50 Undecorated Caboose: unpainted yellow body.	12	20	35
6167-85 Union Pacific Caboose: 1963-66, 1969 unpainted yellow body black heat-stamped markings.	10	16	25
6167-100 Lionel Lines Caboose: 1963-64, unpainted red body.	5	10	14
6167-125 Undecorated Caboose: 1963-64, unpainted red body.	5	7	10
6167-150 Lionel Lines Caboose: 1963-64, unpainted red body.	5	10	14
6167-1967 T.T.O.S. Hopper: (Toy Train Operating Society): 1967, unpainted olive w/metallic gold heat-stamped lettering.	50	65	100
6175 Rocket Flatcar: 1958-61, white plastic rocket load heat-stamped "BUILT BY/ LIONEL" and "U S NAVY" in blue. Unpainted red or black plastic.	40	60	85
6176 Lehigh Valley Hopper: 1964-66, 1969, bright yellow, dark yellow, gray or black.	10	15	20
6219 C & O Work Caboose: 1960, tool compartment and cab painted dark blue.	30	50	75
6220 A.T. & S.F. NW-2: 1949-50, black, die-cast frame. **W**/or *w/out* "6220" stamped on the nose.	150-200	200-325	350-500
6250 Seaboard NW-2: 1954-55, "SEABOARD" lettering applied w/decal, **rubber-stamped** or *wide-spaced rubber-stamping* (about 2-13/16 to 2-23/32 in. long).	175-500	275-675	375-950
6257 Lionel-SP Caboose: 1948-52, painted red, red-orange, tile red or painted dark tile red, as was *smokejack*.	2-200	5-400	8-650
6257X Lionel-SP Caboose: 1948 only.	15	25	35
6257 Lionel Caboose: 1953-55, red body, tile red or dark red.	5	8	10
6257-100 Lionel Lines Caboose: 1963-64, unpainted red body, w/die-cast smokejack.	15	25	40
6262 Wheel Car: 1956-57, unpainted **red** or unpainted *black* body.	50-400	75-1,000	100-1,500
6264 Lumber Car: 1957-58, unpainted red body came w/12 timbers.	30	50	75
6311 Flatcar w/Pipes: 1955 only, unpainted brown, w/three silver-gray plastic pipes.	20	40	65
6315 Gulf Tank Car: 1956-58, w/flat burnt-orange, *glossy burnt-orange*, *true orange* bands, bands painted on the ends.	25-60	55-125	80-175
6315 Lionel Lines Tank Car: 1963-66, all orange tank, **painted** or *unpainted* orange tank.	10-75	20-125	40-225
6315 Gulf: 1968-69, unpainted orange tank.	20	35	75
6342 NYC Culvert Gondola: 1956-58, 1966-69.	15	25	40

6357 Lionel Caboose

6376 Circus Stock Car

6402 Flatcar

6407 Flatcar w/Missile

6414 Evans Auto Loader

6418 Machinery Car

	C5	C7	C8
6343 Barrel Ramp Car: 1961-62.	$25	$40	$65
(6346) Alcoa Covered Hopper: 1956, painted silver, multi-colored ALCOA marking w/adhesive-backed paper label; heat-stamped *blue*, black or **red** heat-stamped lettering.	30-500	50-800	75-**1,200**
6352 Pacific Fruit Express Boxcar: 1955-57, unpainted orange body w/black heat-stamped lettering, **three** or *four* lines of data rubber-stamped on ice compartment door.	75-90	100-150	150-225
6356 NYC Stock Car: 1954-55, painted yellow, **rubber** or *heat*-stamped markings.	25-50	35-75	50-100
6357 Lionel-SP Caboose: 1948-53.	15	22	35
6357 Lionel Caboose: 1953-61, tuscan or maroon, w/*black* or **maroon** die-cast smokejack.	15-275	22-425	35-600
6357-50 A.T. & S.F. Caboose: 1960 only, painted red w/white heat-stamped markings.	600	1,000	1,600
6361 Timber Transport Car: 1960-61, 1964-66 and 1968-69, unpainted *dark* or **light** green body.	40-75	70-125	100-175
6362 Railway Truck Car: 1955-57, *shiny* or **pale** orange.	30-125	45-175	70-250
6376 Circus Stock Car: 1956-57, unpainted white plastic, w/red trim and markings.	60	100	150
6401 Flatcar: 1965, unpainted gray body.	2	5	10
6402 Flatcar: 1962, 1964-66, 1969, gray or brown w/two empty Lionel *cable reels* or 6801-75 **boat** w/blue hull.	8-50	13-65	20-95
6404 Flatcar w/Automobile: black plastic body heat stamped "6404" and "BUILT BY LIONEL" in white, w/*yellow*, red, **Kelly green or brown** auto w/gray bumpers.	40-150	60-200	85-260
6405 Flatcar w/Van: 1961, heat stamped "6405," furnished w/a yellow plastic van w/single rear wheels.	20	35	60

	C5	C7	C8

6406 Flatcar w/Auto: 1961, gray or maroon plastic, unlettered flatcar carrying a single yellow automobile w/gray bumpers.

	$50	$75	$100

6407 Flatcar w/Missile: 1963, w/a large missile w/removable Mercury capsule produced by Sterling Plastics. The Sterling Plastics name always was molded into the base of the capsules.

	300	500	700

6408 Flatcar w/Pipes: 1963, unpainted red plastic flatcar w/five gray plastic pipes held on w/a rubber band.

	15	25	35

6409-25 Flatcar w/Pipes: 1963, unpainted red plastic flatcar w/three gray plastic pipes held on w/a rubber band.

	15	25	35

6411 Flatcar: 1948-50, medium-gray flatcar w/three seven-inch-long wooden 3/8-in. dowels.

	20	30	40

6413 Mercury Capsule Carrying Car: 1962-63, *unpainted blue*, painted blue or unpainted blue-green body.

	100-300	*150-400*	*210-600*

6414 Evans Auto Loader: 1955-66, unpainted red body, black sheet metal superstructure, w/four 4-5/16-in.-long plastic automobiles, metal trucks and one each red, white, yellow and green automobiles.

	75	110	165
AAR-type trucks w/one each red, white, yellow and green automobiles.	70	100	150
"6414" to the left of "LIONEL," four red autos w/gray bumpers.	100	150	200
"6414" to the left of "LIONEL," four yellow autos w/gray bumpers.	200	300	500
"6414" to the left of "LIONEL," four Kelly-green autos w/gray bumpers.	750	1,000	1,500
"6414" to the left of "LIONEL," four brown autos w/gray bumpers.	750	1,000	1,500
Decaled "6414 AUTO LOADER" legend, four light red automobiles w/gray bumpers.	200	400	650

6414-85 Evans Auto Loader: 1964, two yellow and two red automobiles, adaptations from Lionel's slot cars w/molded-in tires.

	450	600	850

6415 Sunoco Tank Car: 1953-55, 1964-66 and 1969.

	10	20	35

6416 Boat Loader: 1961-63, w/four boats w/white-painted hulls, blue-painted cabin and brown-painted interior.

	125	175	250

6417 Pennsylvania Caboose: 1953-57, w/or **w/out** "NEW YORK ZONE."

	20-200	30-300	45-425

6417-25 Lionel Lines Caboose: 1954 only.

	20	30	55

6417-50 Lehigh Valley Caboose: 1954 only, painted *gray* or *tuscan*.

	75-600	125-1,000	175-1,500

6418 Machinery Car: 1955-57, 16-wheel car w/two unnumbered black plastic girders w/"LIONEL" in raised white letters.

	75	100	125
W/two unnumbered orange plastic girders w/"LIONEL" in raised white lettering.	90	115	150
Orange girders w/"LIONEL" in raised black lettering.	75	100	125
Orange girders w/out the raised "LIONEL" having accent color.	75	100	125
Unnumbered, orange plastic girders, painted light gray.	90	115	150
Girders pinkish red-oxide primer color w/raised "U.S. STEEL" lettering outlined in black.	90	115	150
Girders black w/raised "U.S. STEEL" lettering outlined in white.	75	100	125

6419 D.L. & W. Caboose: 1948-50, 1952-55, gray work caboose w/die-cast frame.

	25	35	50

6419 D.L. & W. Caboose

6424 Twin Auto Car

6427 Lionel Lines Caboose

6430 Cooper-Jarrett Van Car

6436 Lehigh Valley Hopper

6440 Pullman

6442 Pullman

6446 N & W Covered Hopper

	C5	C7	C8
6419-25 D.L. & W. Caboose: 1954-55, gray work caboose w/die-cast frame and one coupler.	$25	$35	$50
6419-50 D.L. & W. Caboose: 1956-57, gray work caboose, short die-cast smokejack, bar-end trucks and two magnetic couplers.	25	40	60
6419-75 D.L. & W. Caboose: 1956, gray work caboose identical to the 6419-50, but w/one coupler.	25	40	60
6419-100 N & W Caboose: 1957-58, gray work caboose.	100	150	250
6420 D.L. & W. Caboose: 1948-50, dark gray work caboose w/operating searchlight.	60	100	150
6424 Twin Auto Car: 1956-59, unpainted black plastic, w/automobiles w/chrome bumpers.	30	50	75
6425 Gulf Tank Car: 1956-58, triple dome.	15	30	50
6427 Lionel Lines Caboose: 1954-60, tuscan, numbered "64273."	20	30	45
6427-60 Virginian Caboose: 1958, painted dark blue w/yellow heat-stamped lettering.	125	250	450

	C5	C7	C8
6427-500 Pennsylvania Caboose: 1957-58, painted sky blue and was decorated w/ white heat-stamped lettering, including the number "576427."			
	$200	$350	$525
6428 United States Mail Boxcar: 1960-61, 1965-66, red, white and blue.			
	20	35	50
6429 D.L. & W. Caboose: 1963 only, gray work caboose.			
	150	275	450
6430 Cooper-Jarrett Van Car: 1956-58, unpainted red flatcar w/vans.			
	45	70	100
6431 Piggy-Back Car w/Trailer Trucks and Tractor: 1966, packaged w/two trailers and a road tractor. Car heat stamped 6430, the 6431 number appearing exclusively on the end of the original box.	175	250	375
6434 Poultry Dispatch Stock Car: 1958-59, painted red, illuminated.			
	45	70	100
6436 Lehigh Valley Hopper: 1955-56, 1966, open-top hopper;			
Black, marked "646361," w/out spreader bar.	50	65	90
Black, marked "646361," w/spreader bar.	20	35	50
Maroon, marked "643625," w/out spreader bar.	50	75	100
Maroon, marked "643625," w/ spreader bar.	20	35	50
6436 Lehigh Valley Hopper (Type V): 1963-68, red, cataloged as 6436-110. Stamped w/or *w/out* "NEW 3-55" on sides.	20-35	30-50	50-85
6436 Lehigh Valley Hopper: 1957-58, lilac painted, w/maroon heat-stamped lettering numbered "643657," part of "Girl's Set."	150	250	375
6436-1969 TCA Hopper (Train Collectors Association): 1969.			
	75	90	125
6437 Pennsylvania Caboose: 1961-68.	17	25	40
6440 Pullman: 1948-49, brown sheet metal.	25	40	70
6440 Flatcar w/Piggy-Back Vans: 1961-63, red flatcar w/unpainted gray plastic trailers w/only single rear wheels and no decoration.			
	60	100	140
6441 Observation: 1948-49, brown sheet metal.	25	35	60
6442 Pullman: 1949, brown sheet metal.	30	60	90
6443 Observation: 1949, brown sheet metal.	30	60	90
6445 Fort Knox Gold Reserve: 1961-63.	80	125	175
6446 N & W Covered Hopper: 1954-55, gray or black-painted body and cover, w/out spreader-brace holes, marked "546446."	30	45	60
6446 (-25) N & W: 1955-57, 1963, gray or black-painted body and cover marked "644625."	25	40	60
6446 Lehigh Valley Hopper: (6446-60) 1963, body painted red, roof and hatches unpainted red.	110	175	275
6447 Pennsylvania Caboose: 1963 only.	200	325	500
6448 Target Range Boxcar: 1961-64, red roof and ends w/white side panels or white roof and ends w/red side panels.	18	25	40
6452 Pennsylvania Gondola: 1948-49, numbered "6462" or "6452" on side and rubber stamped "6452" on bottom of the frame.	12	16	25
X6454 A.T. & S.F. Boxcar: 1948, painted orange w/black markings.			
	25	40	60
X6454 Baby Ruth Boxcar: 1948, painted light orange.			
	125	250	375
X6454 Erie Boxcar: 1949-52, brown w/white markings.			
	30	45	70
X6454 N Y C Boxcar: 1948 only, *tan*, brown or **orange** body.			
	20-75	30-125	45-200
X6454 Pennsylvania Boxcar: 1949-52, brown.	30	45	70

X6454 A.T. & S.F. Boxcar

X6454 N Y C Boxcar

X6454 Pennsylvania Boxcar

6456 Lehigh Valley

6460 Bucyrus Erie Crane

6461 Transformer Car

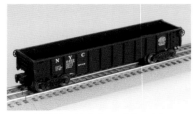

6462 New York Central Gondola

6464-1 Western Pacific Boxcar

6464-25 Great Northern Boxcar

6464-50 Minneapolis & St. Louis

	C5	C7	C8
X6454 Southern Pacific Boxcar: 1949-52, brown.	$30	$45	$70
6456 Lehigh Valley: 1948-55, painted black, maroon, gray or glossy *red*.			
	8-75	10-110	15-175
6457 Lionel Caboose: 1949-52.	15	25	35
6460 Bucyrus Erie Crane: 1952-54, black or red.	40	75	95

	C5	C7	C8

6461 Transformer Car: 1949-50, gray die-cast flatcar w/black transformer load.

$50 — $75 — $100

6462 New York Central Gondola: 1949-56, black, red or *green*.

10-15 — 13-22 — 16-32

6462-500 New York Central Gondola: 1957-58, pink.

150 — 200 — 300

6463 Rocket Fuel Tank Car: 1962-63, painted snow-white w/bright red rubber-stamped lettering.

15 — 25 — 60

6464-1 Western Pacific Boxcar: 1953-54, painted silver, *blue* or red heat-stamped markings.

55-975 — 85-1,600 — 110-2,400

6464-25 Great Northern Boxcar: 1953-54, painted orange w/white heat-stamped lettering.

60 — 75 — 100

6464-50 Minneapolis & St. Louis: 1953-56, four full columns of rivets to the right of the door.

50 — 70 — 100

6464-75 Rock Island: 1953-54, 1969, green-painted body.

60 — 80 — 100

6464-100 Western Pacific: 1954-55, silver (see 6464-250 for orange).

100 — 130 — 190

6464-125 Pacemaker Boxcar: 1954-56, red and gray decorated w/white.

75 — 110 — 150

6464-150 Missouri Pacific Boxcar: 1954-55, 1957, circular Missouri Pacific Lines herald stamped in the panel immediately to the **left of the door**, or in the *fourth panel* from the left end of the car.

75-850 — 125-1,250 — 160-1,900

6464-175 Rock Island: 1954-55, painted silver; markings in *blue* or black.

75-750 — 110-1,000 — 175-1,600

6464-200 Pennsylvania Boxcar: 1954-55, 1969, tuscan-painted doors and body.

75 — 110 — 150

6464-225 Southern Pacific Boxcar: 1954-56.

75 — 110 — 150

6464-250 Western Pacific Boxcar: 1954, 1966, orange stamped 6464-100 or *6464-250*.

130-600 — 200-850 — 275-1,200

6464-275 State of Maine Boxcar: 1955, 1957-59, solid **red door** or *striped door*.

60-100 — 90-165 — 125-250

6464-75 Rock Island

6464-100 Western Pacific

6464-125 Pacemaker Boxcar

6464-150 Missouri Pacific Boxcar

6464-175 Rock Island

6464-200 Pennsylvania Boxcar

6464-225 Southern Pacific Boxcar

6464-250 Western Pacific Boxcar

6464-275 State of Maine Boxcar

6464-300 Rutland Boxcar

6464-325 Baltimore & Ohio Sentinel Boxcar

6464-350 M-K-T (Missouri-Kansas-Texas) Boxcar

6464-375 Central of Georgia Boxcar

6464-400 Baltimore & Ohio Boxcar

	C5	C7	C8
6464-300 Rutland Boxcar: 1955-56, Rutland herald has a **solid dark green** or *yellow* background.	$75-2,000	$125-2,700	$175-3,500
6464-325 Baltimore & Ohio Sentinel Boxcar: 1956 only, painted silver and aqua.	400	625	875
6464-350 M-K-T (Missouri-Kansas-Texas) Boxcar: 1956 only.	200	300	400
6464-375 Central of Georgia Boxcar: 1956-57, 1966.	75	110	150
6464-400 Baltimore & Ohio Boxcar: 1956-57, 1969. Marked "BLT 5-54 BY LIONEL" on one side and "BLT 2-56 BY LIONEL" on the other or *matching built dates.*	70-500	100-850	150-1,200
6464-425 New Haven Boxcar: 1956-58.	40	60	80
6464-450 Great Northern Boxcar: 1956-57, 1966.	75	125	175
6464-475 Boston and Maine Boxcar: 1957-60, 1965-68.	35	50	65
6464-500 Timken Boxcar: 1957-59, 1969.	75	125	175
6464-510 Pacemaker Boxcar: 1957-58, pastel blue.	500	675	950
6464-515 M-K-T Boxcar: 1957-58, pastel yellow.	500	675	950
6464-525 Minneapolis & St. Louis Boxcar: 1957-58, 1964-66.	35	60	100
6464-650 Rio Grande Boxcar: 1957-58, 1966.	75	125	175
6464-700 Santa Fe Boxcar: 1961, 1966.	80	125	185
6464-725 New Haven Boxcar: 1962-66, 1968-69, *orange* or **black** body.	45-200	60-275	100-375
6464-825 Alaska Railroad Boxcar: 1959-60, blue.	175	275	375
6464-900 New York Central Boxcar: 1960-66, jade green.	60	110	150
6464-1965 Train Collectors Association Boxcar: 1965, uncataloged commemorative for the 1965 TCA convention in Pittsburgh, painted blue body.	80	200	250

6464-425 New Haven Boxcar

6464-450 Great Northern Boxcar

6464-475 Boston and Maine Boxcar

6464-500 Timken Boxcar

6464-510 Pacemaker Boxcar

6464-515 M-K-T Boxcar

6464-650 Rio Grande Boxcar

6464-700 Santa Fe Boxcar

6464-725 New Haven Boxcar

6464-825 Alaska Railroad Boxcar

6464-900 New York Central Boxcar

6465 Sunoco Tank Car

6465 Gulf/Lionel Lines Tank Car

6465 Lionel Lines Tank Car

	C5	C7	C8

6465 Sunoco Tank Car: 1948-56, two-dome painted silver, technical data ends w/the word *"TANK"* or "6465." $5-10 $10-15 $15-25

6465 Gulf/Lionel Lines Tank Car: 1958, *gray* or **black** tank.
15-40 18-55 25-85

6465 Lionel Lines Tank Car: 1959, 1963-66, **black** or *orange* tank.
4-15 8-40 12-55

6465 Cities Service Tank Car: 1960-62, painted green.
15 25 35

6467 Miscellaneous Flatcar: 1956 only, molded red plastic body, white heat-stamped "LIONEL 6467." Unpainted black plastic bulkhead, four-spring-steel 2411-4 posts, no load furnished. 30 45 70

6468 Baltimore & Ohio Boxcar: 1953-55, painted *blue* or **tuscan**.
40-250 65-350 100-475

6468-25 New Haven Boxcar: 1956-58, orange body, black doors; "N" of NH logo *black* or **white**. 50-150 75-225 110-325

6469 Liquified Gas Car: 1963 only, unpainted red plastic w/orange tint, heat stamped "Lionel" in white, black molded plastic bulkheads glued in place. The load was a cardboard tube wrapped in glossy white paper. On it, printed in black, was the car number "6469" and an Erie herald. Sheet metal caps were painted white and crimped on each end of the tube. 40 90 140

6470 Explosives Boxcar: 1959-60. 30 50 70

6472 Refrigerator: 1950-53. 25 35 50

6473 Horse Transport Car: 1962-66, 1969. 25 35 50

6475 Pickles: 1960-62, vat car. 25 45 65

6475 Libby's Crushed Pineapple: 1963-64, vats covered in adhesive silver paper w/Libby's logos. 30 40 60

6476 Lehigh Valley Hopper: 1957-69, red, gray or black body.
10 16 22

6476-1 Toy Train Operating Society Hopper: 1969 only, uncataloged.
40 65 110

6476 Lehigh Valley: 1959-63, *red*, **coral pink** or black body.
8-15 10-30 15-50

6465 Cities Service Tank Car

6468-25 New Haven Boxcar

6472 Refrigerator

6473 Horse Transport Car

6480 Explosives Boxcar

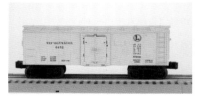

6482 Refrigerator

6512 Cherry Picker Car

656025 Bucyrus Erie

	C5	C7	C8

6476-135 Lehigh Valley: 1964-66, 1968, listed in various catalogs was a yellow 6476 hopper. Be advised, however, that no yellow hopper cars were produced w/the number "6476" stamped on them. Rather, the 6476 number denoted two operating couplers. The cars themselves used various black Lehigh Valley heat stamps, w/ various numbers and built and new dates. SEE OTHER LISTINGS.

6477 Miscellaneous Car w/Pipes: 1957-58, red plastic body, black plastic bulkheads, four spring-steel 2411-4 posts, load of five silver-gray plastic pipes.

	$30	$60	$80

6480 Explosives Boxcar: 1961 only, red.

	30	50	70

6482 Refrigerator: 1957 only, white.

	40	55	85

6500 Beechcraft Bonanza Transport Car: 1962, unnumbered, unpainted black flatcar w/red and white airplane. Four rivets bind each wing together. Red or *white* upper wings and fuselage.

	425-550	550-700	750-950

6501 Flatcar w/Motorboat: 1962-63, boat propelled by pellets of baking soda.

	90	125	175

6502 Steel Girder Transport Car: 1962-63, w/a single unpainted orange girder w/"LIONEL" in raised lettering retained by a 6418-9 elastic band. Unpainted *black* or **red** plastic body.

	20-50	35-80	60-125

6502-50 Steel Girder Transport Car: circa 1963, unlettered, unpainted blue plastic car w/single unpainted orange "LIONEL" girder retained by a 6418-9 elastic band.

	25	40	60

6511 Pipe Car: 1953-56, furnished w/five standard silver-gray plastic pipes and a small envelope containing 13 2411-4 spring steel posts.

	20	45	65

6512 Cherry Picker Car: 1962-63.

	75	100	150

6517 Lionel Lines Caboose: 1955-59, w/or *w/out* underscoring beneath "BLT 12-55" and "LIONEL."

	40-45	60-75	80-100

6517-75 Erie Caboose: 1966 only, bay window caboose.

	250	400	525

6517/1966 TCA Caboose: 1966, uncataloged, commemorative caboose.

	75	125	200

6518 Transformer Car: 1956-58, upper transformer panel heat stamped in white "6518," lower panel heat stamped "LIONEL TRANSFORMER CAR."

	75	115	155

	C5	C7	C8

6519 Allis-Chalmers Heat Exchanger Car: 1958-61 molded medium, dark or *milky orange* plastic. $55-100 $85-140 $125-200

6520 Lionel Lines: 1949-51, simulated generator hid an off-on switch that could be actuated w/a remote control uncoupling track. Beware of reproduction generators.

Tan generator.	425	700	1,000
Green generator.	225	350	475
Orange generator.	35	50	75
Maroon generator.	50	75	100

6530 Firefighting Instruction Car: 1960-62, unpainted red plastic body and unpainted white plastic opening doors.   65   100   150

6536 M & St. L Hopper: (Minneapolis & St. Louis) 1958-59, 1963, this was a large open-topped hopper.   35   55   85

6544 Missile Firing Car: 1960-64, came w/two small envelopes, each containing four 44-40 rockets. Control panel heat-stamped in *white* or **black**.   100-225   140-375   225-550

6555 Sunoco Tank Car: 1949-50, tank painted silver.   20   40   65

6556 M-K-T Stock Car: 1958 only, red.   150   250   450

6557 Lionel Smoking Caboose: 1958-59.   150   250   400

6560 Bucyrus Erie Crane: 1955-64, 1966-69, **gray** or *red* cab.   30-60   45-80   60-110

656025 Bucyrus Erie: 1956, red cab, frame heat-stamped "656025."   65   105   140

6561 Cable Reel Car: 1953-56, unpainted gray or orange reels wound w/solid aluminum wire.   45   65   90

6562 New York Central Gondola: 1956-58, gray, red or black gondola, usually included a load of four red canisters w/"Lionel Air Activated Container" lettering.   28   45   60

6572 Railway Express Agency Refrigerator: 1958-59, 1963, **dark** or *light* green.   65-80   95-125   125-175

6630 Missile Launching Car: 1961, unpainted black plastic body w/pivoting blue plastic launcher base.   75   110   165

6636 Alaska Railroad Hopper: 1959-60, black.   35   55   85

6640 U.S.M.C. Missile Launching Car: 1960, body painted olive drab and was heat-stamped "U.S.M.C. 6640" in white. Unpainted olive drab plastic launcher base w/a black plastic launch rail.   150   225   325

6646 Lionel Lines Stock Car: 1957 only, orange.   25   35   55

6650 Missile Launching Car: 1959-63, unpainted red plastic body heat stamped "6650 LIONEL." Pivoting unpainted blue plastic launcher base w/a black plastic launch rail.   35   50   75

6651 U.S. Marine Corps Cannon Firing Car: 1964-65.   125   225   300

6656 Lionel Lines Stock Car: 1950-53, yellow, **w/or** *w/out* adhesive-backed "Armour" emblem applied to their doors.   18-50   25-75   35-100

6657 Rio Grande Caboose: 1957-58, silver and yellow.   75   125   200

6636 Alaska Railroad Hopper

6736 Detroit and Mackinac Hopper

	C5	C7	C8

6660 Boom Car: 1958, equipped w/a pair of outriggers.

| | $50 | $75 | $115 |

6670 Derrick Car: 1959-60, no outriggers.

| | 40 | 60 | 90 |

6672 Santa Fe Refrigerator: 1954-56, *two* or **three** lines of data to the right of the door.

| | 45-150 | 75-250 | 100-425 |

6736 Detroit & Mackinac Hopper: 1960-62, red.

| | 25 | 45 | 65 |

6800 Airplane Car: 1957-60, unpainted red flatcar, undecorated yellow and black plastic aircraft w/identifying markings molded into the underside of the fuselage. These markings read "NO. 6800-60 AIRPLANE THE LIONEL CORPORATION NEW YORK, N.Y. MADE IN U.S. OF AMERICA." Either black upper surfaces and yellow propeller or yellow upper surfaces w/black propeller. Only three rivets to bind the wing halves.

| | 150 | 200 | 300 |

6801 Boat Car: 1957-60, unpainted red flatcar w/boat in unpainted gray plastic cradle. Metal or plastic trucks, white-hulled boat w/brown deck that had no Lionel markings.

| | 70 | 100 | 150 |

6801-50 Boat Car: AAR-type trucks, yellow boat hull marked "NO. 6801-60 BOAT MADE IN U.S. OF AMERICA" and "THE LIONEL CORPORATION NEW YORK, N.Y."

| | 70 | 100 | 150 |

6801-75 Boat Car: AAR-type trucks, blue boat hull marked "NO. 6801-60 BOAT MADE IN U.S. OF AMERICA" and "THE LIONEL CORPORATION NEW YORK, N.Y."

| | 70 | 100 | 150 |

6802 Flatcar w/Girders: 1958-59, red flatcar w/two black "U.S. STEEL" girders. Car stamped "6802 LIONEL."

| | 20 | 25 | 35 |

6803 Flatcar w/Military Units: 1958-59, w/USMC tank and a truck w/swiveling loudspeakers.

| | 125 | 200 | 300 |

6804 Flatcar w/Military Units: 1958-59, w/USMC anti-aircraft and loudspeaker trucks.

| | 125 | 200 | 300 |

6805 Radioactive Waste Car: 1958-59, w/two illuminated radioactive waste containers painted gray.

| | 75 | 125 | 175 |

6806 Flatcar w/Military Units: 1958-59, w/USMC medical and radar trucks.

| | 100 | 175 | 275 |

6807 Flatcar w/Duck: 1958-59, w/amphibious 2-1/2 ton 6x6 truck.

| | 75 | 100 | 150 |

6808 Flatcar w/Military Load: 1958-59, w/searchlight truck and M19 Gun Motor Carriage.

| | 200 | 275 | 400 |

6809 Flatcar w/Military Units: 1958-59, w/medical van and anti-aircraft trucks.

| | 125 | 200 | 300 |

6810 Flatcar w/Cooper-Jarrett Van: 1958, w/one white Cooper-Jarrett trailer.

| | 35 | 50 | 70 |

6812 Track Maintenance Car: 1959-61, body unpainted red plastic heat-stamped "6812" to the left of "LIONEL" in white serif letters.

| | 50 | 80 | 125 |

6814 Rescue Unit: 1959-61, gray frame w/white tool compartment insert, two molded plastic stretchers, oxygen tank and a blue rubber figure.

| | 50 | 100 | 165 |

6816 Flatcar w/Allis-Chalmers Crawler Tractor: 1959-60, red or *black* flatcar. If dozer has black hood lettering, increase values shown $150-300.

| | 300-1,000 | 475-1,650 | 650-2,700 |

6817 Flatcar w/Allis-Chalmers Scraper: 1959-60, red or *black* flatcar. If scraper has black hood lettering, increase values shown $150-300.

| | 350-1,250 | 450-2,300 | 600-3,600 |

	C5	C7	C8

6818 Flatcar w/Transformer: 1958, red car w/black transformer, heat stamped "6818" on the upper panel. $35 $50 $70

6819 Flatcar w/Helicopter: 1959-61, w/non-operating helicopter w/opaque yellow tail rotor and gray fuselage unmarked or heat stamped "NAVY." 50 75 110

6820 Aerial Missile Transport Car: 1960-61, helicopter equipped w/two huge non-firing missiles. 150 250 400

6821 Flatcar w/Crates: 1959-60, cargo was a modification of the crate load created for the 3444 animated gondolas. 20 30 40

6822 Night Crew Searchlight: 1961-69, black or gray superstructure. 5 40 60

6823 Flatcar w/I.R.B.M. Missiles: 1959-60, carried two matching 6650-type missiles in 6801-64 boat cradles. 40 60 80

6824 U.S.M.C. Caboose: 1960, cab, tool compartment, tool compartment insert and frame all painted olive drab, all markings in white, w/blue rubber figure w/painted hands and face, a white plastic air tank, and two white plastic stretchers. 125 200 300

6824-50 First Aid Caboose: 1964, black frame, no crewman, tool compartment insert, stretchers or oxygen tank. 50 100 150

6825 Flatcar w/Arch Trestle Bridge: 1959-62, w/black HO-sized bridge. 30 50 75

6826 Flatcar w/Christmas Trees: 1959-60, four spring-steel 2411-4 posts keep the foliage load in place. 100 150 215

6827 P & H Power Shovel Car: 1960-63, black flatcar was heat stamped "6827" to the left of "LIONEL" in white. Its cargo was a well-detailed and elaborate kit of a P & H power shovel which was packaged, along w/the booklet, "P & H: The Story of a Trademark" in a special yellow and black P & H box. 125 175 250

6828 P & H Mobile Construction Crane Car: 1960-63, 1966, load was a kit of a crane produced by the Harnischfeger Corp. This kit, in its own yellow and black P & H box, was packaged along w/the flatcar inside a Lionel box. Flatcar was unpainted *black* and **red** plastic. 150-500 225-650 300-1,000

6830 Submarine Car: 1960-61, w/a non-operating Lionel submarine, includes 6830 black heat-stamped numbers on sub. 100 140 200

6844 Missile Carrying Car: 1959-60, rack held six white 44-40 missiles. Unpainted *black* or **red** plastic frames. 45-600 70-750 110-1,200

Unnumbered Flatcar: Gray unpainted 1877-style flatcar w/no markings, no truss rods and AAR-type trucks. Carried either a moss-green tank or moss-green Jeep and cannon, made by Payton Plastics. There is not sufficient information to determine market value. However, an authentic load is key to its scarcity.

Unmarked Hopper: 1963-69 short hopper, yellow, red, black, *gray* or **olive**. 15-50 18-75 25-110

6821 Flatcar w/Crates

6828 P & H Mobile Construction Crane Car

Lionel Postwar Accessories, Track and Transformers

One of the key elements in Lionel's success, both prewar and postwar, was their numerous operating accessories. Joshua Cowen felt it was important to provide a means for children and adults to interact with the trains, as well as providing a semi-realistic setting to operate them in.

Initially the postwar accessories were carryovers of their prewar counterparts. The 45 Gateman, 115 Station, 313 Bascule Bridge, 97 and 164 Coal and Lumber Loaders were all introduced before WWII. Soon, however, new designs poured from the Lionel shops. The 132 Station, 397-Coal Loader and 364 Lumber Loader, all less expensive to produce than their prewar designed counterparts, pushed the earlier models from the catalog.

More than any other component, the development of the vibrator motor allowed Lionel to create a bewildering array of animated yet inexpensive accessories including operating fork lift platforms, animated news stands, culvert loaders and unloaders.

Not all accessories provided action. Bridges crossed gorges; street lamps illuminated the miniature villages of Lionelville and Plasticville. The latter dotted with buildings sold by Lionel, but made by Bachmann.

Today, Lionel's accessories retain their appeal to operators and collectors alike. Children, young or old, still delight in watching day-to-day tasks being performed in miniature by these accessories.

Despite their appeal compared to trains (starter sets in particular), all accessories are relatively scarce. Even the most common of accessories like the 145 Gateman is more difficult to locate than a common train car, such as the 6462 Gondola.

Also cataloged as accessories by Lionel were various easily-lost loads and a few fragile repair parts. Virtually every part of every item was available through Authorized Lionel Service Stations, but the parts cataloged as accessories were available to any Lionel retail outlet. Whereas repair parts typically came in blue and manila envelopes that were hand-labeled as to contents, the "accessory" parts came in conventional retail packaging. It is this retail packaging that warrants the values listed for such items; the items themselves as a rule are easily located. Representative examples of these accessory items are included in the following listings as well. During the 1960s, certain small- to medium-sized accessory items were packaged on blister cards for retail sales. Today, these items in unopened condition are highly sought after collectibles and bring a substantial premium over the prices listed here. For more information about these, as well as more detailed information about the many variations of accessories, consult the "Standard Catalog of® Lionel Trains, 1945-1969."

	C5	C7	C8
022 Remote Control Switches: 1945-66, pair of O-Ga. turnouts.			
	$60	$75	$90
022LH Remote Control Switch: 1950-61, left-hand O-Ga. turnout w/controller.			
	35	45	55
022RH Remote Control Switch: 1950-61, right-hand O-Ga. turnout w/controller.			
	35	45	55
022A Remote Control Switch: 1947, unusual version of a pair of O-Ga. switches built in 1947. Due to material shortages, these switches were built w/out fixed voltage capabilities or bottom plates.	100	150	275
022-500 O-Ga. Adapter Set: 1957-61, allowed the use of O-Ga. switches w/Super 0 track. Much of the value is in the packaging.	2	3	4
025 Bumper: 1946-47, illuminated black-painted die-cast bumper attached to a piece of O-Ga. track.	15	20	30
26 Bumper: 1948, *gray*, 1949-50, red.	10-30	15-40	25-50
30 Water Tower: 1947-50, it had a dark gray die-cast base and a solenoid-lowered plastic spout.	80	125	200
31 Curved Track: 1957-66, Super 0.	1	2	4
31-15 Ground Rail Pin: 1957-66, one dozen pins for outer rails of Super 0 track.			
	1	2	3
31-45 Power Blade Connector: 1961-64, envelope contains 12 copper connectors.			
	1	2	3
32 Straight Track: 1957-66, Super 0.	2	4	6
32-10 Insulating Pin: 1957-60, one dozen insulating pins for use in the outer rails of Super 0 track.	1	2	3
32-20 Power Blade Insulator: 1957-60, this package contained one dozen insulating connectors for use on the center power blade of Super 0 track.			
	1	2	3
32-45 Power Blade Insulator: 1961-66, this package contained one dozen insulating connectors for use on the center power blade of Super 0 track.			
	1	2	3
32-55 Insulating Pin: 1961-66, one dozen insulating pins for use in the outer rails of Super 0 track.	1	2	3
33 Half Curved Track: 1957-66, half section of Super 0 curved track.			
	1	2	3
34 Half Straight Track: 1957-66, half section of Super 0 straight track.			
	1	2	3
35 Boulevard Lamp: 1945-49.	20	35	55
36 Operating Car Remote Control Set: 1957-66, track set includes two control blades, a 90-controller and the needed hook up wire. This allowed operating cars powered through sliding shoes to be operated on Super 0 track.			
	8	12	18
37 Uncoupling Track Set: 1957-66, 1-1/2-in. long Super 0 track section containing an electromagnet. Packaged w/a 90-controller and hook up wire.			
	10	15	20
38 Water Tower: 1946-47, w/internal pump. Supplied w/a turned metal finial to plug the rooftop fill hole, a small funnel and a packet of tablets to use to color the water. Black supporting structure and either brown or dark gray-painted roof or *brown supporting structure and red roof*.	250-275	325-375	500-600
38 Accessory Adapter Tracks: 1957-61, pair of special Super 0 tracks w/only four crossties was needed to allow the attachment of track trips or installation on accessory bases.	8	12	15
40 Hook Up Wire: 1950-51, 1953-63, orange or gray reels, wrapped w/50 ft. of 18-Gauge single conductor wire insulated in either yellow, maroon, blue or white plastic. The earlier production was wrapped in Lionel imprinted cellophane.			
	5	20	40

020 90-Degree Crossover

025 Bumper

30 Water Tower

35 Boulevard Lamp

38 Water Tower

042 Manual Switches

	C5	C7	C8
011-11 Insulating Pins: 1946-60, one dozen insulating pins for O-Ga. track. The collector value of this item is in the packaging.	$1	$2	$3
011-43 Insulating Pins: 1961, one dozen O-Ga. insulating pins.	1	2	3
020 90-Degree Crossover: 1915-61, excluding 1943-45, O-Ga.	5	7	10
020X 45-Degree Crossing: 1915-59, excluding 1943-45.	6	9	14

	C5	C7	C8
042 Manual Switches: 1946-59, pair of manually operated O-Ga. turnouts.			
	$40	$50	$60
43 Power Track: 1959-66, special Super 0 1-1/2-in. track section w/built-in fahnstock clips.	5	7	10
44-80 Missiles: 1959-60, set of four replacement missiles.			
	10	20	30
45 Gateman: 1946-49.	40	50	60
45N Gateman: 1945.	50	65	80
48 Insulated Straight Track: 1957-66, Super 0.	5	7	10
49 Insulated Curved Track: 1957-66, Super 0.	5	7	10
56 Lamppost: 1946-49.	30	45	60
58 Lamppost: 1946-50, Ivory-colored.	35	50	65
61 Ground Lockon: 1957-66, Super 0.	1	2	3
62 Power Lockon: 1957-66, Super 0.	1	2	3
64 Highway Lamppost: 1945-49.	45	60	75
70 Lamppost: 1949-50, has a die-cast tilting head.	25	40	60
71 Lamppost: 1949-59.	15	20	30
75 Goose Neck Lamps: 1961-63, pair of 6-1/2-in. tall black plastic lamps.			
	15	25	40
76 Boulevard Street Lamps: 1956-69, green plastic.			
	15	25	40
88 Controller: 1946-50.	1	2	10
89 Flagpole: 1956-58, stitched-edged flag.	30	50	75
No stitch edge.	25	40	60
90 Controller: 1955-66, w/shiny metal clip retaining a piece of cardstock.			
	3	8	14
No metal clip.	1	2	10
"No. 90 CONTROL" molded into the case.	1	2	10
91 Circuit Breaker: 1957-60.	20	25	30
92 Circuit Breaker Controller:			
Packaged in a manila envelope.	5	10	15
Packed in a traditional box.	5	10	15
Carded blister pack.	—	90	150
93 Water Tower: 1946-49, painted silver.	25	40	65
96C Controller: 1945-54.	1	2	5
97 Coal Elevator:	100	175	225
108 Trestle Set: 1959, packaged in overstamped 1044 transformer box. Only 12 trestle piers provided (two each lettered A-F).	30	45	85
109 Trestle Set: 1961, set of 12 piers.		No value established.	
110 Trestle Set: 1955-69.	18	22	35
111 Trestle Set: 1956-69, set of 10 "A" piers.	15	25	35
112 Super 0 Switches: 1957 only, pair.	55	90	100
112R Super 0 Switches: 1958-66, pair.	65	100	125
112-125 Super 0 Switch: 1957-61, left hand remote control w/022C controller.			
	40	60	80
112-150 Super 0 Switch: 1957-61, right hand remote control w/022C controller.			
	40	60	80
112LH Super 0 Switch: 1962-66, left hand remote control turnout w/a 022C controller.	40	60	80
112RH Super 0 Switch: 1962-66, right hand remote control turnout w/a 022C controller.	40	60	80
114 Newsstand with Horn: 1957-59.	75	115	150
115 Lionel City Station: 1946-49.	250	350	500
118 Newsstand w/Whistle: 1957-58.	60	100	125

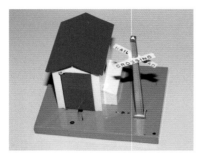

45 Gateman

64 Highway Lamppost

71 Lamppost

93 Water Tower

76 Boulevard Street Lamps

97 Coal Elevator

110 Trestle Set

	C5	C7	C8

40-25 Cable Reel: 1955-57, orange reel holding 15 in. of the same black four-conductor wire as used on Lionel remote control track sections. It came packaged in a preprinted manila envelope, and it is that envelope that actually has the values listed here. $75 $150 $300

40-50 Cable Reel: 1960-61, this orange reel holding 15 in. of the same black three-conductor wire as used on Lionel switch controls. It came packaged in a preprinted manila envelope, and it is that envelope that actually has the values listed here. 75   150   300

	C5	C7	C8
119 Landscaped Tunnel: 1957-58, 14 in. long, 10 in. wide and eight in. high, vacuformed plastic tunnel. Too infrequently offered in Lionel packaging to establish value.			
120 90-Degree Crossing: 1957-66, 90-degree Super 0 crossing.	$5	$10	$15
121 Landscaped Tunnel: 1959-66, Styrofoam tunnel. The Lionel packaging is essential to its value as a Lionel collectable. Too infrequently offered in Lionel packaging to establish value.			
123 Lamp Assortment: 1953-59.	150	250	400
123-60 Lamp Assortment: 1960-63.	200	300	500
125 Whistle Shack: 1950-55.	25	45	60
128 Animated Newsstand: 1957-60.	125	175	225
130 60-Degree Crossing: 1957-66, Super 0 60-degree crossing.	10	14	18
131 Curved Tunnel: 1957-66, Styrofoam tunnel. Lionel packaging is essential to its value as a Lionel collectable. Too infrequently offered in Lionel packaging to establish value.			
132 Illuminated Station w/Automatic Train Control: 1949-55, brick red chimney.	75	110	150
133 Illuminated Passenger Station: 1957, 1961-62, 1966, green chimney.	50	75	100
138 Water Tank: 1953-57, unpainted gray plastic roof.	100	150	175
140 Automatic Banjo Signal: 1954-66, packed in a box.	30	40	55
142 Manual Switches: 1957-66, pair Super 0 manual turnouts.	30	40	55
142-125 Super 0 Switch: 1957-61, single left-hand Super 0 manual.	20	30	40
142-150 Super 0 Switch: 1957-61, single right-hand Super 0 manual.	20	30	40
142LH Super 0 Switch: 1962, separate sale left-hand Super 0 manual turnout.	20	30	40
142RH Super 0 Switch: 1962, separate sale right-hand Super 0 manual turnout.	20	30	40
145 Automatic Gateman: 1950-66.	30	40	55
145C Contactor: 1950-60, SPST pressure-activated normally open momentary contact switch collectable value is in the box.	1	2	10
147 Whistle Controller: 1961-66, contained a D-cell battery.	2	4	10
148 Dwarf Signal: 1957-60, furnished w/148C switch.	50	65	100
150 Telegraph Pole Set: 1947-50, set of six brown plastic poles w/metal base clips.	40	60	75
151 Semaphore: 1947-69.	20	28	40
152 Automatic Crossing Gate: 1945-49, main and pedestrian gates painted silver.	20	40	55
153 Automatic Block Signal and Control: 1945-59.	30	40	50
153C Contactor: single pole, double throw pressure-activated momentary contact switch. Collectable value is in the box.	1	2	10
154 Automatic Highway Signal: 1956-69.	30	40	50
155 Bell Ringing Signal: 1955-57, no "feet."	45	60	75

111 Trestle Set

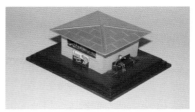

114 Newsstand w/Horn

115 Lionel City Station

118 Newsstand w/Whistle

123 Lamp Assortment

123-60 Lamp Assortment

125 Whistle Shack

128 Animated Newsstand

	C5	C7	C8

156 Illuminated Station Platform: 1946-51, two sections of black plastic picket fence between roof supports and provided w/a separate fence section to connect two or more platforms together. Four lithographed tin miniature billboards hung from the fences. $60 $85 $125

157 Illuminated Station Platform: 1952-59, four lithographed tin miniature billboards hung from fences.   30   45   60

161 Mail Pickup Set: 1961-1963.   65   100   140

163 Single Target Block Signal: 1961-69, packaged in box.   30   40   55

164 Log Loader: 1946-50, power terminals protruded through the top of the base, adjacent to the loading bin.   150   225   350

167 Whistle Controller: 1946-57.   4   8   15

175 Rocket Launcher: 1958-60.   125   250   400

175-50 Extra Rocket: 1959-60, replacement rockets for the 175 Launcher and 6175 Flatcar. Prices shown are for original six-pack box.   150   225   400

182 Triple Action Magnet Crane: 1946-49, a nicely detailed electro-magnet, which lifted the 182-22 scrap steel supplied w/the crane, was marked "Cutler Hammer." Note: The cab of the 182 ALWAYS had a smokestack, and the smokestack was NEVER molded as part of the cab.   150   250   325

192 Operating Control Tower: 1959-60.   150   200   275

193 Industrial Water Tower: 1953-55, w/flashing red warning light.   85   115   160

195 Floodlight Tower: 1957-69.   45   60   75

195-75 Eight-Bulb Floodlight Extension: 1957-60, this was a standard eight-bulb array from a 195 Floodlight Tower, plus two extension posts. This could be used to increase the light output from a 195.   20   35   60

196 Smoke Pellets: 1946-47, contained 100 smoke pellets made of ammonium nitrate for use in bulb-type smoke units only.   40   75   125

197 Rotating Radar Antenna: 1957-59, *orange* or gray platform structure.   80-100   100-125   150-190

132 Illuminated Station w/Automatic Train Control

138 Water Tank

140 Automatic Banjo Signal

145 Automatic Gateman

152 Automatic Crossing Gate

150 Telegraph Pole Set

151
Semaphore

153 Automatic Block
Signal and Control

154 Automatic Highway
Signal

155 Bell Ringing Signal

156 Illuminated Station Platform

157 Illuminated Station Platform

	C5	C7	C8
199 Microwave Relay Tower: 1958-59.	$40	$75	$120
206 Artificial Coal: 1946-59, half-pound cloth bags lettered w/red "No. 206," "ARTIFICIAL COAL" and Lionel markings filled w/ground Bakelite "coal."	5	10	15
214 Plate Girder Bridge: 1953-69, metal base, plastic sides.	15	20	30
252 Crossing Gate: 1950-63.	25	30	40
253 Automatic Block Signal: 1956-59.	20	30	45
256 Freight Station: 1950-53, dark or *light green* roof.	40-75	60-125	75-175
257 Freight Station w/Diesel Horn: 1956-57, the correct base has "257" molded into it. Dark or *light green* roof.	60-75	75-125	100-175
260 Bumper: 1951-69, red-painted die-cast metal or *unpainted black plastic*.	15-30	20-40	25-50
262 Highway Crossing Gate: 1962-69, packaged in box.	50	75	100
264 Operating Fork Lift: 1957-60.	250	325	400
282 Gantry Crane: 1954-55, electromagnet has blackened sheet metal housing, crane cab screwed in place.	140	190	250
282R Gantry Crane: 1956-57, electromagnet housing bright metal, crane cab was snapped in place.	140	190	250
299 Code Transmitter Set: 1961-63, packaged w/a 299-25 telegraph key.	100	125	175
308 Railroad Sign Set: 1945-49, included five different die-cast signposts.	35	50	75
309 Yard Sign Set: 1950-59, nine plastic signs w/die-cast metal bases.	20	30	45
310 Billboard: 1950-68, five unpainted green plastic billboard frames furnished w/ perforated die-cut sheets of cardboard billboards.	5	10	40
313 Bascule Bridge: 1946-49, L-shaped gearbox. Supplied w/a black steel alignment frame.	300	525	675
313-82 Fiber Pins: 1946-60, one dozen 027 insulating pins.	1	2	3
313-121 Fiber Pins: 1961, one dozen 027 insulating pins.	1	2	3
314 Plate Girder Bridge: 1945-50, gray rounded-end die-cast girder sides rubber-stamped "LIONEL" in black.	25	35	50
315 Illuminated Trestle Bridge: 1946-47, w/red light mounted mid-span.	75	100	125
316 Trestle Bridge: 1949.	25	40	55
317 Trestle Bridge: 1950-56.	25	35	50

164 Log Loader

175 Rocket Launcher

182 Triple Action Magnet Crane

195 Floodlight Tower

199 Microwave Relay Tower

206 Artificial Coal

214 Plate Girder Bridge

256 Freight Station

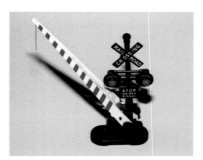

262 Highway Crossing Gate

264 Operating Fork Lift

	C5	C7	C8
321 Trestle Bridge: 1958-64, sheet metal base w/unpainted gray plastic sides and top. It was shipped unassembled and the buyer was to assemble it.	$20	$35	$50
332 Arch Under Bridge: 1959-66, gray plastic sides w/black-painted metal deck. It was shipped unassembled and the buyer was to assemble it.	30	45	60
334 Dispatching Board: 1957-60.	175	250	310
342 Culvert Loader: 1956-58, came w/6342.	200	275	350
345 Culvert Unloading Station: 1957-59, came w/6342.	250	350	425
346 Operating Culvert Unloader: 1965-66, manual version of the 345.	100	150	250
347 Cannon Firing Range Set: 1964.	200	600	1,000
348 Operating Culvert Unloader: 1966-69, manual version of the 345. Came w/6342.	125	175	250
350 Engine Transfer Table: 1957-60.	150	325	450
350-50 Transfer Table Extension: 1957-60.	125	175	225
352 Ice Depot: 1955-57, came w/6352 ice car.	175	250	325
353 Track Side Control Signal: 1960-61.	20	30	45
356 Operating Freight Station: 1952-57, dark green roof. W/one each dark green and orange baggage carts. Early production came w/a colorful lithographed tin insert for one of the baggage carts, add $75 to values listed for this item. W/dark green and orange baggage carts or *one tomato red baggage cart and one light green baggage cart*.	60-125	95-160	140-220
362 Barrel Loader: 1952-57, commonly w/blue rubber man, if white rubber man, add $25 to listed values.	70	100	150
362-78 Barrels: 1952-57, box of six brown-stained small wooden barrels.	5	10	20
364 Lumber Loader: 1948-57, *dark crackle gray* finish or light gray hammer tone finish.	90-100	125-150	175-200
364C On-Off Switch: 1959-64.	2	8	16
365 Dispatching Station: 1958-59.	80	115	140
375 Turntable: 1962-64.	125	175	225
390C Switch: 1960-64.	5	10	20
394 Rotary Beacon: 1949-53, unpainted aluminum or painted red or *dark green.*	20-50	30-75	45-100
395 Floodlight Tower: 1949-56, unpainted aluminum or painted red, silver, green or *yellow.*	25-100	40-140	60-200
397 Coal Loader: 1948-57, *yellow* or blue GM motor housing.	125-250	175-350	225-450

309 Yard Sign Set

299 Code Transmitter Set

313 Bascule Bridge

334 Dispatching Board

342 Culvert Loader

345 Culvert Unloading Station

346 Operating Culvert Unloader

347 Cannon Firing Range Set

350 Engine Transfer Table

352 Ice Depot

	C5	C7	C8
410 Billboard Blinker: 1956-58.	$30	$50	$70
413 Countdown Control Panel: 1962 only.	45	75	100
415 Diesel Fueling Station: 1955-67.	100	145	200

	C5	C7	C8
419 Heliport: 1962 only, included yellow helicopter.	$175	$425	$600
443 Missile Launching Platform w/Exploding Ammunition Dump: 1960-62.	25	40	80
445 Operating Switch Tower: 1952-57.	40	75	100
448 Missile Firing Range Set: 1961-63, w/6448 Target Range Car w/red sides and white lettering, roof and ends. Accessory packaged w/lichen "bushes."	90	175	250
450 Signal Bridge: 1952-58, included two signal heads.	50	65	80
450L Signal Bridge Head: 1952-58, blackened die-cast twin lamp socket. Much of the value is in the small traditional box it was packed in.	40	60	100
452 Gantry Signal Bridge: 1961-63.	75	110	150
455 Operating Oil Derrick: 1950-54, furnished w/four turned solid aluminum oil drums and a separate sign reading "SUNOCO OIL DERRICK No. 455."	175	225	275
456 Coal Ramp: 1950-55, supplied w/a special 456-100 controller, a 3456 operating hopper car, 456-83 maroon plastic receiving bin, two 456-85 coal pin mounting posts, a 456-84 coal bin door and a bag of 206 coal. *Dark gray, braided steel wire handrails* or dark or light gray w/handrails made of fishing line.	150-200	225-275	300-350
460 Piggy Back Transportation Set: 1955-57, came w/3460 flatcar and trailers. W/two green plastic "LIONEL TRAINS" trailers w/"FRUEHAUF" and "DURAVAN" signs on the front.	100	150	175
460P Piggy Back Platform: platform only w/out trailers or flatcar. The box must be present in order for this to have any real value.	300	500	700
461 Platform w/Truck and Trailer: 1966, lacks depressions molded into the top to receive trailer wheels. Came w/a white single axle Lionel-made trailer and a red die-cast tractor made by Midge.	100	150	200
462 Derrick Platform Set: 1961-62, w/two 6805-type containers w/out illumination but w/wire bales attached to handles.	200	275	350
464 Lumber Mill: 1956-60.	125	175	225
465 Sound Dispatching Station: 1956-57, came w/a gray plastic microphone equipped w/two red buttons.	100	140	175
470 Missile Launching Platform w/Exploding Target Car: 1959-62, came w/ exploding 6470 Target Car.	100	150	210
494 Rotary Beacon: 1954-66.	30	40	50
497 Coaling Station: 1953-58.	125	160	230
671-75 Special Smoke Bulb:	10	20	30
703-10 Special Smoke Bulb:	15	30	45
760 072 Track: 1950, 1954-58, box of 16 sections of 072 track.	50	75	120
902 Elevated Trestle Set: 1959-60, came packaged in a paper sack printed w/the label "902 ELEVATED TRESTLE SET."	—	100	250

356 Operating Freight Station

364 Lumber Loader

394 Rotary Beacon

395
Floodlight
Tower

397 Coal Loader

410
Billboard
Blinker

419 Heliport

443 Missile Launching Platform w/Exploding
Ammunition Dump

445
Operating
Switch Tower

448 Missile Firing Range Set

	C5	C7	C8
908 Railroad Terminal: circa 1964.	Too rarely traded to establish value.		
909 Smoke Fluid: 1957-68.	$5	$20	$45
910 U. S. Navy Submarine Base: 1961, made entirely of cardboard.	Too rarely traded to establish value.		
919 Artificial Grass: 1946-64, half-pound bag of green-dyed sawdust.	7	7	25
920 Scenic Display Set: 1957-58.	40	100	150
920-2 Tunnel Portals: 1958-59, set of two "HILLSIDE" gray plastic tunnel portals.	20	35	50
920-3 Green Grass: 1957-58, the clear plastic bag of green-dyed sawdust "grass."	2	10	30
920-4 Yellow Grass: 1957-58, the clear plastic bag of yellow-dyed sawdust "grass."	2	10	30
920-5 Artificial Rock: 1957-58, expanded vermiculite.	5	30	50
920-8 Lichen: 1958.	5	25	50
927 Lubricating and Maintenance Kit: 1950-59.	10	30	60
928 Maintenance and Lubricant Kit: 1960-63.	20	40	70
943 Exploding Ammunition Dump: 1959-61.	30	60	90
950 U.S. Railroad Map: 1958-66, packed in a tube.	60	90	150
951 Farm Set: 1958.	125	175	400
952 Figure Set: 1958.	125	175	400
953 Figure Set: 1959-62.	125	175	400
954 Swimming Pool and Playground Set: 1959.	125	175	400
955 Highway Set: 1958.	125	175	400
956 Stockyard Set: 1959.	125	175	400
957 Farm Building and Animal Set: 1958.	125	175	400
958 Vehicle Set: 1958.	150	250	475
959 Barn Set: 1958.	150	250	475
960 Barnyard Set: 1959-61.	125	175	400

450 Signal Bridge

455 Operating Oil Derrick

456 Coal Ramp

462 Derrick Platform Set

460 Piggy Back Transportation Set

464 Lumber Mill

465 Sound Dispatching Station

497 Coaling Station

902 Elevated Trestle Set

920 Scenic Display Set

928 Maintenance and Lubricant Kit

943 Exploding Ammunition Dump

	C5	C7	C8
961 School Set: 1959.	$125	$175	$400
962 Turnpike Set: 1958.	175	275	500
963 Frontier Set: 1959-60.	150	250	475
963-100 Frontier Set: 1960.	300	450	700
964 Factory Site Set: 1959.	150	250	475
965 Farm Set: 1959.	125	175	400
966 Fire House Set: 1958.	125	175	400
967 Post Office Set: 1958.	125	175	400
968 TV Transmitter Set: 1958.	150	250	475
969 Construction Set: 1960.	150	250	475
970 Ticket Booth: 1958-60, 46 in. tall, 22 in. wide, 11 in. deep cardboard ticket booth.	—	125	175
971 Lichen: 1960-64.	75	175	300
972 Landscape Tree Assortment: 1961-64.	150	300	500
973 Complete Landscaping Set: 1960-64.	300	1,000	1,500
974 Scenery Set: 1962-63.	700	2,500	4,000
980 Ranch Set: 1960.	125	200	400
981 Freight Yard Set: 1960.	125	200	400
982 Suburban Split Level Set: 1960.	125	200	400
983 Farm Set: 1960-61.	125	200	400
984 Railroad Set: 1961-62.	125	200	400
985 Freight Area Set: 1961.	125	200	400
986 Farm Set: 1962.	125	200	400
987 Town Set: 1962.	400	700	1,000
988 Railroad Structure Set: 1962.	150	275	450
1008 Uncoupling Unit: 1957-62.	1	2	5
1008-50 Uncoupling Track Section: 1957-62.	1	2	5
1009 Manumatic Uncoupler:	1	2	5
1010 Transformer: 1961-66, 35-watt.	10	20	25
1011 Transformer: 1948-52, 25-watt.	10	15	20
1011X Transformer: 1948-52, 25-watt, 125-volt, 25-cycle.	10	15	20
1012 Transformer: 1950-54, 35-watt.	20	30	40
1014 Transformer: 1955, 40-watt.	15	25	40
1015 Transformer: 1955-60, 45-watt.	25	35	45
1016 Transformer: 1959-60, 35-watt, 110-volt primary transformer had a speed control and circuit breaker, but no fixed voltage taps or whistle control. It was available 1959-60.	10	20	30
1019 Remote Control Track Set: 1946-50, 027 uncoupling track.	5	8	10
1020 90-Degree Crossing: 1955-69, 027 90-degree crossing.	2	4	7
1021 90-Degree Crossing: 1945-54, 027 90-degree crossing.	2	4	8
1022 Manual Switches: 1953-69, pair of 027 turnouts.	15	20	30
1022LH Manual Switch: 1953-69, manual 027 left-hand turnout.	8	10	16
1022RH Manual Switch: 1953-69, manual 027 right-hand turnout.	8	10	16
1023 45-Degree Crossing: 1956-69, 027 crossing.	3	6	10
1024 Manual Switches: 1946-52, pair of metal-based 027 manual turnouts.	10	20	25
1025 Illuminated Bumper: 1946-47, die-cast black illuminated bumper, attached to a section of 027 straight track.	10	15	20

953 Figure Set

968 TV Transmitter Set

971 Lichen

972 Landscape Tree Assortment

974 Scenery Set

981 Freight Yard Set

	C5	C7	C8
1025 Transformer: 1961-66, 1969, 45-watt.	$25	$35	$45
1026 Transformer: 1961-64, 25-watt.	10	15	20
1032 Transformer: 1948, 75-watt.	20	35	60
1032M Transformer: 1948, 75-watt, 125-volt, 50-cycle.	30	45	70
1033 Transformer: 1948-56.	40	60	90
1034 Transformer: 1948-54, 75-watt.	20	35	60
1035 Transformer: 1947, 60-watt.	5	10	15
1037 Transformer: 1946-47, 40-watt.	10	15	25
1041 Transformer: 1945-46, 60-watt.	20	35	50
1042 Transformer: 1947-48, 75-watt.	25	40	60
1043 Transformer: 1953-58, 50-watt.	20	35	50
1043-500 Transformer: ivory-colored case, white cord and gold-colored handle, 60 watts.	75	125	175
1043M Transformer: 1953-58, 50-watt, 125-volt, 25-cycle.	40	55	75
1044 Transformer: 1957-69, 90-watt.	40	65	90
1044M Transformer: 1957-69, 90-watt, 125-volt and 25-cycle.	40	65	90

	C5	C7	C8
1045 Operating Watchman: 1946-50.	$20	$35	$50
1047 Operating Switchman: 1959-61.	90	125	170
1053 Transformer: 1956-60, 60-watt.	20	35	45
1063 Transformer: 1960-64, 75-watt.	25	40	60
1063-100 Transformer: 1961, 75-watt.	30	45	65
1073 Transformer: 1961-66, 60-watt.	20	30	50
1121 Remote Control Switches: 1946-51, pair of 027 turnouts.	20	35	45
1122 Remote Control Switches: 1952-53, pair of 027 turnouts.	17	30	35
1122E Remote Control Switches: 1953-69, pair of 027 turnouts.	20	35	45
1122LH Switch: 1955-69, single left-hand 027 turnout.	12	18	25
1122RH Switch: 1955-69, single right-hand 027 turnout.	12	18	25
1122-234 Fiber Pins: 1958-60, one dozen 027 insulating pins.	1	2	3
1122-500 027-Gauge Adapter: 1957-66, conversion pins to use 027 switches w/ Super 0 track.	1	2	3
1144 Transformer: 1961-66, 75-watt.	10	20	40
1232 Transformer: 1948, 75-watt, 220-volt primary.	50	100	150
1241 Transformer: 1947-48, 60-watt, 220-volt primary.	50	100	150
1244 Transformer: 1957-66, 90-watt, 220-volt primary.	50	100	150
1640-100 Presidential Special: 1960, bag of plastic people and paper signs for passenger cars indicating Secret Service, Press Corps and both political parties.	100	225	400
3330-100 Operating Submarine Kit: 1960-61, packaged in cardboard box w/ elaborate artwork.	100	200	300
6009 Uncoupling Section: 1953-55, 027.	3	6	10
6019 Remote Control Track: 1948-66, 027.	4	6	10
6029 Uncoupling Track Set: 1955-63, 027.	3	5	7
6149 Remote Control Uncoupling Track: 1964-69, 027.	1	5	7
6418 Bridge: See 214.			
6800-60 Airplane: 1957-58, individually boxed for separate sale.	150	350	450
A Transformer: 1947-48, 90-watt.	20	40	50
A220 Transformer: 1947-48, 90-watt, 220-volt.	50	70	100
AX Transformer: 1947-48, 90-watt, 110-volt, 25-hertz primary.	20	40	50
CTC Lockon: 1947-69.	—	—	1
ECU-1 Electronic Control Unit: 1946-49.	40	75	100
KW Transformer: 1950-65, 190-watt.	100	150	200
LTC Lockon: 1950-69, illuminated.	2	5	12
LW Transformer: 1955-56, 125-watt.	75	100	125
OC Curved Track: 1945-61, O-Ga.-curved track.	—	.50	1
OC-18 Steel Pins: 1946-60, one dozen steel pins for O-Ga. track. The collectable is the envelope, not the pins.	—	—	1
OC-51 Steel Pins: this small envelope, available only in 1961, contained one dozen steel pins for O-Ga. track. The collectable is the envelope, not the pins.	—	—	1

1033 Transformer

1034 Transformer

1043
Transformer

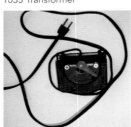

1043-500 Transformer

1047 Operating Switchman

1640-100 Presidential Special

CTC Lockon

ECU-1 Electronic Control Unit

SP
Smoke
Pellets

KW Transformer

	C5	C7	C8
OS Straight Track: 1945-61, O-Ga. straight track.	$.50	$1	$2
OTC Lockon:	1	2	4
Q Transformer: 1946, 75-watt.	20	40	60
R Transformer: 1946,100-watt, 1947, 110-watt.	50	75	100
RCS Remote Control Track: 1946-48, O-Ga.	5	10	15
R220 Transformer: 1948, this transformer was the same as an R, but was adapted for the European market by the use of a 220-volt primary coil rather than the standard 110-volt US-type coil.	50	100	150
RW Transformer: 1948-54, 110-watt.	50	75	100
S Transformer: 1947, 80-watt.	20	35	60
SW Transformer: 1961-66, 130-watt.	60	90	125
SP Smoke Pellets: 1948-69, bottle of 50 pills.	10	20	30
TOC Curved Track: 1962-69, O-Ga. curved track.	—	.50	1
TOC-51 Steel Pins: 1962-69, one dozen steel pins for O-Ga. track. The collectable is the envelope, not the pins.	—	—	1
TOS Straight Track: 1962-69, O-Ga. straight track.	.50	1	2
TW Transformer: 1953-60, 175-watt.	75	125	150
T020 90-Degree Crossover: 1962-69, 90-degree O-Ga. crossing.	5	7	10
T022-500 O-Ga. Adapter Set: 1962-66, allows the use of O-Ga. switches w/Super 0 track. Much of the value is in the packaging.	2	3	4
UCS Remote Control Track: 1949-69, O-Ga.	8	14	18
UTC Lockon: 1945-46, fits Standard-Gauge track as well as 027 and O-Ga. track.	1	2	4
V Transformer: 1946-47, four-throttle, 150-watt.	100	125	150
VW Transformer: 1948-49, four-throttle, 150-watt.	120	140	175
Z Transformer: 1945-47, four-throttle, 250-watt.	100	125	150
ZW Transformer: 1948-49, 250 watts, 1950-66, *275-watt.*	100-150	150-225	250-300

TW Transformer

UCS Remote Control Track

UTC Lockon   V Transformer

ZW Transformer

MARX

Toy trains bearing the name Marx dominated the shelves of dime stores and other economy retailers for much of the 20th Century. Initially, Marx's toys were actually produced by others and only sold by Marx. The first trains were produced by the Girard Model Works. They were sold by Marx as "The Joy Line." Joy Line trains were sold through 1936.

Marx bought the Girard plant in 1935, and trains continued to be produced there until 1975, three years after Quaker Oats bought the company.

	C6	C8

Joy Line
Marx sold Joy Line trains from 1927 through 1936.

Steam

(101) Steam: 0-4-0, 1930-31, black, cast iron, electric w/headlight.

	C6	C8
	$155	$210

(102) Steam: 1930-31, black, cast iron, mechanical and screw or *slip-on key*.

	50-65	75-100
(103) Steam: 1933-35, red, mechanical.	45	80
(104) Steam: 1933-35, black, mechanical, sparkler, dummy or battery-operated headlight.	40	80
(105) Steam: 1932-35, red body, black frame, mechanical, dummy or battery-operated headlight.	40	80
(106) Steam: 1932-35, black body, red frame and electric.	50	100
(107) Bunny Locomotive: 1935-36, pink and blue, mechanical.	800	1,200
350 Steam: 0-4-0, 1927-30, yellow, black, red, blue, mechanical.	300	425

(106) Steam

(107) Bunny Locomotive

357 Coach

458 Observation

M10000 Union Pacific

M10000 Union Pacific

M10000 Union Pacific

(657) Union Pacific "Coach"

(658) Union Pacific "Coach Buffet"

(735) Mechanical

(791) Mechanical or Electric

	C6	C8

Rolling Stock

351 Tender: 1927-35, yellow and blue, black or red, long or short body, "351 *Koal Kar*" or no number. $25-75 $45-125

352 Gondola: 1927-36, "Venice Gondola," blue, or red or orange floor toy. 40 80

(352) Gondola: 1935-36, "Bunny Express," frame lavender or light blue or green. 150 250

353 Tank: 1927-34, "Everful Tank Car," gold body, red or black ends, blue or black frame. 50 75

354 Side Dump: 1927-34, "Contractor Dump Car," yellow body, blue or black ends, blue or black frame. 50 80

355 Boxcar: 1927-34, "Hobo Rest," red body, blue or black frame, blue, yellow, black or orange roof. 40 80

(356) Caboose: 1926-34, "Eagle Eye Caboose," red body, blue or black frame, yellow, black or orange roof. *Illuminated* or non-illuminated. 40-80 75-115

357 Coach: 1931-34, "The Joy Line Coach," green body, blue or black frame, red, orange or *yellow roof*. 50-75 65-100

458 Observation: 1931-34, "The Joy Line," green lithography, red or orange roof, w/or w/out illuminated "Joy Line" drumhead. 40-150 50-200

Articulated Streamliners
M10000 Power Cars

M10000 Union Pacific Power Car: electric, 1934-37, many variations. 30 80

M10000 Union Pacific Power Car: mechanical, 1934-37, many variations. 30 80

Passenger Cars for M10000 Sets

(657) Union Pacific "Coach": 1934-37, two- or four-wheel. Many variations matching M10000 power car. 25 50

(658) Union Pacific "Coach Buffet": observation, 1934-37, w/or w/out illumination. Many variations matching M10000 power car. 25 50

M10005 Power Cars

(732) Mechanical or Electric: 1936-40, cream w/green and orange trim. 40 60

(732GMD) Electric: 1948, white w/green and orange trim, pin or tab coupler. 30 60

(735) Mechanical: 1946-50, yellow and brown, w/or w/out reverse. 40 80

(735D) Dummy: 1951-53, yellow and brown w/orange trim, tab coupler on front. 30 70

(791) Mechanical or Electric: 1940, 1948-52, silver w/red and blue trim. 20 40

Passenger Cars for M10005 Sets

(657G) Union Pacific: 1936-40, cream w/green roof, orange trim, "*RPO*," "*REA/RPO*" or Coach lettered either Los Angeles, Omaha or Denver. 15-30 30-60

(658G) Union Pacific: 1936-40, "Squaw Bonnet," observation, matches (657G). 20 30

(757) Union Pacific: 1937-40, yellow, brown roof, orange trim, "RPO," "REA/RPO," *Diner* or Coach lettered Los Angeles, Omaha or Denver. 20-200 40-400

(757A) Union Pacific: 1948-50, white w/green roof, or *silver, red and blue*, "RPO, REA/ RPO," Observation or Coach lettered either Los Angeles, Omaha or Denver. 15-40 30-80

21 Santa Fe E7 Diesel

(52) Union Pacific E7 Diesel

54 KCS Diesel

81 Monon Diesel

(902) Western Pacific Diesel

1798 Cape Canaveral Express Diesel

1095 Santa Fe Diesel

	C6	C8

(758) Union Pacific: 1937-40, "Squaw Bonnet," observation, matches (757).

	C6	C8
	$25	$35

(758A) Union Pacific: 1945-50, "Squaw Bonnet," observation, white, green and orange, or silver, red and blue. — 20 — 30

Passenger Cars for Mercury Sets

(657) New York Central: 1938-40, gray body and roof (various shades),"US Mail-Bag," "Toledo," "Coach," *"Cleveland,"* *"Coach,"* "Chicago." — 40-60 — 80-125

(657CQ) New York Central: 1939-47, brass body and roof, black trim, illuminated or non-illuminated,"US Mail-Bag," "Toledo," "Coach," "Cleveland," "Coach," "Chicago," "Coach." — 50 — 100

(657RA) New York Central: 1937-40, 1948, "Coach," red body and roof, white trim. "Toledo," "Cleveland" or "Chicago." — 40 — 100

(658) New York Central: 1940, observation, gray, "Detroit." — 45 — 90

(658CQ) New York Central: 1939-41, observation, brass, "Detroit." — 60 — 100

(658RA) New York Central: 1937-40, observation, red and "Detroit." red. — 50 — 100

	C6	C8

Diesel Locomotives

21 Santa Fe E7 Diesel: 1950-54, A-unit, tin lithographic, silver, red, *powered* or dummy. $25-30 / $50-60

(51) Allstate Diesel: 1957-59, plastic, A-unit, orange, black, powered or dummy. 110 / 150

(51) Allstate Diesel: 1957-59, plastic, B-unit, orange, black. 100 / 160

(52) Union Pacific E7 Diesel: 1960, plastic, A-unit, powered orange. 125 / 175

(52) Union Pacific E7 Diesel: 1960, plastic, B-unit, powered orange. 150 / 200

54 KCS Diesel: 1956-60, tin lithographed, A-unit powered or dummy, red, black, yellow. 80 / 125

(55) KCS Diesel: 1957-60, B-unit, four- or eight-wheel. 50 / 100

62 B & O Diesel: 1953-54, 1958, 1967, tin, A-unit, silver, blue, powered or dummy. 40 / 80

81 Monon Diesel: 1955-56, 1958-59, tin, A-unit, powered or dummy, two- or four-wheel, gray, red, "81F." 50 / 80

(82) Monon Diesel: 1958-59, B-unit, four- or eight-wheel. 40 / 75

99 Rock Island Diesel: 1958-74, plastic, A-unit, powered or dummy, black, red. 50 / 80

(99X) Rock Island Diesel: 1958-61, B-unit. 40 / 75

112 LV Diesel: 1974-76, switcher, red. 20 / 40

588 New York Central Diesel: 1958-62, switcher, black, maroon, *gray*. 25-50 / 50-75

702 Western Pacific Diesel: 1972-74, switcher, green w/gold, yellow or *cream* trim. 30-60 / 50-80

799 Rock Island Diesel: 1959-65, switcher, black and red. 30 / 45

799 Western Pacific Diesel: switcher, 1959-65, green and yellow. 60 / 80

(800) Missouri Pacific Diesel: switcher, 1975-76, blue. 50 / 90

(801) Illinois Central Gulf Diesel: switcher, 1974-75, w/or w/out reverse mechanism, orange and white "Split Rail" scheme. 30 / 60

901 Western Pacific Diesel: E-7A, 1956-60, plastic, powered or dummy, green and yellow or *gray and yellow*. 50-90 / 75-125

(902) Western Pacific Diesel: E-7 B-unit, 1957-58, green and yellow or *gray and yellow*. 60-100 / 85-135

1095 Santa Fe Diesel: plastic, E-7 A-unit, 1952, gray, red, yellow, powered or dummy. 40 / 75

(1096) Santa Fe Diesel: E-7 B-unit, catalog no. 1095B, 1955-71. 25 / 40

1798 Cape Canaveral Express Diesel: switcher, 1959-64, red, white and blue. 85 / 110

(1998) Allstate Diesel: 1959, blue, eight-wheel. 130 / 220

1998 A.T. & S.F. Switcher: 1955-62, eight-wheel, maroon or *black*. 40-80 / 85-125

1998 Rock Island Diesel Switcher: 1962, gray and red, eight-wheel, powered or dummy, black or *silver trucks*. 80-100 / 115-140

1998 Union Pacific Diesel: 1955-62, dark or *lemon* yellow, eight-wheel, powered or dummy. 80-110 / 115-140

1998 A.T. & S.F. Switcher

1998 Union Pacific Diesel

(2002) Handcar

2002 New Haven Diesel

2124 B & M Diesel

6000 Southern Pacific Diesel

1 Steam

333 Steam

400 Steam

490 Steam

(494/495) Steam

500 Steam

	C6	C8
(2002) Handcar:	$30	$45
2002 New Haven Diesel: plastic, E-7 A-unit, 1960-74, black, white, orange "McGinnis scheme," powered or dummy. Powered.	50	75
Dummy.	60	74
(2003) New Haven Diesel: E-7 B-unit, 1960-74, black, white, orange "McGinnis scheme."	50	75
2124 B & M Diesel: RDC, 1958-59, silver gray.	200	275
4000 New York Central Diesel: 1953-55, 1959-69, 1971-74, plastic, black and white, powered or dummy, many variations.	85	150
4000 Penn Central Diesel: 1971-73, plastic, E-7 A-unit, powered or dummy, turquoise green, w/or w/out white stripe and painted grilles.	175-275	225-400
4000 Seaboard Diesel: 1955-62, tin, A-unit, green, yellow, electric, mechanical or dummy.	50	75
(4001) Seaboard Diesel: 1962, B-unit, four-wheel.	175	225
6000 Southern Pacific Diesel: 1952-54, tin, A-unit, power or dummy, orange, silver or *white* stripe.	25-35	40-60

Steam Locomotives
Electric

	C6	C8
1 Steam: 1959-60, Wm. Crooks locomotive, plastic, 4-4-0 w/smoke, 1973, 0-4-0 no smoke, plastic.	75	100
(198) Steam: 0-4-0, 1962, plastic, Marlines, *red* or black.	40-80	60-115
333 Steam: 4-6-2, 1949-53, die-cast, black, w/or w/out smoke.	60	100
391 Steam: 2-4-2, 1938, 1942, 0-4-0 1939-41, all black or *black w/red trim*.	40-60	75-100
396 Steam: 0-4-0 or 2-4-2, 1941-42, sheet metal, black or *copper*.	40-50	60-75
397 Steam: 2-4-2, 1941, *copper* or black boiler.	60-70	85-100
400 Steam: 0-4-0, 1953-54, locomotive, plastic, black or *olive drab*.	15-50	20-75
490 Steam: 0-4-0, 1962-75, black or gray.	20	25
(494/495) Steam: 0-4-0 or 2-4-2, 1939-41, 1946-52, Marlines, numbered "3000," many variations, the most valuable of which included a *red cab and boiler*.	25-80	50-120
500 Steam: 0-4-0 or 2-4-2, 1938-42, Army, olive drab.	75	100
(591) Steam: 0-4-0, 1953-60, electric, black.	10	20
(593) Steam: 0-4-0, 1953-60, electric.	10	20
(595) Steam: 0-4-0, 1959-60, electric.	10	20
(597) Steam: 0-4-0, 1934-52, Commodore Vanderbilt, black, red, gray, *olive drab*.	25-150	50-250
(635) Steam: 0-4-0, 1938-41, Mercury, *black*, red, gray.	35-60	60-110
666 Steam: 2-4-2, 1955, die-cast, black or *olive drab*.	25-60	35-85
(833) Steam: 0-4-0, 1947-52, black.	15	20
897 Steam: 0-4-0, 1939, lithographed black or *olive drab*.	60-125	85-200

666 Steam

897 Steam

1829 Steam

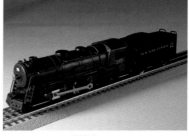

999 Steam

	C6	C8
898 Steam: 0-4-0, 1946-52, black.	$15	$20
994 Steam: w/or w/out number on cab.	25-40	50-80
(995) Steam: 0-4-0, same as 994, black or *red*.	25-150	50-250
999 Steam: 2-4-2, 1941-42, 1947, black, die-cast, *open*, closed or embossed pilot.	25-75	50-125
1666 Steam: 2-4-2, plastic, w/or w/out smoke, black or *gray*.	20-50	25-75
1829 Steam: 4-6-4, black, w/or w/out smoke.	40-50	70-100
3000 Steam: 0-4-0 or 2-4-2, 1939-41, 1946-52, many variations, all equal value except *red* boiler w/light blue, silver and black running board apron.	55-75	100-150
3000: See (494/495).		

Mechanical Steam Locomotives

	C6	C8
(1) Steam: 0-4-0, 1962, Wm. Crooks, black.	50	100
(198) Steam: 0-4-0, 1962, Marlines, plastic, black or *red*.	30-60	50-100
(232) Steam: 0-4-0, 1934-48, Commodore Vanderbilt, black, red, green, gray or *silver*.	40-225	50-300
(233): See (635).		
400 Steam: 0-4-0, 1952-56, 1958, 1965-76, black, many variations, all equal value except *w/rubber bulb smoke puffer*.	15-30	20-60
(401) Steam: 0-4-0, 1962, Marlines, black.	8	12
(591) Steam: 0-4-0, 1950-58, black.	10	20
(635) Steam: 0-4-0, 1938-40, Mercury, black, gray, red or *blue*.	50-100	75-175
666 Steam: 0-4-0, mechanical, uses same body as does electric 999.	500	1,000
734 Steam: 0-4-0, 1950-52, Mickey Mouse locomotive.	175	225
(735) Steam: 0-4-0, 1950-52, black.	15	30
(833) Steam: 0-4-0, 1947-52, black.	15	25
897 Steam: 0-4-0, 1940, tin lithographed, black and white or *olive drab*.	60-175	100-250
898 Steam: 0-4-0, 1940, 1946-48, black.	20	40
994 Steam: 0-4-0, black.	20	40
3000 Steam: 0-4-0, Canadian Pacific, maroon or *blue and white* sideboards.	125-150	175-200

Tenders

	C6	C8
(198A) Marlines Tender: used w/198 Steam, black or *blue* plastic.	25-40	40-60
(451) Canadian Pacific Tender: 1937-41, six in., four-wheel frame silver, red, maroon or lettered Pennsylvania.	20	50
(461) CP Tender: 1935-39, six in., eight-wheel frame, automatic couplers, silver, maroon or *light blue*.	30-50	60-75
500 (851 M) Army Supply Train Tender: 1935-40, six in., four-wheel, olive drab or lime-olive body.	50	75

	C6	C8

(551) New York Central: 1934-36, Commodore Vanderbilt wagon top tender, four-wheel, black, *silver*, blue, red, gray, copper. $10-*150* $15-*250*

(941) Tender: 1949-52, four-wheel frame, lithographed tin, *red* or black NKP or red, green and yellow "Mickey Mouse."   10-*100*   15-225

(951) Tender: 1939-42, 1951-58, four- or eight-wheel, New York Central or *NKP*.   15-*100*   20-*160*

952 Olive Drab Tender: "Army Supply Train," 1940, four-wheel.   150   175

(961) Eight-Wheel Slope Back Tender: 1962-64, 1967-68, 1972, 1974, black, plastic or *gray*, assorted road names.   15-25   20-30

(971) New York Central Tender: 1938-48, two-wheel, articulated, pin couplers, brass, gray and red.   50   75

(1951) Tender: black plastic, 1952-74, four- or eight-wheel, assorted road names, including *Canadian Pacific*.   10-50   15-75

(2451) CP Tender: 1937-38, 1941, six in., eight-wheel frame, hook couplers, *light blue* or maroon, yellow or gold lettering.   40-50   60-75

(2551) New York Central: 1938-40, Commodore Vanderbilt, eight-wheel frame and rivets.   15   30

2731 Santa Fe Tender: 1953, 1955, 1959-60 black plastic used w/1829.   25   40

(3551) Union Pacific: New York Central or "*1st Div. S.P.&P.R.R.*" tender, 1955-57, 1959, six in., four-wheel frame, formed metal.   15-50   20-75

(3651) William Crooks Tender: 1959-62, 1973 black plastic, "Tales of Wells Fargo," or "1st Div. St. P. & P.R.R."   20   40

(3661): See (198A).

(3991) New York Central: 1949-54, die-cast, black.   40   70

Early Six-Inch Cars

201 Observation: 1934-35 cherry red, Joy Line couplers.   50   65

245 Pullman: 1934-36, "Bogota," cherry red.   20   40

246 Coach: 1934-36, "Montclair," cherry red.   20   40

547 Baggage: New York Central, 1934-35, cherry red, Joy Line couplers.   45   65

(550) Crane: 1934-35, New York Central, orange cab, red boom, red or black crane cab base, Joy Line couplers.   20   40

245 Pullman

246 Coach

694 Caboose

5011-5026 Baggage/Mail Car

37960-37975 PRR

4485-4500 BAR

37960-37975 PRR

90171 B & LE

90171 B & LE

384299 B & O

3824 UP

556 New York Central

31055 Monon

	C6	C8
(551) Wagon Top Tender: 1934-36, New York Central Commodore Vanderbilt, four-wheel, black, *silver*, blue, red, gray and copper.	$10-*150*	$15-*250*
552 Gondola: CRI & P, 1934-36, cherry red.	20	30
553 Tank Car: Santa Fe, 1934-36, bright yellow.	15	30
(559) Double Floodlight Car: w/two nickel or black lights.	75	150
694 Caboose: New York Central, 1934-36, cherry red.	15	30
817: See 91453.		
1678 Hopper: Northern Pacific, 1934-35, olive-bronze, Joy Line couplers.	20	35
1935 Mail Car: New York Central, 1934-36, dark green, Joy Line couplers.	45	90
91453 Refrigerator Car: C & S, 1934-35, yellow, Joy Line couplers.	30	50

Six-Inch Four-Wheel Cars

The "six-inch" four-wheel cars, (actually 6-3/4 in. long) were sold from 1934 into 1942. After a break due to World War II, the car returned in 1946 and remained in the line through 1972. Plastic couplers were introduced on part of the line about 1953.

Baggage, Express, Mail Cars

	C6	C8
547 Baggage/Mail Car: New York Central, 1936-37, red body, yellow, silver or *black lettering*.	35-45	60-85
1935 "U.S. Mail Car": New York Central, 1936-37, green or red body.	40	90
5011-5026 Baggage/Mail Car: New York Central, 1957, blue and gray body.	35	60

Boxcars

	C6	C8
4485-4500 BAR: "State of Maine Products," 1960, 1962, blue, white and red, solid doors.	50	75
37960-37975 PRR: "Merchandise Service," 1954, gray and red, solid doors; also produced w/out number on side in 1965.	15	30
46010 SSW: "Cotton Belt Route," 1940, Cobalt blue, *orange, yellow*, brown, crimson red, candy apple red.	30-65	75-*125*
51998 C & NW: "400 Streamliners," 1939-40, Cobalt blue, *orange, yellow*, brown, crimson red, candy apple red.	30-65	75-*125*
90171 B & LE: 1940, 1948, 1953, 1955, Cobalt blue, *orange, yellow*, brown, crimson red, candy apple red, caramel, Salmon red.	30-55	75-*115*
174580-174595 New York Central: pacemaker, red and gray body, white and black detail, sliding doors.	75	125
384299 B & O: 1940, 1954-55, 1957, cobalt blue, *orange, yellow*, brown, crimson red and candy apple red.	30-65	75-*125*

Cabooses

	C6	C8
556 New York Central: red, w/or w/out illumination.	15-50	20-*125*
694 New York Central: dark red, many variations.	20	30
956 SAL: green and yellow.	50	75
3824 UP: yellow and brown body, orange, *brown* or black frame.	15-25	20-*40*
5563 KCS: red, yellow and black.	75	125
20102 New York Central: red and gray, w/or w/out illumination.	5-90	10-*175*
31055 Monon: red and gray.	75	125

(561) Searchlight

552 CRI & P

554 NP "General Coal Co."

554 NP "General Coal Co."

28500 LV High-Sided

91257 Seaboard RR

241708 B & O

1678 Northern Pacific

(552M) (298/6) Gondola

(557M) Coach

Marx
243

	C6	C8

Flatcars and Miscellaneous Work Cars

Note: If loads listed are missing, value of car should be reduced 75 percent or more.

(550) Crane: 1934-35, New York Central, orange cab, red or black crane cab base. — $20 / $40

(559) Double Floodlight: no lettering or lithography, black or *red frame*, brass, black or *red deck*, black or *nickel lights*. — 20-50 / 40-90

(561) Searchlight: w/single large brass, red-painted metal or red plastic light. — 25 / 65

(562) Flatcar: black, w/dump or stake truckload. — 125 / 175

(563) Lumber Car: w/load of four pieces of square lumber. — 40 / 60

(566) Cable Car: black, w/wooden cable reel wound w/rope. — 50 / 75

(572A) Airplane Car: black car w/various colors of airplanes as load, red most common. — 125-150 / 200-275

(574) Barrel Car: black, w/seven wooden barrels. — 50 / 75

(663) Pole Car: black, w/15-dowel load. — 40 / 50

Unnumbered Rail Transport Cars: (sold as a pair), black, w/rail load. — 175 / 225

Unnumbered Wheel Car: w/wheel load. — 100 / 125

Gondolas

548 CRI & P "Guernsey Milk": 1939-40, turquoise, cream, wood milk cans held by cardboard insert. — 75 / 125

552 CRI & P: 1937-38, 1940, red, green or blue. — 15 / 25

552G CRI & P: "Groceries and Sundries," yellow, brown, w/box load. — 50 / 100

554 NP "General Coal Co.": 1935-40, 1946, 1950, blue w/red interior or red w/yellow interior. — 15 / 25

28500 LV High-Sided: green and silver, 1953, 1960. — 10 / 20

86000 DLW High-Sided: iridescent blue, red, 1956. — 30 / 50

91257 Seaboard RR: 1957, red, brown, *dark blue*. — 15-50 / 20-85

241708 B & O: 1953, yellow exterior, w/*black*, gray or red interior. — 5-20 / 15-50

738701 PRR: 1940, 1952, 1954 high-sided, red. — 20 / 35

Hoppers

1678 Northern Pacific: "General Coal Co.," 1936, olive-bronze, red interior. — 30 / 40

86000 DLW: "Lackawanna," 1953, blue. — 20 / 25

738701 PRR Hopper: "Pennsylvania," 1940 tuscan w/tuscan or *black* interior. — 15-20 / 25-35

Military Cars

(552M) (298/6) Gondola: "Ordnance Dept," olive w/or w/out bullet load. — 60-100 / 110-200

(557M) Coach: "Army Supply Train," "Radio Car," olive lithographed body, w/or w/out antennas. — 50-75 / 75-100

(558M) Observation: "Army Supply Train," "Official Car," olive lithography, w/or w/out illumination, nickel or brass platform rail. — 50 / 100

(561M) Searchlight Car: olive drab; 1939, red, black or olive handle; mirror lens and *dummy searchlight* 1941. — 35-100 / 65-125

(572) Field Gun Car: 1940, olive drab. — 70 / 100

(572A) Flatcar: w/olive or red airplane, 1940. — 150 / 250

(572D) Flatcar: olive dump or cargo truck. — 150 / 225

(572G) Siege Gun Car: 1940, cannon has 5/8-in. bore, olive drab. — 125 / 150

(558M) Observation

(561M) Searchlight Car

(572G) Siege Gun Car

(572AA) Anti-Aircraft Gun Car

(572MG) Machine Gun Car

245 Pullman

246 Pullman

2071 Coach

Unnumbered "Bogota"

Unnumbered "Montclair"

	C6	C8
(572M) Flatcar: olive, 1940, 1957, various metal or plastic truck loads.	$60	$80
(572AA) Anti-Aircraft Gun Car: 1940, cannon has 5/16-in. bore, olive drab.	100	125
(572MG) Machine Gun Car: 1940, olive drab.	100	125
(572ST) Flatcar: w/tank, 1940, various tanks used, including *tumbling* and sparkling; painted and lithographed.	125-225	250-425

Passenger Cars

	C6	C8
201 "Observation": 1934-36, cherry red.	50	75
245 Pullman: 1934-36, cherry red, "Bogota."	25	40
246 Pullman: 1934-36, cherry red, "Montclair."	30	50
246 Coach: Canadian Pacific, 1938-40, wine-maroon body, "Montreal."	125	250
247 Coach: Canadian Pacific, 1938-40, wine-maroon body, "Toronto."	125	250
248 Coach: Canadian Pacific, 1938-40, wine-maroon body, "Quebec."	125	250
249 Coach: Canadian Pacific, 1938-40, wine-maroon body, "Ottawa."	125	250
250 Coach: Canadian Pacific, 1938-40, wine-maroon body, "Winnipeg."	125	250
251 Coach: Canadian Pacific, 1938-40, wine-maroon body, "Vancouver."	125	250
252 Coach: Canadian Pacific, 1938-40, wine-maroon body, "Calgary."	125	250
253 Coach: Canadian Pacific, 1938-40, wine-maroon body, "Hamilton."	125	250
2071 Coach: New York Central, silver.	40	75
2072 Observation: New York Central, matches 2071.	70	100
Unnumbered "Bogota": commonly w/red body, sometimes w/*blue and white* or green and yellow, lithographed body, silver, red, blue or black frame, w/or w/out illumination.	20-75	40-125
Unnumbered "Montclair": commonly w/red body, sometimes w/*blue and white* or green and yellow, lithographed body, silver, red, blue or black frame, w/or w/out illumination.	20-75	40-125
Unnumbered "Observation": commonly w/red body, sometimes w/*blue and white* or green and yellow, lithographed body. Silver, red, blue or black frame, w/or w/out illuminated interior and drumhead.	20-75	40-125

Unnumbered
"Observation"

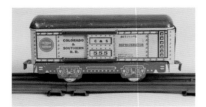

555 "Colorado & Southern Refrigerator"

567 Side Dumping Ore Car

59 Stock Car

553 Tank Car

553 Tank Car

553 Tank Car

19847 Tank Car

19847 Tank Car

556 New York Central

552 CRI & P

554 NP "General Coal Co."

(2552M) Gondola

	C6	C8

Refrigerator Cars

555 "Colorado & Southern Refrigerator": 1937-42, 1953-54, cream body, blue or
   red roof, red, black or *silver frame*, sliding doors or *man in door*. $20-175 $40-275

10961-10976 FGEX: 1940-49, 1954-56, yellow car w/sliding doors and gray roof.
                                                                          150   275

91453 "Colorado & Southern Refrigerator": 1936-38, yellow w/sliding doors.
                                                                           25   40

Side Dump Cars

567 New York Central: "Side Dumping Car," yellow w/brass, brown or copper deck.
                                                                           20   40

Stock Cars

59 Stock Car: Union Pacific, *slotted* or solid lithographed tuscan car sides.
                                                                        20-40   35-60

Tank Cars

553 Tank Car: Santa Fe, 1934-36, bright yellow or silver, flat or domed ends.
                                                                           15   30

553 Tank Car: UTLX, silver, black or tin dome and ends.   20   30
19847 Tank Car: SDRX, black or *green*.   20-30   30-80

Six-Inch Eight-Wheel Cars

Offered from 1936 into 1942, these cars used the same bodies as their four-wheel counterparts, but were equipped with swiveling four-wheel trucks.

Baggage, Express, Mail Cars

547 Baggage/Mail Car: New York Central, 1936-37, red body, yellow lettering.
                                                                           70   100

1935 "U.S. Mail Car": New York Central, 1936-37, red body.   60   90

Boxcars

46010 SSW: "Cotton Belt Route," 1940, cobalt blue, *orange, yellow*, brown, crimson red.
                                                                        30-65   75-125

51998 C & NW: "400 Streamliners," 1939-40, cobalt blue, *orange, yellow*, brown,
   crimson red.   30-65   75-125

90171 B & LE: 1940, cobalt blue, *orange, yellow*, brown, crimson red, caramel and
   Salmon red.   30-55   75-115

384299 B & O: 1940, cobalt blue, *orange, yellow*, brown, crimson red.
                                                                        30-65   75-125

Cabooses

556 New York Central: red, w/black or *red frame*.   15-25   25-50

Flatcars and Miscellaneous Work Cars

Note: If loads listed are missing, value of car should be reduced 75 percent or more.

(2550) Crane: New York Central, orange cab, red or black crane cab base.
                                                                           30   65

(2561) Searchlight: w/*illuminated* or dummy lamp.   60-75   100-125
(2562) Flatcar: black or *red*, w/dump or stake truckload.   125-175 175-225
(2563) Lumber Car: black or *red*, w/load of four pieces of square lumber.
                                                                        40-80   60-175
(2566) Cable Car: black, w/wooden cable reel wound w/rope.   50   75
(2574) Barrel Car: black, w/seven wooden barrels.   50   75
(2663) Pole Car: black or *red*, w/15-dowel load.   30-80   60-175

	C6	C8

Gondolas

548 CRI & P: "Guernsey Milk" 1939-40, turquoise, cream, wood milk cans held by cardboard insert. — $100 / $150

552 CRI & P: 1937-38, 1940, green w/black or *red frame*. — 15-25 / 25-45

552G CRI & P: "Groceries and Sundries," yellow, brown, w/box load. — 75 / 150

554 NP "General Coal Co.": 1936-40, red w/yellow interior. — 15 / 35

738701 PRR: 1940, high-sided, red. — 20 / 35

Military Cars

(2552M) Gondola: "Ordnance Dept." olive w/or w/out *bullet load*. — 60-100 / 110-200

(2561MD) Searchlight Car: olive drab, 1939, dummy searchlight. — 100 / 150

(2572) Field Gun Car: 1940, olive drab. — 125 / 175

(2572G) Siege Gun Car: 1940, cannon has 5/8-in. bore, olive drab. — 125 / 175

(2572MG) Machine Gun Car: 1940, olive drab. — 175 / 250

(2572ST) Flatcar w/Tank: 1940, painted olive or lithographed red and yellow tank. — 300 / 400

Passenger Cars

246 Coach: Canadian Pacific, 1938-40, wine-maroon body, "Montreal." — 125 / 250

247 Coach: Canadian Pacific, 1938-40, wine-maroon body, "Toronto." — 125 / 250

248 Coach: Canadian Pacific, 1938-40, wine-maroon body, "Quebec." — 125 / 250

249 Coach: Canadian Pacific, 1938-40, wine-maroon body, "Ottawa." — 125 / 250

250 Coach: Canadian Pacific, 1938-40, wine-maroon body, "Winnipeg." — 125 / 250

251 Coach: Canadian Pacific, 1938-40, wine-maroon body, "Vancouver." — 125 / 250

252 Coach: Canadian Pacific, 1938-40, wine-maroon body, "Calgary." — 125 / 250

253 Coach: Canadian Pacific, 1938-40, wine-maroon body, "Hamilton." — 125 / 250

Unnumbered "Bogota": black or *red frame*. — 30-50 / 50-70

Unnumbered "Montclair": black or *red frame*. — 30-50 / 50-70

Unnumbered "Observation": black or *red frame*. — 30-50 / 50-70

Refrigerator Cars

555 Colorado & Southern Refrigerator: 1937-42, cream body, blue or red roof, red or black frame. — 30 / 60

Side Dump Cars

567 New York Central "Side Dumping Car": yellow w/brass, brown or copper deck. — 20 / 40

Stock Cars

59 Stock Car: Union Pacific, *slotted* or solid lithographed tuscan car sides. — 20-40 / 35-60

Tank Cars

553 Santa Fe: silver, flat- or dome-shaped ends, black or *red frame*. — 20-25 / 35-45

	C6	C8

Marx Seven-Inch Cars

Marx produced the cars in this series for 10 years, beginning in 1949.

Boxcars

1476 "Mickey Mouse Train": 1950-57, yellow.	$90	$165
4484 BAR: "State of Maine," 1956-57.	20	30
37950-37959 PRR: "Merchandise Service," 1950-55, red and gray.	15	25

Cabooses

C-504-C-518 B & O: 1955-57, blue, gray and black, four- or eight-wheel.		
	45	65
956 Nickel Plate Road: 1950-58, red and gray.	15	25
969-980 KCS: 1956-57, yellow, red and black.	125	175
1235 SP: 1952-55, red, maroon and silver.	15	20
1951 A.T. & S.F.: 1951-53, red and black.	15	20
3855 Monon: 1956-57, red, gray and white.	30	75
20110-20124 New York Central: 1954-58, "Pacemaker."	20	30
691521 "Mickey Mouse Train Meteor": 1950-51.	70	110

Gondolas

36000 C & O: 1956-57, brown.	20	35
80982 Wabash: 1950-53, yellow.	15	20
Unnumbered "Mickey Mouse Train": 1950-51, blue and yellow.	75	115

4484 BAR

37950-37959 PRR

C-504-C-518 B & O

956 Nickel Plate Road

1235 SP

3855 Monon

20110-20124 New York Central

80982 Wabash

	C6	C8

Passenger Cars (1860 PERIOD)

1 Combine: St. Paul & Pacific, 1959-60, 1962, yellow w/black roof, four- or eight-wheel. $40 $75

3 Coach: St. Paul & Pacific, 1959-60, 1962, yellow w/black roof, four- or eight-wheel. 40 75

174580 New York Central

20102 New York Central

92812 Reading

71499 NYC & St. L NKP

254000 B & O

13079 LNE Hopper

234 Coach

234 Vista Dome

	C6	C8

Marx 3/16 Metal Scale Cars

Note: Most of the freight cars in this series used scale-like trucks, the exceptions are noted.

Boxcars

1950 GAEX: green w/GAEX-DF or DF on yellow stripe, scale-like or high metal trucks. — $15 — $25

3200 NYNH & H: — 25 — 40

9100 Union Pacific: "The Challenger," black or *red ends.* — 25-110 — 40-225

70311 PRR: brown. — 25 — 35

174580 New York Central: "Pacemaker," w/or *w/out rivet detail* on sides, scale-like or high metal trucks. — 20-25 — 30-35

Cabooses

In addition to the cabooses listed below, seven-inch cabooses came in certain sets otherwise composed of 3/16-cars. These cabooses are listed in the seven-inch section.

20102 New York Central: w/or w/out illumination. — 15-90 — 20-175

92812 Reading: red. — 25 — 35

Flatcars

Note: If loads listed are missing, value of car should be reduced 75 percent or more.

2700 NYC & St. L NKP: black, w/or *w/out provision for stakes*, used scale-like or high metal trucks. — 25-50 — 50-75

3773 B & M: black w/U-stakes, scale-like, high metal or deluxe, plastic trucks were used on this car. — 25 — 60

80410 C & O: came w/three U-stakes, scale-like or high metal trucks. — 40 — 60

Gondolas

17899 T & P: lettered *"Texas & Pacific"* or "T & P," light blue-gray. — 30-40 — 55-65

44572 C & O: black, high-sided, w/or *w/out rivet detail.* — 10-15 — 15-20

71499 NYC & St. L NKP: black. — 20 — 35

254000 B & O: light gray or light blue-gray, came w/either scale-like, high metal or deluxe plastic trucks. — 10 — 20

347000 PRR: gondola, black. — 20 — 30

Hoppers

13079 LNE Hopper: gloss or crackle black, w/or w/out end brace. — 25-35 — 50-60

Military Cars

(2572H) Ramp Car: w/olive tank, 1940. — 500 — 1,000

(2572I) Ramp Car: w/dark red tank, same car as above. — 500 — 1,000

(2572J) Ramp Car: "Deluxe Delivery" w/trailer load. — 500 — 1,000

Passenger Cars

Note: Only NEW YORK CENTRAL cars are on scale trucks. All others are on high metal or deluxe plastic trucks.

234 Coach: New York Central, two-tone gray, windows w/silhouettes; illuminated, scale-like trucks. — 35 — 60

234 Vista Dome: New York Central, two-tone gray, short dome, scale-like trucks. — 35 — 60

(236) New York Central: "Meteor," obs., two-tone gray, windows, w/silhouettes; illuminated, scale-like trucks. — 35 — 60

1007 Observation: Western Pacific, silver, windows w/silhouettes, illuminated, high metal or deluxe plastic trucks. — 60 — 100

1217 Coach: Western Pacific, silver, high metal or deluxe plastic trucks. — 80 — 110

(236) New York Central

3152 Vista Dome

3152 Coach

3197 Observation

35461 PFE

53941 PRR

256 NIAX

	C6	C8
1217 Vista Dome: Western Pacific, silver, full-length dome, high metal or deluxe plastic trucks.	$60	$100
3152 Vista Dome: A.T. & S.F., silver, full-length dome, illuminated, deluxe plastic trucks.	40	60
3152 Vista Dome: A.T. & S.F., silver, half-length dome, w/or w/out illumination, w/or w/out silhouettes, w/or w/out punched windows, plastic trucks.	20	50
3152 Coach: lithographed windows or punched windows w/silhouettes.	25	50
3197 Observation: A.T. & S.F., "El Capitan," silver, lithographed windows or punched windows w/silhouettes.	25	50
3557 Coach or Vista Dome: New York Central, silver body, *lithographed* or illuminated windows w/silhouettes.	125-225	175-325
3558 Observation: New York Central, "Meteor," silver, *lithographed* or illuminated windows w/silhouettes.	125-225	175-325

Refrigerator Cars

35461 PFE: yellow w/black or *red ends*.	30-175	50-300

Stock Cars

13549 A.T. & S.F.:	40	60
53941 PRR: brown.	250	325

	C6	C8

Tank Cars
256 NIAX: "Niacet Chemical Corp.," silver tank, black or *silver dome*.

	C6	C8
	$15-35	$20-60
552 SCCX: "Shell," orange tank, black dome, scale-like or high metal trucks.	25	40
2532 CSOX: "Cities Service," green.	25	40

Work Cars
	C6	C8
(3550) New York Central: gray or *red body*.	25-75	40-115
(3591A) Searchlight: w/red plastic lamp.	50	80

Plastic 3/16-Inch Freight Cars
	C6	C8
504 Caboose: B & O, blue.	150	250
2532 Tank Car: CSOX, green.	25	40
(03556S) Caboose: SP, red.	25	40
(03563S) Flatcar: Erie, maroon.	25	40
13975 A.T. & S.F. Stock Car: *yellow*, red or brown.	15-25	30-50
347100 Gondola: PRR, gray.	15	30
467110 Boxcar: B & O, orange.	25	35

Marx Plastic Freight Cars
Produced from 1952 through 1975, some of the same tooling is in use today by new owners.

Boxcars
	C6	C8
2858 "USAX Ordnance": olive drab.	225	400
3280 Santa Fe: four-wheel, orange or white.	15	20
5595 "Farm Master Brand": 1959, automatic boxcar, cream or white.	25	40
13975 A.T. & S.F.: four- or eight-wheel, brown, red or *yellow*.	15-25	20-60
18918 Great Northern: brown.	50	90
20053 Seaboard: 1957, 1959, four-door boxcar, tuscan or *red*.	60-115	85-165
34178 Great Northern: 1961, 1975, lime or *dark green*.	15-25	20-40
43461 Pacific Fruit Express: 1955, white.	15	20

5595 " Farm Master Brand"

5595 "Farm Master Brand"

20053 Seaboard

43461 Pacific Fruit Express

77003 Boston and Maine

176893 New York Central

635 New Haven

643 Western Pacific

1977 A.T. & S.F.

2225 Santa Fe

4427 Santa Fe

(4556) Southern Pacific

18326 New York Central

18326 Penn Central

	C6	C8
54099 Missouri Pacific: 1956-57, 1960, 1974, *orange, green or yellow,* or red automatic.		
	$25-125	$40-200
77003 Boston and Maine: 1952, 1955, 1957, blue.	20	30
147815 Rock Island: 1952-59, red or *tuscan.*	20-45	45-70
161755 New York Central: 1952, yellow, four-wheel.	15	20
174479 New York Central: "Pacemaker," green, four-wheel.	30	50
176893 New York Central: 1973-74, dark green.	30	50
186028 Union Pacific: 1955, dark red.	30	60
249319 Marlines Operating Boxcar: operating, 1955, 1959, red or white.		
	30	50
259199 Canadian Pacific: tuscan.	100	125
467110 B & O:	15	20
Unnumbered Marlines: 1952, red or blue.	30	60

Cabooses

	C6	C8
45 SP-Style Caboose: 1973, dark brown.	35	45
234 "US Army": 1957, olive drab.	30	50
C350 Monon: maroon or red, four- or eight-wheel.	25	35
X467 "Rocket Computing Centre" Caboose: red, four-wheel.	40	55
504 B & O: 1953, blue, four-wheel.	190	250
564 "Allstate": 1959.	5	20
586 Rock Island: work caboose, brown.	20	30
635 New Haven: maroon, brown or black, white and orange "*McGinnis scheme,*" four- or eight-wheel.	15-25	20-40
643 Western Pacific: SP-style caboose, green, four-wheel.	20	30
643 Western Pacific: bay window caboose, 1973, green.	65	115
969 KCS: red, four- or eight-wheel.	50	75
1015 ICG Work Caboose: 1974, black, orange, white.	35	50
MP1231 "Missouri Pacific System": 1974, white, four-wheel.	30	50
1500 Rio Grande: 1974, orange.	65	90
1963 USAX: 1963, work caboose.	100	150
(1972) Santa Fe: 1974, brown or red.	10	15
1977 A.T. & S.F.: 1973-75, red, maroon or *red, silver and yellow,* four- or eight-wheel.		
	10-15	15-25
1988 B & LE: 1974, orange.	25	50
2130 USA Work Caboose: olive drab.	125	225
2225 Santa Fe: 1958-66, bay window, maroon.	50	75
(2225) "Allstate": 1953-59, bay window, orange or turquoise blue.	80	125
2366 Canadian Pacific: maroon.	75	100
3824 Union Pacific: 1956, 1962, bay window, maroon.	60	85
3900 Union Pacific: 1974-75, orange, brown, *yellow* or orange and black, four- or eight-wheel.	10-30	15-50
4427 Santa Fe: 1952-59, red.	15	25
4546 New York Central Caboose: dark red, large-type, 74.	20	30
(4556) Southern Pacific: 1953-75, red or brown.	10	15
(4564) New York Central: red or brown.	15	20
4586 Union Pacific: 1957-58, work caboose, red, w/or *w/out searchlight.*		
	25-30	35-50
(4587) Santa Fe: 1962, work caboose w/light, maroon.	30	50
(4588) "Allstate": 1955, work caboose w/light, tuscan.	30	60
(4589) New York Central: 1957, track-cleaning work caboose.	75	125
(4590) A.T. & S.F.: 1955-62, *red,* brown, or brown and red.	15-20	20-30
5586 Western Pacific: 1957, work caboose, dark red.	20	30
17858 Rock Island: 1958-59, SP-style caboose, tuscan, four- or eight-wheel.		
	15	25

Unnumbered New York Central

4571 WECX

4583 GEX

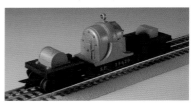

39520 SP

51100 Southern

51170 Erie

21429 Lehigh Valley

28236 Virginian

	C6	C8
17858 Rock Island: bay window, maroon.	$35	$70
18326 New York Central: 1956-74, *black, white and green* or numerous other colors, four- or eight-wheel.	15-30	20-50
18326 Penn Central:	15	25
95050 Lehigh Valley: 1974, red, four-wheel.	7	12
Unnumbered Marlines: 1952, 1974, red, four-wheel.	25	50
Unnumbered W.T. Grant: 1972, light orange, similar to 4556.	20	30

Cranes

5590 New York Central: black plastic cab, die-cast base, *w/or w/out* searchlight.	40-75	50-115
IC-1020X35 Illinois Central: brown and orange.	25	45
Unnumbered New York Central: gray and black or black.	15	25

Dump Cars

967(A) New York Central: 1957-58, blue or *black*, four-wheel.	100-125	175-225
Unnumbered Erie: eight-wheel log dump w/five-log load, maroon or blue mechanically operated or maroon electrically operated.	20	35

	C6	C8

Flatcars
Note: If loads listed are missing, value of car should be reduced 75 percent or more.

	C6	C8
24 Illinois Central: w/searchlight, 1974, black.	$25	$40
56(A) Brown: 1973, w/yellow fence and wood load.	25	35
586 Erie: maroon.	5	10
586 USA: olive drab, various silver military loads.	50	90
1024 Illinois Central Gulf: 1974, black, yellow rails.	25	50
1796 Rocket Launcher: 1959-60, white or blue and gray, four- or eight-wheel.	100	175
2246 USA: 1957, olive drab, w/two silver plastic military loads, six different individual possible cargo items.	75	125
2824 "US Army": 1957, depressed center car, olive drab, missiles and launcher.	100	200
4528A Erie: 1956, maroon or *orange* w/red, *gray or green* tractors.	40-150	75-275
4566 CWEX: 1955, blue depressed center car (various shades) w/gray or *yellow* cable reels.	50-100	75-250
4571 WECX: 1955-65, red depressed center car w/gray searchlight and generator.	25	50
4581 BKX: red, w/two lights and a generator.	50	75
4583 GEX: 1955, black.	50	100
5545 CB & Q: 1957, red or maroon, commonly w/black girder marked.	35	60
5545 CB & Q: also came w/two each of a variety of trailers, including Allstate, *Walgreens*, Burlington, Western Auto, or New York Central.	125-200	175-275
(5561) WECX: 1956-57, red, depressed, w/gray searchlight.	40	65
39520 SP: 1958, depressed center, black or maroon w/generator.	40	75
44535 SAL: gray, w/eight-piece pipe load.	35	60
51100 Southern: 1955-73, auto loader, red or maroon or *blue base* w/gray or yellow rack and four cars.	25-30	55-65
74563 ACL: 1961, red, w/red rails and a four-piece lumber load.	60	90
Unnumbered Erie: four- or eight-wheel, w/lumber, cable reel, two autos, two tractors, Atomic Light Generator, a generator or variety of trailers of which *Walgreens* and *Western Auto* are the most valuable.	20-125	25-200

Gondolas
Note: If loads listed are missing, value of car should be reduced 75 percent or more.

	C6	C8
1799 USAX: 1959, *red*, *eight-wheel* or blue, four-wheel, w/missile load.	65-80	110-125
2236 USA: 1957, olive drab, w/missile load.	50	80
2824 Missile Launcher: 1961-62, yellow.	50	75
5532 "Allstate": 1959-62, light or dark blue, eight- or *four-wheel*.	15-35	20-65
20309 L & N: 1959, 1961, brown or yellow.	60	125
51170 Erie: black, blue, *orange* or gray.	15-80	20-150
131000 SCL: 1973, yellow or blue, four-wheel.	15	20
39234 Canadian Pacific: 1957, 1960-62, brown, black, tuscan, removable ends.	50	70
347100 PRR: 1952-73, four- or eight-wheel.	10	20
715100 New York Central: 1970-74, four- or eight-wheel.	15	20
Unnumbered Marines: 1952, yellow, four-wheel.	20	30

Hoppers

	C6	C8
21429 Lehigh Valley: 1965-76, many variations.	20	30
21913 Lehigh Valley: 1965-74, many variations.	10	20
28236 Virginian: 1955, 1974, *red* or brown.	15-75	30-150

(5543) Flat w/Two Tanks

(5553) Allstate

Tank Cars

	C6	C8
246 "Chemical Rocket Fuel": cream or white.	$15	$25
284 UTLX: 1954, 1964, three-dome.	15	25
2532 "Cities Service": 1966-70, green, four- or eight-wheel.	10	15
(5543) Flat w/Two Tanks: 1955-74 Cities Service, Allstate or *Gulf*.	25-125	50-225
(5553) Allstate: Exxon or "*Milk*," three-dome, 1960-74.	25-225	50-300
(9553) "Allstate": "Allstate Rocket Fuel" or *Gulf*, 1959-74, single-dome, four- or eight-wheel.	15-35	25-60
X-246 "Chemical Rocket Fuel": four-wheel.	15	20

(404) Block Signal

(414) Crossing Bell

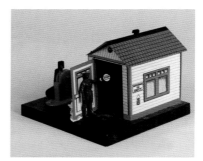
(1439) Crossing Shanty

Marx Accessories

Marx marked no numbers on the accessories they produced, requiring reference to catalogs for proper identifications. For that reason, they are listed here in alphabetical order.

(3832) Airport: plastic.	30	50
(3741) Army Barracks: plastic.	30	50
(3861) Barn: plastic barn and silo.	15	25
(3862) Barn:	15	25
(1456) Barrel Loader: automatic.	50	75
(6102) Battery Box: black.	15	20
(0446) Beacon: rotating.	20	30
(0226) Billboard: plastic, *yellow lighted* or green non-illuminated, two-piece set.	10-20	20-35
(404) Block Signal: two lights, 6-1/2 in. tall.	5	10
(404) Block Signal: three lights, 6-1/2 in. tall.	5	10

	C6	C8
(405) Block Signal: with rheostat and three lights.	$15	$20
(434) Block Signal: 1952, single target eight in. tall.	12	20
(434) Block Signal: three lights, black, 6-1/2 in. tall.	12	20
(454) Block Signal: 1952, two lights, black, seven in. tall.	5	10
(464) Block Signal: plastic, 1957, double target type, gray or black.	1	15
(1402) Block Signal: two lights, black, 6-1/2 in. tall.	5	10
(1404) Block Signal: position type, metal, five lights, nine in. tall.	75	100
(1404) Block Signal: position type, plastic.	30	40
(1405) Block Signal: three lights, w/control.	60	80
Unnumbered: block signal, green.	10	15
(1303) Bridge: black, "Erie."	8	15
(1304) Bridge: girder, metal.	10	15
(1305) Bridge:	15	30
(1310) Bridge: girder, metal.	15	35
(1320) Bridge: 18-in. through-truss.	10	25
(1324) Bridge: similar to 1320 w/beacon added.	30	50
(1350) Bridge: silver, 24 in. long.	10	20
(1380) Bridge: silver, 24 in., w/beacon added.	30	50
(6110) Buildings: cardboard, set of eight.	30	50
(505) Bumper: non-illuminated, red or black metal or gray or white plastic.	5	10
(605) Bumper: illuminated, metal or plastic, black.	5	10
(304) Cattle Corral: metal, black or silver.	20	30
(3856) Chicken Coop: lithographed.	25	35
(3851) Church: plastic.	20	25
(3852) Church: 1952, identical to 3851.	20	25
(409) Circuit Breaker: 25-watt.	5	10
(415) Circuit Breaker: 50-watt.	5	10
(419) Circuit Breaker: 30-watt.	5	10
(420) Circuit Breaker: black.	10	15
(420A) Circuit Breaker: black.	5	10
(425) Circuit Breaker:	5	10
(424) Control Tower: metal.	25	45
(6101) Controller:	3	5
(1601) Coupler Adapter:	5	10
(409) Crossing Flasher: red or black.	12	18
(414) Crossing Bell: 7-1/2 in. tall.	15	20
(417) Crossing Sign: red and chrome.	12	18
(317) Crossing Gate: manual, black or red, eight inches.	8	12
(064) Crossing Gate: plastic.	3	5
(428) Crossing Gate: automatic, seven-in., gray or black plastic.	5	10
(0217) Crossing Gate: gray plastic.	3	5
(1438) Crossing gate: 1952, w/double arms.	12	20
(321) Crossing Set: four-piece.	12	25
(430) Crossing Set: three pieces.	10	20
(1420) Crossing Shanty: 1957, w/gate and attendant.	25	50
(1439) Crossing Shanty: w/gate and attendant.	25	50
(1440) Crossing Shanty: illuminated, w/gate and attendant.	40	65

(2960) Girard Whistling Station

(438) Crossing Signal

(416)
Floodlight
Tower

	C6	C8
(314) Crossing Sign: "Caution," "High Speed Trains."	$5	$10
(067) Crossing Signal: plastic.	2	5
(069) Crossing Signal: plastic.	2	5
(418) Crossing Signal: 1952, w/bell.	10	15
(421) Crossing Signal: plastic, w/flashing lights.	10	15
(423) Crossing Signal: 1952, black and chrome, w/flashing lights.	10	15
(438) Crossing Signal: w/automatic gate, 1952, black or red.	10	15
(1426) Crossing Signal: banjo-type, plastic, w/flashing light.	10	15
(0218) Crossing Watchman Shed: 1956, red.	10	15
(412) Derrick: black and red or orange.	25	40
(422) Derrick: black and red lithographed.	30	50
(0442) Derrick: gray and red plastic.	10	15
(1450) Diesel Fuel Station:	50	75
(3771) Diner: plastic.	22	35
(1614) Dump Unit:	75	100
(1615) Dump Unit: identical to 1614.	75	100
(403) Dwarf Signal:	25	40
(3812) Factory:	25	35
(316) Fence: black or silver (value per section).	5	7
(6111) Fence and Ramp:	10	15
(782) Figure Set: plastic.	7	12
(6114) Figure Set: farm animals, lithographed, eight-piece set.	30	60
Unnumbered Figure Set: soldiers and tents.	30	50
(3781) Firehouse: plastic.	10	25
(416) Floodlight Tower: 1952-53, four lights, plastic, 13-1/2 in. tall.	15	25
(0436) Floodlight Tower: 1952-53, gray and black, plastic, 13-1/4 in. tall.		
	10	15
(416) Floodlight Tower: twin lights, black, *green*, red or silver.	10-15	20-35
(416A) Floodlight Tower: twin lights, 11-1/2 in. tall.	15	25
(5420) Freight Station: 1952, lithographed metal.	75	100
(5424) Freight Station: same as 5420, w/accessories, 1953-54.	100	125
(1460) Gantry Crane: 1955-57.	65	100
(2959) Girard Whistling Station: red and gray.	25	45
(2960) Girard Whistling Station: red and gray.	25	45

	C6	C8
(2970) Girard Whistling Station: illuminated.	$30	$50
(1600) Glendale Freight Station:	50	75
(1900) Glendale Station: w/warning signal.	50	75
(2900) Glendale Station: w/lamp and signals.	75	100
(3880) Glendale Station: plastic.	15	25
(4116) Glendale Station: kit, lithographed.	50	75
(4412) Glendale Station: lithographed metal.	50	75
(4416) Glendale Station: w/light and accessories.	50	75
(4418) Glendale Station: talking station.	75	100
(066) Grade Crossing: brown plastic stamped "RR."	1	3
(6103) Grade Crossing: brown, stamped "RR Crossing."	2	5
(2940) Grand Central Terminal: lithographed, buff-yellow.	75	100
Unnumbered Grand Central Terminal: blue, yellow or tan, red.	45	60
(068) High-Tension Poles: brown plastic, set of six.	10	15
(3802) House: colonial.	10	20
(500) Key: for mechanical locomotives.	2	8
(062) Lamppost: plastic, six in. tall.	1	2
(072) Lamppost: plastic, six in. tall.	1	2
(073) Lamppost: set of three, 6-1/4 in. tall.	10	15
(074) Lamppost: plastic, 6-1/4 in. tall.	3	5
(078) Lamppost: plastic, 6-1/2 in. tall.	3	5
(308) Lamp: street, metal body, seven in. tall, battery operated, assorted colors.	10	25
(408) Lamp: street lamp, black or red.	10	15
(419) Lamp: street lamp, 7-1/2 in. tall, black or red.	10	15
(426) Lamp: street, gray, plastic, 7-1/2 in. tall.	5	10
(429) Lamp: street, 1952.	10	15
(1392) Lift Bridge: silver, Illinois Central herald.	45	80
(B-25) Light: extension.	10	15
(X-5) Light Bulb Kit: five replacement 12-volt bulbs.	10	20
(X-10) Lubricant: tube.	2	5
Unnumbered Newsstand:	5	10
(2979) Oak Park Station: yellow and green.	40	70
(2980) Oak Park Station: yellow and green.	40	70

(429) Lamp   (410) Searchlight   (439) Semaphore

	C6	C8
(2990) Oak Park Station: w/light.	$60	$90
(3721) Police Station:	10	20
Unnumbered Power House: w/transformer inside.	60	125
(0161) Power Pole: set of 12 plastic.	5	10
(3871) Ranch House: plastic.	10	15
(3872) Ranch House: identical to 3871.	10	15
(3792) Ranch Set: plastic.	15	25
(421) Rheostat:	5	10
(6112) Rocket Accessories Set: Cape Canaveral.	50	75
(390C) Railroad Accessory Set: consists of a 390 tunnel and two 313 telltales.		
	18	25
(399) Railroad Accessory Set: consists of a 390 tunnel, two 313 telltales and one 1310 girder bridge.	30	45
(6106) Scale: plastic.	5	10
(3822) School: plastic.	10	25
(436) Searchlight Tower: black.	15	25
(310) Searchlight: battery-operated, green.	17	30
(410) Searchlight: square pedestal, 5-1/4 in. tall.	15	25
(063) Semaphore: plastic, six in. tall.	10	15
(311) Semaphore: manual, red or black, 9-1/2 in. tall.	10	15
(312) Semaphore: manual, green base, 9-1/2 in. tall.	10	15
(439) Semaphore: black, illuminated, 9-1/4 in. tall.	10	15
(0211) Semaphore: plastic, manual.	2	5
(3891) Service Station: plastic.	10	20
(3892) Service Station: plastic, identical to 3891.	10	20
(6108) Shovel:	10	20
(1624) Sign: "Uncouple Here."	1	2
(Unnumbered) Sign: "40."	2	5
(Unnumbered) Sign: "Notice, No Trespassing, RR Property."	2	5
(Unnumbered) Sign: "Reduce Speed."	2	5
(Unnumbered) Sign: "W."	2	5
(Unnumbered) Sign: "Curve."	2	5
(348) Sign Set: 1953-55, five-piece, right-of-way.	15	20
(1136) Sign Set: seven signs.	10	20
(1180) Sign Set: 12 signs.	15	25
(1182) Sign Set: 12 signs.	15	25
(1281) Sign Set: 12 signs.	15	25
(1282) Sign Set: 12 right-of-way signs.	15	25
(1434) Signal: overhead bridge, silver.	30	50
(0221) Signal Set: automatic.	8	15
(430) Signal Set: 29 pieces, plastic.	15	25
(406) Single Bull's-Eye Crossing Signal:	10	15
(333F) Smoke Refill: green glass bottle.	2	5
(0405) Spotlight: black and red, plastic.	5	10

	C6	C8
(2899) Station: whistling lithographed.	$25	$40
(3881) Station: w/accessories and figures.	10	20
(3882) Station: identical to 3881.	10	20
(3381) Station and Accessory Set: plastic.	10	20
(6104) Station Platform: plastic, six people.	10	15
(6109A) Suitcase: tan lithographed.	50	75
(3841) Supermarket: plastic.	15	20
(3842) Supermarket: plastic identical to 3841.	15	20
(413A) Switchman Tower: metal.	20	30
(2920) Switchman Tower: plastic.	25	35
(2939) Switchman Tower: plastic, illuminated.	25	35
(2940) Switchman Tower: 1952-58, w/two moving men.	35	50
(061) Telephone Pole Set: 12 brown plastic poles.	5	10
(313) Telltale: paper or rubber tales.	10	15
Track: curved or straight.	.10	.25
(464/C) Track Connection Package: four pieces.	1	3

Transformers

Prices typically are .25 per watt of rated output.

	C6	C8
(299) Trestle Set: eight-piece.	15	25
(612) Trestle: black.	2	5
(615) Trestle: black.	2	5
(1414) Trestle: graduated and bridge set.	10	15
(6113) Trestle and Bridge Set: w/plastic tunnel.	10	15
(1412) Trestle Set: 24-piece plastic.	7	12
(4376) Trestle Set: 14-piece plastic.	5	10
(6105) Baggage Truck: four-wheel, plastic.	5	10
(6107) Baggage Truck: two-wheel, plastic.	10	15
(6109) Trunk: steamer, lithographed.	30	50
(309) Tunnel: red, green, yellow.	30	50
(390) Tunnel: 1939-53, metal or fiber.	5	10
(392) Tunnel: 1950, lithographed.	5	10
Various Numbers Turnout: manual or remote, w/controller if applicable.	5	10
Various Numbers Uncouplers:	1	2
(1830) Union Station: blue and red.	40	60
(1430) Union Station: blue and yellow.	35	55
(0165) Water Tower: gray plastic.	10	15
(065) Water Tower: plastic, w/spout, black, gray and red or *green and yellow*.	15-25	20-40
(465) Water Tower: bubbling, gray, 14-1/2 in. tall.	35	50
(1379) Water Tower: identical to 0165.	8	12
(700) Whistle: two-tone.	5	10
(701) Whistle: two-tone.	5	10

UNIQUE

The Unique Art Manufacturing Co. was a toy manufacturer based in Newark, N.J. The company's strength was attractively lithographed mechanical toys, which it had produced since 1916. These toys came in a variety of forms, including cars and typewriters. Particularly popular were sophisticated dancing musical wind-up toys, which are quite sought after today. Under the direction of Samuel I. Berger, wind-up trains were added to the product line in 1949, and electric trains thereafter. The company's established distribution channels, the booming train market and the local availability of tooling, no doubt at a bargain price from the 15-year-defunct Dorfan firm, led to the decision to enter this market. The Dorfan tooling was not used as is, but rather was

742 Engine

2000 Engine

	C5	C7	C8
Control Tower: lithographed tin, two-story building containing power supply, cream w/green roof, some have reverse button, 3x2x4 inches.	$15	$30	$60
High Side Gondola: tin, orange w/red inside, w/out punched out sides, black lettering reads "Unique Lines," 7-1/2 in. long.	30	45	60
Hobo Boxcar: lithographed tin, clockwork, rolls along floor w/dog biting hobo.	500	750	1,000
100 Boxcar: tin, silver w/red lettering reads "Unique Lines" and "3509," 7-1/2 in. long.	40	60	80
101 Hopper Car: tin, orange w/red inside, black lettering reads "Unique Lines," 7-1/2 in. long.	25	38	50
102 Passenger Car: nine-inch long tin, blue body w/silver roof, white and black lettering reads "Pullman" and "City of Joplin."	100	150	200
102 Passenger Car: tin, blue body w/silver roof, white and black lettering reads "Pullman" and "Garden City," nine in. long.	100	150	200
105 Caboose: tin, red w/yellow lettering reads "Unique Lines," 7-1/2 in. long.	30	45	60

modified to create cars that minimized the labor required to assemble.

However, another lithographed toy manufacturer took Unique's incursion into train manufacturing very seriously. Louis Marx & Co. responded to Unique's entry by developing a line of cars to compete directly with the newcomer. Faced with this stiff competition, plus a materials shortage due to rationing during the Korean War, Unique withdrew from the toy train market in 1951. During their brief production history, Unique produced a few items that are coveted by collectors today, including their Circus Set and its 105 Animated Caboose.

	C5	C7	C8
105 Caboose: tin, red w/yellow w/swing-out, lettering reads "Unique Lines" and "Benny the Brakeman" on the rear platform, 7-1/2 in. long.	$40	$65	$100
107 Cattle Car: tin, red w/yellow roof, marked "Unique Lines," 7-1/2 in. long.	50	75	100
109 Circus Car: tin, mostly red w/open roof, marked "Jewel T Circus," elephant in center panel, 7-1/2 in. long, hard to find.	100	150	200
109 Circus Car: tin, mostly red w/yellow roof, marked "Jewel T Circus," lion in center panel, 7-1/2 in. long.	50	75	100
109 Circus Car: tin, mostly red w/open roof, marked "Jewel T Circus," lion in center panel, 7-1/2 in. long, desirable.	100	150	200
109 Circus Car: tin, mostly red w/yellow roof, marked "Jewel T Circus," elephant in center panel, 7-1/2 in. long.	50	75	100
515 Hillbilly Express: lithographed tin, clockwork, runs back and forth along inclined track.	100	150	200
702 Finnegan the Baggage Man: lithographed tin, clockwork, package has cutout cardboard luggage.	50	75	100
742 Engine: tin, clockwork, multicolored and gray w/tender, marked "Unique Lines," 7-1/2-in. long tender, 10-in. long engine.	40	60	90
1950 Engine: tin, electric w/reverse and headlight, multicolored and blue, w/tender, marked "Unique Lines," 7-1/2-in. long tender, 10-in. long engine.	30	45	80
1950 Engine: tin, multicolored and blue, w/tender, marked "Unique Lines," 7-1/2-in. long tender, 10-in. long loco.	30	45	80
2000 Engine: tin, diesel, powered A and dummy A, multicolored and maroon, marked "Rock Island," 14 in. long.	30	45	80

WYANDOTTE

The All Metal Products Co. was formed in Wyandotte, Mich. in 1920 for the purpose of manufacturing automotive parts. By the fall of the following year however the owners, William F. Schmidt and George Stallings, broadened their horizons. Their sights were soon set, as the pun goes, on the toy gun business. With the sale of toy pistols to S.S. Kresge forming the foundation of this new trade, by 1921 the company had expanded operations to include two manufacturing facilities in Wyandotte. At that time the business' hometown was adopted as a trade name for the burgeoning line of fanciful weaponry, and Wyandotte Toys was born.

Concurrently, upper-level management was expanded, among them Arthur Edwards, who later bought shares in the firm. Edwards eventually became president of the company.

Shown here are typical examples of Wyandotte's lithographed train production. At the top is a 2000 locomotive, with its corresponding tender at bottom, where it is joined by a caboose. Wyandotte, upon taking over Hafner, sold the existing inventory of Hafner-marked items. On the center shelf are three Hafner-Wyandotte gondolas.

By the 1930s, the firm's offering had expanded into a bewildering array of guns, cars, trucks, airplanes, and miniature sweepers and doll carriages. During this time the company adopted the slogan, "Wyandotte Toys are Good and Safe." In 1935, the company boasted of producing 5.5 million toy guns and over 7 million other toys—but no trains.

The absence of trains continued until 1951, when Wyandotte purchased the inventory and tooling of Hafner. Initial sales for Wyandotte were limited to existing Hafner inventory, but ultimately the firm began new production as well. Initially, production was in Wyandotte; however, the company relocated to Piqua, Ohio, in 1955—becoming Piqua Products—and only shipped a few trains before failing in 1956. Subsequently, Louis Marx & Co. purchased the Wyandotte and former Hafner dies—most likely merely to keep them from competitor's hands.

	C5	C7	C8
Wyandotte marketed several items using the original Hafner name and numbers—only those believed, or known to have been sold by Wyandotte are listed here.			
Caboose: No. 41021.	$5	$10	$15
Caboose: No. 614333.	10	15	20
Gondola: No. 91746.	10	15	20
Hopper: No. 13788.	15	20	25
Locomotive: No. 109.	20	40	60
Locomotive: No. 112.	40	75	100
Locomotive and Tender: 970.	15	30	45
Locomotive and Tender: No. 2000.	15	40	60
Santa Fe Boxcar: BX32.	10	15	25
115041 Train Set: 1952, Freight, w/No. 2000 Locomotive, 78100, 91746, BX32, 41021.	60	120	140
2155 Train Set: Freight, w/No. 970 Locomotive, stop-start mechanism, 78100, 91746, 41021.	75	100	150
2157 Train Set: Freight, w/No. 970 Locomotive, no stop-start mechanism, 78100, 91746, 41021.	60	120	140
2158 Train Set: Freight, w/No. 970 Locomotive, stop-start mechanism, headlight, figure-eight track, 78100, BX32, 91746, 41021.	60	120	140

GLOSSARY

AAR: Association of American Railroads, an industry standards and lobbying group.

Archbar truck: Trucks constructed with side frames consisting of two strips of bar iron or steel, called Arch Bars. These bars are bent so that placed mirrored to each other they roughly form a diamond shape with extended ends. Between these ends are the axle journal boxes. These trucks were banned from interchange service in 1939.

Bakelite: A brand of hard, brittle thermoset plastic. Heating Bakelite does not soften it, making it popular for electrical components. Lionel also used Bakelite occasionally for car bodies.

Commutator: An insulated segmented copper plate connected to the coils of direct-current and universal electric motors. Current flows from the carbon brushes to the commutator segments. This allows for the reversal of current into the coils of the motor

Cupola: The raised structure on the roof of a caboose that allowed a clear view of the sides of the train, making dragging equipment and "hot boxes" easily spotted regardless of the height of the remainder of the train.

Coupler: The device for mechanically interconnecting the individual cars of a train and transmitting the draft forces. Modern railroad couplers are of the "knuckle" type, but previously link and pin as well as other types were used.

Die-casting: Manufacturing process that involves forcing molten metal, usually a zinc alloy, into a mold, called a die, under high pressure. Rugged, detailed, precisely made parts can be mass-produced in this manner.

E unit: Two meanings. A) In Lionel trains, the electromechanical switch that selects motor contacts, and thus the motor's direction of rotation, is called an "E-unit." They are usually cycled by interrupting the current flow to the track. These come in two position (forward-reverse) or three-position versions, as well as a manual version which is two position, but requires hands-on operation by the operator. Three-position E-units are the most common, and their sequence of operation is forward-neutral-reverse-neutral-forward, and so on. B) In real railroading, E-unit is slang for a General Motors Electro-Motive Division E-series twin-engine diesel that rode on two A-1-A trucks. The two terms are not generally confused as Lionel did not build a miniature E-unit during the postwar era.

Gauge: The distance between the tops of the rails. On most real U.S. railroads this is 4 feet 8 1/2 inches. For Lionel's most popular size of trains this width is 1 1/4 inches.

Heat-stamping: A decorating process whereby a heated die is used to transfer and adhere a colored decoration to the subject piece. When used on plastics, heat stamping often leaves an impression, the depth of which varies with the temperature of the tool and the duration of contact.

Hot box: Early railroad wheel bearings were lubricated with oil-soaked cotton called "waste." If the lubrication ran dry, the bearing would overheat, setting fire to the waste. If the train continued to operate, the bearing would fail, derailing the train.

House car: A term used for enclosed freight cars such as box, stock, refrigerator, and poultry cars. These cars are used for lading requiring protection from weather.

Magnetraction: This feature was intended to better keep the locomotive on the track and increase its pulling power by using powerful Alnico magnets to magnetize the wheel, "sticking" the train to Lionel's tin-plated steel track

Rubber stamping: A decorating process which uses an engraved rubber block that is inked and then pressed to the subject. Rubber stamping tends to not be as bold, or as permanent, as heat-stamping. However, rubber stamping can be used on irregular surfaces, which heat-stamping cannot, and the set up cost is considerably less.

Scale: A numeric ratio describing the relative size of a miniature to an original.

Siderail: Handrail extending alongside a locomotive or railcar.

Silk screening: A labor-intensive decorating process. A piece of sheer fabric (originally silk, now polyester) is stretched tight. A thin sheet of plastic with holes cut out to reveal where ink is to appear on the work piece is placed over the screen. The screen is pressed to the work piece ink, then forced through the openings in the plastic, and through the screen onto the work surface. Multi-color designs require multiple screens, and the inks are applied sequentially starting with the lightest color and moving up to the darkest.

Sintered iron: Sintering is a metallurgical process whereby powdered metal is poured into a mold and subjected to heat and pressure, forming it into a single piece.

Smokejack: The railroad term for the smokestack found on cabooses and other freight and passenger cars.

Tack board: Wooden panels on an otherwise steel door that provide a place to attach notes.

Tender: The tender of a real steam locomotive is semi-permanently linked to the locomotive by means of a drawbar. The tender carries the water supply for the steam locomotive as well as the fuel, be it coal, oil or wood.

Truck: The structure consisting of paired wheels with axles, side frame, bolster, and suspension system beneath railroad cars. Referred to as a "bogie" in Europe.

NATIONAL TOY TRAIN MUSEUM

Headquarters for the Train Collectors Association

Many of the trains shown in this volume are from the collection of the National Toy Train Museum, headquarters for The Train Collectors Association. The TCA is an international organization of men and women dedicated to collecting and preserving toy trains.

The Train Collectors Association, was born from a 1954 meeting in the Yardley, Pennsylvania barn of Ed Alexander. The TCA has grown to nearly 32,000 members today. A national office, along with a museum, was built in Strasburg, Pennsylvania to accommodate the growing needs. The building has undergone 3 expansions since that time.

Toy trains are presented in a colorful and exciting turn-of-the-century setting. The Museum's vast collection of floor toys, electric trains and train-related accessories includes those from the mid-1800s through the present. See Lionel, American Flyer, Marx, Marklin, LGB and many, many others.

The National Toy Train Museum offers five operating layouts: Standard, "0", "S", "G" and HO gauges. The Standard gauge layout highlights tinplate trains from the 1920s and 1930s. The "0" gauge layout presents trains from the 1940s through current production items. The "S" gauge layout highlights American Flyer trains manufactured during the 1950s. The "G" gauge layout shows what one can do with large, durable modern trains which are made for indoor or outdoor use. The HO gauge layout was professionally built by Carstens Publications, Inc. for a series of articles published in its Railroad Model Craftsman magazine.

A continuously running video show in The Museum's Theater area features cartoons and comedy films about toy trains. The Museum Gift Shop offers a wide and unusual selection of toy train-related gifts.

Also housed in the Museum is an extensive Toy Train Reference Library, which is open to the public. On file are catalogs, magazines and books devoted to toy trains from 1900 to the present.

Come to Strasburg and visit the National Toy Train Museum where we have 5 different gauge layouts operating and displays of trains dating from 1840 until the present. If you are a person with a few trains or a house full, come join us.

OPEN:

- Weekends in April, November and December
- Daily — May through October
- 10:00 a.m. - 5:00 p.m.

visit their website at

www.traincollectors.org

for additional information.